Ovid

Heroides XIV

Edited by Arthur Palmer

Ovid

Heroides XIV
Edited by Arthur Palmer

ISBN/EAN: 9783337190279

Printed in Europe, USA, Canada, Australia, Japan

Cover: Foto ©ninafisch / pixelio.de

More available books at **www.hansebooks.com**

P. OVIDII NASONIS

HEROIDES

XIV.

EDITED BY

ARTHUR PALMER, M.A.,
FELLOW OF TRINITY COLLEGE, DUBLIN.

LONDON: GEORGE BELL AND SONS.
CAMBRIDGE: DEIGHTON, BELL, AND CO.
DUBLIN: E. PONSONBY.
1874.

VEN. ARTHVRO PALMER, A. M.,

HVNC QVALEMCVNQVE LIBELLVM

DEDICAMVS.

PREFACE.

THE title given by Ovid to this work was probably simply *Heroides*, or *the Heroines:* not *Epistolae Heroidum*. Priscian, lib. x. 9, cites the work under the former title; and so, Heinsius informs us, does the scholiast on the Metamorphoses, *passim*. It has been inferred by some from Art. iii. 345, that *Epistolae* was the original title: Ovid there says, speaking of his compositions,

> Vel tibi composita cantetur Epistola voce
> Ignotum hoc aliis ille novavit opus.

This does not however prove anything. On the other hand, addressing his wife, the poet says, Trist. I. vi. 33, lamenting his feebleness to sing her praise as she deserved:—

> Prima locum sanctas heroidas inter haberes:

where he appears to allude to his published work "The Heroines." In the MSS. the epistles are entitled *Epistolae sive Heroides, Epistolae Heroidum*, or *Epistolae heroides*, a discrepancy which shows uncertainty as to the title. The last

Title. of these titles appears to make *herois* an adjective, and it is in this sense that Loers seems to understand the word, when he calls *Herois* "carminum genus." There appears to be no authority for this use of the word. There certainly is not in Ovid. He uses the word "herois" four times: Am. II. iv. 33; Art. i. 713; Trist. v. v. 43; Trist. I. vi. 33, always in the sense of "Heroine," ἡρωΐνη, never in the sense of "Heroic epistle."

Spurious Epistles. Twenty-one epistles are generally published as the Heroides of Ovid. The present edition contains but fourteen: and even of these, the authorship of the last two, Laodamia and Hypermnestra, is questionable. The last nine epistles have all been condemned by some eminent German scholars, while it may be said of the last seven that their condemnation at the present day is all but universal. When Lachmann and Madvig, perhaps the two greatest Latinists of the century, join in condemning them as spurious, I have sufficient authority for excluding them from this edition. A brief recapitulation of the arguments commonly urged against them is all that is here necessary. We must in the first place make a division even of these last epistles. All of them except the epistle of Sappho, the verses of the epistle of Paris which are numbered in the edition of Heinsius 39–142, and the epistle of Cydippe from vs. 13 ad fin., are included with the most ancient MS. of the Heroides. Of these portions Lachmann thus writes : . . . 'neque ullam excusationem habet inepta editorum vel recentissimorum *superstitio*, qui epistolam Sapphus et eos versus qui apud Heinsium his numeris notati sunt, xvi. 39–142, xxi. 13–248, noluerint aut eicere aut circumscribere.'

Spurious Epistles.

The epistle that since the time of Heinsius has been classed as the fifteenth is condemned by Lachmann, and by every scholar possessed of common sense. It need not detain us long, but a brief summary of the arguments against it is necessary. It does not appear in any MS. of the slightest value—none earlier than the fifteenth century. Before the time of Heinsius it was placed last of the series, after the epistle of Cydippe, both in the old editions, and also the manuscripts in which it appears. In some MSS. it is published along with the poems of Tibullus, and other poets, instead of Ovid. It is a skilful cento of Ovidian expressions, but abounds in lines such as Ovid could scarcely have written, such as these:

Sappho.

40. Nulla futura tua est: nulla futura tua est.
184. Convenit illa mihi: convenit illa tibi.
198. Plectra dolore tacent: muta dolore lyra est.

Lachmann has pointed out that the author lived later than the time of Lucan, as 'furialis Erictho,' vs. 139, is derived from the Thessalian witch of that name in the sixth book of the Pharsalia. Some critics have gone so far as to place the composition of this epistle far in the middle ages. I think, myself, the author was

Sappho. familiar with the writings of Juvenal. I may add that vs. 117, 'Gaudet et e nostro crescit maerore Charaxus,' condemns the epistle, as Ovid does not use the word 'maeror,' rare in poetry of the Augustan age: that 'rependo' in vs. 32, could not have been written by Ovid: vid. ad. xi. 123. The verses inserted in the sixteenth epistle, and the completion of the twenty-first, have even less external authority than the epistle of Sappho.

There remain the five epistles from the sixteenth to the twentieth inclusive, and the first twelve verses of the twenty-first.

Epp. xvi.-xxi. These epistles are never mentioned by Ovid in any part of his voluminous writings. They differ in character from the early epistles, in containing replies from men to epistles from women. They differ from the early ones in being much more prolix, in being copied chiefly from Alexandrine writers such as Callimachus and others instead of the old classical models, Homer and the tragedians: most important of all, in their lax, creeping, and mawkish tone. To these general differences should be added the occurrence at the end of pentameters of *pudicitiae*, xvi. 288, *superciliis*, xv. 16, *deseruit*, xix. 202. Ovid, as Lachmann remarks, at the time when he composed the Heroides, always closed his pentameters with dissyllables. Lachmann also points out *qui* for *quo modo*, in xvii. 213, a usage not found in Ovid. [He is wrong, however, as Merkel has pointed out, in stating that

PREFACE.

nihil occurs nowhere else in Ovid, with both syllables shortened, besides xix. 170. Cf. Trist. v. 8, 2.] Such are the arguments, which appear to me decisive, against the authenticity of the last seven epistles: if cause has been shown for their rejection it will not be matter of regret, but of satisfaction, and Ovid will be vindicated from the charge of having produced a mass of prolix and tedious stuff which has little merit beyond smooth versification.

Sappho.

In Am. II. xviii. 21, seqq. Ovid enumerates most of the genuine Heroides. He does not, however, profess to give a complete list, and yet this is tacitly assumed by those who impugn the epistles not here enumerated.

Ovid's Enumeration.

> Aut quod Penelopes verbis reddatur Ulixi,
>   Scribimus, et lacrimas, Phylli relicta, tuas:
> Quod Paris et Macareus et quod male gratus Iaso
>   Hippolytique parens Hippolytusque legant,
> Quodque tenens strictum Dido miserabilis ensem
>   Dicat, et Aeoliae Lesbis amica lyrae.

Here Ovid enumerates nine epistles at least: or ten, if we include, as I think we should, both epistles to Jason, that of Hypsipyle, and that of Medea. Accordingly, of the first twelve epistles none have, I believe, ever been questioned except those which are believed not to have been enumerated in the above list. The genuine epistle of Sappho having perished, there remain four which have been subjected to scepticism. These are the letters of Briseïs, Hermione, Deianira, and Medea. The authenticity

Lachmann's opinions.

Briseis.

of all these has been questioned by no less a personage than Lachmann,[1] of whose opinion Merkel says that it is 'nulla membranarum auctoritate inferius,' an extravagant compliment.

The third epistle is not absolutely rejected by Lachmann, and the grounds of his objection to it are trivial in the extreme. He asks 'quis unquam puerilius in eodem schemate quater repetendo perstitit quam hic poeta, qui ita scripserit in epistola Briseïdos? 3-10:

> *Quascumque aspicies lacrimae fecere lituras;*
> *Sed tamen et lacrimae pondera vocis habent.*
> *Sit mihi pauca queri de te dominoque viroque :*
> *Fas est de domino pauca viroque queri.*
> *Non ego poscenti quod sum cito tradita regi*
> *Culpa tua est : quamvis haec quoque culpa tua est.*
> *Nam simul Eurybates me Talthybiusque vocarunt*
> *Eurybati data sum Talthybioque comes.*

The epanalepsis in these lines is, it is true, offensive, but it is made more remarkable than it really is by Lachmann's adopting a false reading of 5, 6, and although when the blemish is pointed out, it is apparent, yet most readers, even careful readers of Ovid, will peruse the lines in question without perceiving it. Such as it is, this is the only objection which Lachmann has brought against the

---

[1] As Lachmann's tract, published Ind. Lect. Berol., 1848, is difficult to obtain, I have given rather a full résumé of its contents. I obtained a copy through the kindness of Professor Gneist, Rector of the University of Berlin.

PREFACE.

epistle, a composition which appears to me *Briseis.*
most thoroughly Ovidian, full of poetry and
spirit, and perhaps contains more beauty in
individual lines than any other of the Heroides.
The objection of Lachmann, grounded as it is
on a charge of want of poetic taste, will seem in-
conclusive in deed when the composition against
which it is urged contains such lines as these,
full of the true ring of poetry,

    Vs. 45. Diruta marte tuo Lyrnesia moenia vidi.
    Vs. 88. Et preme turbatos Marte favente viros.
    Vs. 93.   Fratribus orba
        Devovit nati spemque caputque parens,

or that truly fine line,

    Vs. 106. Qui bene pro patria cum patriaque iacent,

the effect of which on a poetic mind is equal and
similar to that produced by the first two lines of
Collins' Ode :

        How sleep the brave who sink to rest
        By all their country's wishes blest!

The next epistle whose claims to its place are *Hermione.*
canvassed by Lachmann, is the eighth. Lach-
mann condemns it altogether as spurious. His
condemnation rests exclusively on metrical
grounds derived from two lines : vv. 71, 78.
The first is

        Orabat superos Leda suumque Iovem.

The second,

        Castori Amyclaeo et Amyclaeo Polluci.

The objection to the first line is the shortening
of the final syllable of *Leda*. Lachmann ob-

Hermione. serves that Ovid wrote *Ledc*, and always lengthened the final syllable of feminine nominatives of Greek proper names of the first declension.¹ Accordingly he condemns, and condemns rightly, as not from the pen of Ovid, Her. xvii. 150 :

> Et quasdam voces rettulit Aethra mihi.

His objection to the second line is, chiefly, the elision at the end of *Castori*. Ovid, he urges, never elides a long vowel at the end of a dactyl. [In connexion with this subject, Lachmann remarks that Ovid never allowed a dissyllable forming an iambus, ending in a vowel, to precede another word beginning with a vowel. So Her. xvii. 97 is not Ovidian: 'Disce meo exemplo formosis posse carere.' Nor is Am. II. xix. 20: 'Saepe time insidias, saepe rogata nega,' where, as Lachmann remarks, 'time insidias' is nonsense. Perhaps we should read there 'saepe tamen sedeas': cf. Prop. III. v. 14: 'Nec mihi ploranti lenta *sedere* potest'; *sedere* was a vox amatoria opposed to *venire*. And the old reading in Trist. ii. 295, ' Stat. Venus ultori iuncta viro ante fores' 'multis nominibus absurdum est.']

I agree with Lachmann that vv. 71 and 78, if genuine, are enough to condemn the eighth epistle, but they are in my opinion spu-

---

¹ The rule, however, is not absolute. In Am. ii. 442, we have 'Leda fuit nigra conspicienda coma,' a passage where Lachmann wished to change ' Leda' to 'Lyda.'

PREFACE.   xiii

rious. I must give the passage at length; it *Hermione.*
has been certainly grossly interpolated.

> Non ego fluminei referam mendacia cygni
>   Nec querar in plumis delituisse Iovem.
> Qua duo porrectus longe freta distinct Isthmos,
>   Vecta peregrinis Hippodamia rotis.
> *Castori Amyclaeo et Amyclaeo Polluci*
>   *Reddita Mopsopia Taenaris urbe soror.*
> Taenaris Idaeo trans aequora ab hospite rapta
>   Argolicas pro se vertit in arma manus.
> *Vix equidem memini, memini tamen: omnia luctus*
>   *Omnia solliciti plena timoris erant.*
> *Flebat avus Phoebeque soror fratresque gemelli*
>   *Orabat superos Leda suumque Iovem.*
> Ipsa ego *non longos etiam tum scissa capillos*
>   *Clamabam 'sine me, me sine, mater, abis?'*
> *Nam coniunx aberat.* Ne non Pelopeia credar
> Ecce Neoptolemo praeda parata fui.

The portions italicised are probably spurious.
How is the 11th line to be translated? *My
grandfather, and her sister Phoebe,*[1] is the
meaning, but the change of subject is not war-
ranted by the Latin. 'Nam coniunx aberat'
means *her* husband was absent, and it ought
to mean *my* husband was absent. And where
do we find a picture of the rape of Helen similar to this one, the most ridiculous point in
which is perhaps the poor figure cut by the
weeping Dioscuri. With this tissue of absurdities compare what we know the poet to have

---

[1] As I reject this passage as spurious, I must of course resign the introduction of Phoebe as an argument in favour of my emendation of xii. 149.

Hermione. said, iv. 53, sqq., when speaking of family fate in the case of Phaedra.

> Forsitan hunc generis fato reddamus amorem
>   Et Venus ex tota gente tributa petat.
> Iuppiter Europen, prima est ea gentis origo,
>   Dilexit tauro dissimulante deam :
> Pasiphae mater decepto subdita tauro
>   Enixa est utero crimen onusque suo.
> En ego nunc ne forte parum Minoia credar
>   In socias leges ultima gentis eo.

What the poet should have said in the corresponding passage in the eighth epistle ought to be then something like this :

> Num generis fato quod nostros errat in annos
>   Tantalides matres apta rapina sumus ?
> Non ego fluminei referam mendacia cygni
>   Nec querar in plumis delituisse Iovem.
> Qua duo porrectus longe freta distinet Isthmos,
>   Vecta peregrinis Hippodamia rotis.
> Taenaris Idaeo trans aequora ab hospite rapta
>   Argolicas pro se vertit in arma manus.
> Ipsa ego nunc ne forte parum Pelopeïa credar
>   Ecce Neoptolemo praeda parata fui.

If the absurdities and incongruities of the passage are excised, the metrical solecisms are excised along with them. The passages obelised have all the appearance of interpolations, as they are introduced in a manner peculiarly appropriate to interpolations, the first two verses repeating the mention of Helen, and the latter lines introducing an unseemly digression.

I have no great disposition to defend the authenticity of the Hermione, as it treats of an uninteresting subject in an uninteresting manner. I am, however, convinced that it is from the pen of Ovid, for the following reason. One of the most remarkable features in this poet's compositions is the manner in which his imitated compositions reflected the conception of the sources from which they were taken: a feature by which he is distinguished from his contemporaries, and indeed from most poets, except Shakspeare. Thus his Phaedra is Euripides' Phaedra repeated over again, contending between passion and shame: his Jason is the smooth-tongued, ungrateful Jason of Euripides: his Dido is Virgil's Dido, a little softened. But no idea was realised more exactly by Ovid than that which dominates in so many Greek tragedies—namely, the idea of a certain fate attaching itself to some unhappy family or race. Ovid, as a true poet, embraced this truly poetical idea, and constantly recurs to it. So we find poor Phaedra sullenly exclaiming—

> Forsitan hunc *generis fato* reddamus amorem,
> Et Venus ex tota gente tributa petat.

So Deianira:—

> Heu! *devota domus!* solio sedet Agrius alto,
> Oenea desertum nuda senecta premit;
> Exulat ignotis Tydeus germanus in oris:
> Alter fatali vivus in igne fuit:
> Exegit ferrum sua per praecordia mater:
> Impia quid dubitas Deianira mori!

Ovid alone of the Roman poets entered thoroughly into this conception; and in the

Hermione. eighth epistle, which I am now discussing, it appears brought forward in the most forcible manner:—

> Num *generis fato* quod nostros ERRAT in annos
> Tantalides matres apta rapina sumus?

No other poet but Ovid could have written the first line, with the remarkable word 'errat.' I will repeat here what I have said in my note, ad loc: that, by 'errat,' Ovid, more than probably, intended to represent the word ἐξορίζεται, which occurs in the Hippolytus of Euripides, a word by which the Greek poet forcibly emphasises his conception of a curse arising from ancestral crime descending to remote generations.

Deianira. Lachmann's objections to the ninth epistle are also based on metrical grounds. He objects to *insani Alcidae* in vs. 133, on the ground that a hiatus of this sort is only allowed by Ovid where either the fourth or fifth foot is a dactyl. But the reading *insani* has long been condemned as corrupt, and *Aonii* has been, with great probability, restored by Merkel. Lachmann impugns vs. 131, 141.

> Forsitan et pulsa Aetolide Deianira

> Semivir occubuit in letifero Eveno.

He asserts that Ovid only admitted hiatus of this sort (that is, in the middle of the verse), in two cases: (1) where the same vowel begins the second word which ends the first; (2) where the second word is either of the conjunctions *et* or *aut*. The second line is objectionable, according to Lachmann, on account of the lengthening of the last syllable of *occubuit*. Lachmann lays down that Ovid only lengthens a final short syllable in the middle of the line in two cases: (1) where either of the conjunctions *et* or *aut* follows a caesura in third foot of the hexameter: (2) where a Greek word follows. Now, both these rules would demand a very large induction to establish that there cannot be any exception to them, and the instances quoted by Lachmann, chiefly from the Metamorphoses, certainly do not suffice to sustain such apparently unreasonable canons. We may well acquiesce in the conclusion of Merkel, that Ovid, in these instances, allowed himself the license, if license it is to be called, common enough among other poets; but that when writing his epic poem, the Metamorphoses, he bound himself by stricter rule, according to Greek custom. I do not think the authenticity of the ninth epistle has ever been questioned by any scholar of real eminence except Lachmann[1]; and, for my part, I would

---

[1] Of course it has been attacked by some of the numerous band of remodellers, revisers, and would-be Bentleys which the German land, rich in impostors, produces. But as their criticisms generally do more harm to themselves than the objects of their attack, there is no reason why they should not be allowed to continue them. Thus L. Müller, attacking the four-

Deianira. as soon think of questioning the existence of the poet himself.

Medea. The next epistle cavilled at by Lachmann is the twelfth. He does not reject it, and the only reason for questioning it is, that it possesses 'molestam quandam et exuberantem orationis abundantiam.' This being the only fault Lachmann's microscopic eye has been able to detect in it, we may leave this epistle to speak for itself. I doubt if many readers will say of its vigorous, abrupt opening, for instance, which is thoroughly in Ovid's manner —

> At tibi Colchorum, memini, regina, vacavi,

that it possesses any offensive superfluity or prolixity. The poem is a very beautiful one, and contains one line that is worthy of being quoted:—

> Hoc ipsum ingratus quod potes esse meum est.

And that word *ingratus* recalls one argument of a positive kind that this epistle is from the pen of Ovid. In his enumeration he includes 'quod male gratus Iason legat.' Now, Hypsipyle says nothing about Jason's ingratitude. The word 'ingratus' is not to be found in the sixth epistle. But ingratitude is the head and front of Jason's offending against Medea. It is her theme from first to last; and naturally

---

teenth epistle, has exposed an amount of careless incompetence almost incredible in a person possessed of his reputation.

PREFACE.

so, for she had saved his life at the price of her own exile. Hence we have in the twelfth epistle :— *Medea.*

vs. 21. Est aliqua ingrato meritum exprobrare voluptas.
vs. 124. Debuit ingratis Scylla nocere viris.
vs. 206. Hoc ipsum ingratus quod potes esse meum est.

The objections to the authenticity of the thirteenth appear to me to be more formidable, although Lachmann condemns it only on account of 'exilis ingenii vena.' In the first place, this epistle was evidently from the same hand that wrote the letters from Paris to Helen, and Helen to Paris, the sixteenth and seventeenth epistles in ordinary editions. I do not think any one who reads the three carefully will deny this. The same smooth versification, the same prolix and nerveless style, joined with numerous similarities in diction which are common to the three, demonstrate that they must stand or fall together. The question who was their author seems, at first sight, capable of an easy answer, from Ovid's words, Am. II. xviii., where, addressing his friend Macer, he says :— *Laodamia.*

> Nec tibi qua tutum vati, Macer, arma canenti,
>   Aureus in medio marte tacetur amor.
> Et Paris est illic et adultera nobile crimen
>   Et comes extincto Laodamia viro.
> Si bene te novi non bella libentius istis
>   Dicis et a vestris in mea castra venis.

In this passage Macer is all but said to have written the thirteenth, sixteenth, and seventeenth. It has, however, been pointed

Laodamia. out to me by Professor Maguire, who stoutly upholds the authenticity of all the epistles, except that of Sappho, that Ovid here is speaking of episodes on these subjects introduced by Macer in his epic poem on the Trojan war. This, he urges, is shown by *illic*, which refers to the words *in medio marte*. This view is plausible and ingenious. The authorship of the poems, however, is a question I do not feel called upon to answer; and whether it was Macer, Sabinus, or some other friend of Ovid's, the argument that they never formed a part of the Heroides of Ovid remains unaffected.

Hypermnestra. Lachmann pointed out *generis*, ending vs. 62: and *potitur*, with the middle syllable lengthened, contrary to Ovidian usage, in vs. 113. But, curiously enough, neither of these lines is to be found in the best MS., and both are certainly interpolations. This fact ought to strengthen our belief in the authenticity of the epistle, although there is enough still left to make us doubt. I have ejected one barbarism in vs. 42, and I ought to have marked as spurious 103, 104, containing *Io*, with the first syllable short. There remains *mittit*, without an accusative, in vs. 1, the curious expression *funere digna* in vs. 32, and a general inaccuracy of detail as regards the legend, which I have pointed out in my notes. The imitations of Horace need not make us falter, as Ovid would have followed his treatment of the story of Hypermnestra as closely as he did Virgil's treatment of the story of Dido. There is, too, a rough strength in the poetry, especially in vss. 14, 120, which should rather incline us to the belief that this epistle is from the pen of Ovid, but lacking the benefit of careful revision, perhaps one of those compositions of which he writes (Trist. I. vii. 30):—

Hypermnestra.

Defuit et scriptis ultima lima meis.

The tiro in criticism could not possibly have a better introduction to that art than a careful study of the Heroides, for several reasons. In the first place he there has exhibited to him in the strongest light the difference between a good and a bad manuscript, and learns to hold to the one and despise the other. He finds that the very corruptions in a single good MS. are more precious than the concurrent voice of a hundred later and inferior ones, in which correction has taken the place of corruption. Take for instance iii. 100. By steadfastly fixing his gaze on the corrupt *negateta* of the codex Puteaneus, and refusing to believe that *negata meo* could possibly have come out of it, he at last succeeds in extracting in a perfectly legitimate manner the words *negante data*, thereby restoring sense and poetry to a passage which has been misread for a thousand years. Again, xiii. 116, 122, he finds to his satisfaction that in both passages the bad or awkward Latin of the vulgate is not supported by his MS., and

Critical Study of the Heroides.

Study of the Heroides. that by a careful scrutiny of the corruption he can restore the passage in accordance with his ideas of what Ovid should have written. It is only when he comes to deal with a poet like Propertius that he fully realises the loss of such a faithful friend as the Puteaneus. When shocked by bad Latin, or unpoetic language, or amazed by extreme obscurity, the critic has in the latter case no good, though it may be corrupt MS., whose corruptions he can decipher for himself, but he must fall back upon the solutions arrived at by the poor scholars who formed the copyists of the fourteenth and fifteenth centuries. He must either reject them or adopt them, and if he reject them, his own emendation must, in order to be accepted, have on its side an overpowering amount of self-evidence, inasmuch as it can appeal to no MS. authority in its favour. For instance, let us examine a passage which, I believe it will be admitted, is the most difficult in Propertius, It is III. xxvi. 83 (ed. Paley). He is there addressing Virgil, and after depreciation of his own light poems in comparison with the higher efforts of his friend, goes on to say that, after all, his own poetry will find readers. We shall, I think, agree that the passage should run as follows:—

> Tale facis carmen, docta testudine quale
> Cynthius impositis temperat articulis.
> Non tamen *haec* ulli venient ingrata legenti
> Sive in amore rudis sive peritus erit.

PREFACE.

> Nec minor *his* AUDIS, aut si minor, ore canorus
>   Anseris indocto carmine cessit olor.
> *Haec* quoque perfecto ludebat Iasone Varro
>   Varro Leucadiae maxima flamma suae.

'However, these light poems of mine will not be ungrateful to any reader, whether he be a tiro or an adept in love: nor have *you*, Virgil, *less fame in this sort of composition* than I have, or if you have, the tuneful swan is worsted by the rude cackle of the goose.' That this is the simple, easy, and certain restoration, I have not the slightest doubt, confirmed as it is by the whole tenor of the passage, both prior and subsequent to the portion I have quoted. But this restoration has to be made without help from MSS., for they all read *animis* for *audis*, the result of which has been that no modern has ever understood the passage, although a few have honestly persuaded themselves that they have done so. Now had we a MSS. like the Puteaneus, we should probably have been assisted in restoring *audis* by a corruption *avidis*, but as it is, the passage has to be restored in the teeth of the MSS. And this is unfortunately often the case in emending Propertius.

Secondly, the Heroides form an easy introduction to criticism, because of the excellent and thorough recension of the best MSS. published by Merkel, from the collation of H. Keil. That this recension is thorough and faithful, is shown by the fact that Keil thought it worth his while to record such apparently unmeaning

Critical Study of the Heroides. corruptions as those in ii. 100, xiii. 110, 122, and many others. That these give the key to restorations, I have shown in my notes, and I must express the deep obligations I am under to this collation, without which this edition would have had little value. For the recension of Jahn is by no means thorough as regards P, and Heinsius generally only recorded its variants, where he was able to build something on them himself.

The third reason why the Heroides form a good *rudimentum* in criticism is derived from the nature of Ovid's poetical genius. He is essentially devoid of conceit, more so than any other Latin poet, and always writes in the same easy style. He is also the most voluminous of Latin poets. From the former quality the critic derives a negative, from the latter fact a positive advantage. He can say with more confidence in the case of Ovid than he could in the case of any other poet, that this or that passage could never have been written by him. He could not venture to assert even this in the case of Virgil, much less in the case of poets like Persius or Statius. On the other hand, the large amount of Ovid's poetry that we possess supplies us with the means of restoring the true reading in such passages, as there are few idioms that he has not often repeated. When it is added that more than an average share of corruption has fallen to the lot of these epistles, it will be conceded that they possess, in a high degree, the qualities requisite for testing and training the critical acumen of a student.

    The recension of the text in this edition is based upon the critical apparatus given by Merkel, supplemented only occasionally by readings of the later MSS., taken from the editions of Jahn and Loers. Merkel's recension is exclusively based on two MSS. (1) P, which I sometimes call by its old name of Puteaneus. This is a manuscript of the ninth or tenth century, and is, Merkel observes, one of the best classical manuscripts in existence. It is now in the National Library at Paris, Cat. No. 8242. (2) G, called Guelferbytanus I. in other editions, placed by Merkel about the beginning of the twelfth century. I cannot but think that Merkel has attached too much weight to this codex, and I am glad to find I am supported in this estimate by the judgment of Dilthey (Cydippa, p. 134), 'Omnino hunc codicem a Merkelio iusto pluris esse factum crediderim'). In fact, the true division of the MSS. is into two classes. They are—first, the Puteaneus; second, all other manuscripts. The latter class number, probably, some hundreds, of dates varying from the twelfth to the fifteenth century. But the Puteaneus alone is worth all the rest put together: it is first, and the rest nowhere. Heinsius, who first collated it, called it his 'sacra ancora.'¹ I cannot see, after careful

---

¹ 'Puteaneus ad quem frequenter recurrimus tanquam ad sacram ancoram.' Note on xii. 17.

MSS. consideration of the question, that G is deserving of any extraordinary pre-eminence among the more recent MSS. I believe, contrary to the opinion of Merkel, that G was copied from P, either directly or indirectly; for there is hardly a single passage where a reading of any importance, hopelessly lost in P, is regained in G. On the other hand, the corruptions in P are the very places where G either goes wrong, or supplies an obvious correction. For instance, let the reader examine vi. 140, vii. 71, 152, ii. 100, and he can hardly avoid coming to any other conclusion. Here and there G and his younger brethren are unfortunately not only useful, but absolutely necessary, as there are two or three gaps in P. These are all, Ep. i. to vs. 14 of Ep. ii.: from iv. 48 to iv. 103: from v. 97 to vi. 49.

Faults in P. In awarding such high praise to this manuscript, I do not mean to be understood to say that it is free from faults, but that it is comparatively free from the greatest of faults—namely, alteration. It frequently goes wrong in unimportant points, where the scribe, who was evidently a very unlearned man, trusted himself to make a small correction. But this does not occur in important passages, or where the reading is one of difficulty. There the corruptions of the archetype are handed down to us unchanged, while, where the copyist has gone wrong himself, it is by making mistakes easily corrected.

Perhaps the most striking feature in the Codex Puteaneus is the omission of one of two similar syllables or words in juxtaposition. This habit of copyists is well known to critics, and so important is a knowledge of it, that it may be called the chief aid of the emendator. Any one ignorant of its value who will turn over the pages of Mr. Munro's Lucretius, in which the omitted syllables are printed in italics, will derive an instructive lesson respecting this habit. It arises from the very nature of copying, and is by no means confined to ancient scribes. Every one who has corrected proofs for his printer will remember how often he has had returned to him such slips as these : *vit* for *vivit*, *eleïdes* for *eleleïdes*, *commissaque dextrae* for *commissaque dextera dextrae*, all of which actually were sent in to the editor in the preparation of this edition. The law may be thus stated : wherever in poetry there is a deficiency of syllables or words in a line, or where in prose there is a deficiency in sense, probably the deficiency arises from the omission of a syllable or word, the same as, or similar to, a syllable or word, next to which it originally stood. This habit in its most elementary form is seen exemplied in a remarkable manner in the MS. we are speaking of. Take for instance the following defective lines : —

Avoidance of dittography.

vi. Hanc o demens Colchisque ablate venenis.

iv. Praeposuit Theseus nisi manifesta negemus.

xiii. Troas invideo quae sic lacrimosa suorum.

e

Avoidance of dittography.

XIII. Cur venit a verbis multa querela tens.

XVII. Et dabo cunctas tempore victa manus.

From not recognising the common cause of the corruptions these passages are very badly corrected in later MSS. Here are the corrections, which have been allowed to disfigure the pages of many editions :—

Hanc *tamen* o demens Colchisque ablate venenis.

Praeposuit Theseus nisi *nos* manifesta negemus.

Troadas invideo quae sic lacrimosa suorum.

Cur venit a verbis multa querella *tuis*.

Et dabo *coniunctas* tempore victa manus.

The student, from the mere enunciation of the above law, will supply the deficiencies better himself. There are many other instances in P, not quite so simple, which will be found explained in the notes.

I have remarked that this principle is very well known to critics; but it does not seem to me to have been so thoroughly applied as it might be. Its application is quite as effective in Greek as in Latin. By its use my friend Mr. Tyrrell has made, in my opinion, a certain and brilliant restoration in the Bacchae of Euripides. The MS. gives :—

ἴθ', ὦ βάκχε θηραγρέταν βακχᾶν.

Mr. Tyrrell, by the insertion of a second θήρ, at once restores metre and poetry.

ἴθ', ὦ βάκχε θήρ, θηραγρέταν βακχᾶν.

PREFACE.

The following emendations will not be out of place in illustrating the carrying out of this law.   *Avoidance of dittography.*

Eur. Frag. 674.

χαίρω γέ σ' ὦ βέλτιστον Ἀλκμήνης τέκος
. . . . τόν τε μιαρὸν ἐξολωλότα.

The passage is an illustration of the use of χαίρω with accusative. In the lacuna Heath proposed ἐλθόντα, Cobet σωθέντα. But neither of these words could well have been omitted. Apply the law of the accidental omission of similar words, and read:—

ἔτ' ὄντα τόν τε μιαρὸν ἐξολωλότα.

'I'm glad, Hercules, you're alive, and the rascal slain.' ἔτ' ὄντα fell out before τόν τε.

Eur. Frag. 254.

This fragment should run thus:—

ἐκ τῶν δικαίων γὰρ νόμοι τ' αὐξήματα
μεγαλὰ φέρουσι πάντα δ' ἀνθρώποις τάδε.
τάδ' ἐστὶ χρήματ' ἤν τις εὐσεβῇ θεόν.

For ἐκ in the first line, the MSS. have εἰ, and τάδε is left out in verse three before the following τάδε. 'From justice law is strengthened, and justice is everything to man: *justice* is *money*, if a man be pious.' The repetition of τάδε is in accordance with a universal custom, by which a word is repeated from the end

Avoidance of dittography. of a preceding line to emphasise a climax. Thus Hor. Ep. i. xi. 30 :—

> Quod petis hic est:
> *Est Ulubris*, animus si te non deficit aequus.

Eur. Frag. 652.

Πόλλ' ἐλπίδες ψεύδουσι καὶ ἄλογοι βροτούς.

καὶ λόγοι is proposed by Dindorf; but λόγοι has no business here. If the form καλόλογος can exist I would read :—

Πόλλ' ἐλπίδες ψεύδουσι καλόλογοι βροτούς.

'Fine talking hopes' (castles in the air). According to the law, καλόλογοι became καλογοι = καὶ ἄλογοι.

Tacitus, Annals, i. 51.

'Incessitque itineri et proelio.' I cannot but think that this is too pregnant a construction even for Tacitus. 'He advanced [prepared alike] for marching and fighting.' Orelli defends it by Ann. xiii. 40: 'qui viae pariter ac pugnae composuerat exercitum.' But this is nothing like so strong an expression. Substitute 'in' or 'ad' with the accusative for the datives in the latter passage, and there is nothing unusual to strike a reader. Make the same substitution in the first passage, and the construction is nearly as harsh as before the substitution. I cannot help believing, inasmuch as the word *pars* begins the next sentence, that a contracted form of *paratus*, resembling *pars*, has dropped out. Read: 'Incessitque itineri et proelio paratus. Pars,' etc.

So Curtius iii. 8, 'itineri simul paratus et proelio.' *Avoidance of dittography.*

I will conclude this subject with an application of this principle which may fail to convince the reader, although it has convinced me.

Propertius, III. xxxi. 5.

Hic equidem Phoebo visus mihi pulchrior ipso
Marmoreus tacita carmen hiare lyra.

The poet is describing a statue of Apollo. The reading above has two glaring faults:—
(1) *Equidem* is properly only used with the first person; (2) *Marmoreus* has nothing to agree with. Read:—

Hic Phoebus Phoebo visus mihi pulchrior ipso
Marmoreus tacita carmen hiare lyra.

'Here a marble Apollo, more beautiful it seemed to me than Apollo himself, oped his his lips, accompanying his silent lyre.'

Phoebus was lost before *Phoebo*, and *equidem* was just the word that a half learned scribe would select to make up a line with.

This edition being in the main critical, I have never shrunk from altering the text where an emendation appeared necessary. In doing so I have bound myself by three conditions:—(1) to avoid needless[1] alterations: (2) to adhere as closely as possible to the best *Alterations of the text.*

---

[1] Madvig's condemnation of causeless alterations is pithy and just: 'coniecturis non necessariis, id est, malis,' Adv. Lat., p. 45.

PREFACE.

Alterations of the text.

MSS. (3) to take care that my emendation should be in keeping with Ovidian usage. While adhering to these three rules, I have, I flatter myself, been fortunate enough to relieve the text of several barbarisms.

The following is a complete list of deviations from Merkel's text, which are either proposed for the first time in this edition, or are defended on original grounds:—

 i.   1. *haec* for *hanc.*
 i. 40. *vigil* for *dolo.*
 ii. 100. *negante data* for *negata meo.*
 iv. 86. *militia* for *materia.*
 vi. 54. *nauta—fui* for *causa—fuit.*[1]
 vi. 55. *iuvi* for *vidi.*
 vi. 100. *cavet* for *favet.*
 vi. 118. *dotales* for *res tales.*
 vi. 131. *hanc, hanc,* for *hanc tamen.*
 vii. 45. *quid non censeris* for *quod non verearis.*
 vii. 71. *ut tum* for *totum.*
 vii. 152. *remque,* or *iamque,* for *haneque.*
 viii. 120. *se* for *sic.*
 xii. 123. *mersisset* for *misisset.*
 xii. 149. *Cum clamore Pheres* for *cum minor e pueris.*
 xii. 170. *Et—abit* for *nec—habet.*
 xiii. 110. *muta querella latens* for *multa querella tuis.*
 xiii. 122. *refecta* for *referre.*
 xiv. 42. *plena soporis* for *vina soporis.*

---

[1] See *Corrigenda.*

The majority of these readings approach *Alterations* more closely than those hitherto adopted to *of the text.* the best MS., and nearly all are easily deducible from it, according to established critical rules: while in those instances where an arbitrary change has seemed necessary, that change has been as slight as possible, as, for instance, in the substitution *cavet* for *favet*, vi. 100. The only case in which I can be charged with audacity is in my conjecture on xii. 149. I have, however, introduced it into the text, which I should not have ventured to do had any reading previously suggested appeared even tolerable.

The above, with one or two other suggestions of less importance, constitute the sum of what I have been able to do for the text of the Heroides. I am indebted to Mr. Tyrrell for *hac* instead or *hinc*, in i. 103: and in vi. 156 will be found an an emendation of Lindemann's, which I looked upon as certain, until I saw Madvig's defence of the MS. reading, which is, however, substantially the same as regards meaning.[1]

These are all the points of difference from Merkel's text due to modern scholars. Those derived from Heinsius, and the ancient commentators, are pointed out in the notes.

As Professor Madvig in his Adversaria Graeca, *Madvig's* published in 1871, had anticipated me in a very *emendations.*

See infra, p. xxx.

Madvig's emendations important emendation on vii. 71, I looked forward with much interest to the appearance of his second volume, the Adversaria Latina, which have lately been given to the world. I find that he has hit upon the same conjecture as I had on two passages —namely, on xii. 17, and xiii. 122.[1] My sheets, however had been printed some months before the appearance of the Adversaria Latina, so it was too late to mention this fact in the notes, as I had done on vii. 71. It is, doubtless, highly satisfactory to find one's judgment confirmed by such an authority. I look upon Madvig as by far the greatest critic of the present generation, differing not only in degree of excellence, but in kind, from the numerous emendators of the Herwerden and Lucian Müller type. Madvig's emendations are, for the most part, so pointed, so thoroughly do they address themselves to the real weakness of the text, so replete are they with common sense, and withal so felicitous, that the short perusal I have been able to give to his second volume has been one of the richest intellectual treats I have enjoyed for a very long time. But though confirmation by such an authority is to be coveted, yet there is probably more disappointment than pleasure in being anticipated in a certain emendation, no matter by whom: and therefore I confess it

---

[1] In this restoration I find, from the Delphin edition, that we have both been anticipated by one Francius.

was with a feeling of relief I found that I had been left a good deal of my own. Madvig has, he says, given more pains to the Heroides than any other of the poems of Ovid. I subjoin a list of his emendations (which had not also occurred to me), so far as they were not previously known from other sources.

Madvig's emendations.

ii. 105. Madvig reads '*Atque* tibi excidimus nullam puto Phyllida nosti.' This is, of course, possible; but an emendation is not, I think, absolutely necessary here.

iii. 19. This verse Madvig would punctuate thus:—

Si progressa forem, caperer ne, nocte, timebam;

joining 'nocte' with 'progressa forem:' wrongly in my opinion.

iii. 136. For 'tuis' Madvig reads *patris*. In this he is probably right, although the occurrence of 'pater' in the previous line does not at first sight seem to favour the change.

iv. 137. I am glad to find Madvig finds a difficulty in this passage, although his reading does not appear to me to clear up anything: he reads:—

Nec labor est celare: licet: pete munus ab *ipsa* (Venere).

The latter part of my English note on this should be cancelled, as the alteration there proposed is much too extravagant. I would mark the couplet as spurious. The words 'pete munus ab illa' seem to be imported from Art. ii. 575, where they have a meaning. They have none here.

f

Madvig's emendations.

vi. 100. For 'se favet' Madvig reads *Scse avet:* suggested to me some time ago by Mr. S. Allen, for want of a better. This is a most un-Ovidian expression, and I believe my own emendation is right.

vi. 140. Admirers of Madvig will be truly sorry to see him assenting to a modification of the reading of G, which involves a false quantity. He proposes :—

> Quodlibet *ad facinus iste* dat arma dolor.

Ovid would on no account allow the last syllable of the first penthemimer to be short; and the only line of this sort now left standing by Mr. Paley in Propertius, II. viii. 8 :—

> Vinceris aut vincis : haec in amore rota est,

should be corrected—

> Vinceris aut vincis : *sic* in amore rota est.

vi. 156. The reading of the best MSS. is, I think, here defended with justice by Madvig.

> A totidem natis orba sit illa viro :

i. e. 'after having so many children, may she be bereft of her husband.' For 'a' or 'ab' = 'after,' Madvig quotes Livy, XXIV. xxii. 6; XXXI. viii. 1, 'ab hac contione,' 'ab hac oratione;' and in Ovid, Art. iii. 226; Met. xii. 578; Pont. IV. xv. 4; and other passages. The passage from the Metamorphoses best defends the idiom :—

> A sermone senis repetito munere Bacchi.

Lindemann, however, whose emendation I

have adopted in the text, is not to be defrauded of his due merit of having first seen the meaning of the passage, although he substituted *cum* for 'a,' through forgetfulness of the Ovidian use of the latter preposition, pointed out by Madvig.

Madvig's emendations.

vii. 33. Here Madvig reads:—

> Aut ego, quae coepi—neque enim dedignor—*amorem*,
> Materiam curae praebeat ille meae.

This is the best emendation yet proposed, and gives the meaning ;' but I do not believe in it. I do not think 'praebere amorem' is a likely expression : *praebere* is too material.

vii. 45. Madvig reads :—

> Non ego sum tanti—quid nos *metiris* inique ?

But *metior* is never used by Ovid, except of spacial mensuration. And Madvig's reading is objectionable on account of *nos*, which he is obliged to understand to mean Dido and Aeneas ('Inique et se et Aeneam aestimari dicit'). But there is nothing in the passage which allows us to suppose that Aeneas is blamed for forming a false estimate of himself. Madvig does not attempt to take *nos = me*, I suppose on account of the awkward change from *ego*.

I prefer my own reading if *censeris* may stand for *aestimas*, which I still believe it may; but

---

'The sentiment of these lines is well expressed in Byron's lines :—
"'Tis time this heart should be unmoved,
Since others it hath ceased to move.
Yet though I cannot be beloved,
Still let me love !"

Madvig's emendations. if it may not, then a better reading than Madvig's is—

> Non ego sum tanti—quid non *mentiris*, inique?

If I were re-writing my note, I think I should give this the preference. 'Inique' in this case would be the vocative. 'Mentiris' occurs again in the epistle, vs. 81. Another obvious suggestion, not devoid of merit, is:—

> Quid non *mercaris* inique?

vii. 85. Madvig suggests:—

> Haec mihi narraras: *di me monuere:* merentem Ure, cet.

This is quite devoid of value, in my opinion.

vii. 159. He proposes:—

> Sic superent quoscumque tua de gente *reportat*
> Mars ferus, et damni sit modus ille tui.

'hoc est: sic vivant et salvi maneant, quos ferus Mars ex excidio Troiano superstites fecit et reportat, *nec plus cladis ac damni patiare*. Mars quos in bello et proeliis non delet, reportat.'

This is an excellent conjecture, and I would adopt it. But, strange to say, Madvig does not seem to see the point of his own emendation. It clearly is: 'Let *Mars* (war) be the limit to your disasters, not *Neptune* (the sea) [with whose storms Dido had been threatening Aeneas, vs. 60 seqq.].'

vii. 172, Madvig reads,

> Nunc levis *evectam* continet alga ratem.

This emendation appears to me to rob the line of its poetry.

PREFACE. xxxix

ix. 106, he reads (P giving 'quem')   *Madvig's emendations.*

Quum tu non esses, iure vir illa fuit.

This may be true; it is probable, however, that the copyist of P wrote 'quem' instead of 'quod,' taking it for the relative agreeing with 'vir.'

ix. 141. Madvig reads '*lentifero* Eveno.' G (according to Iahn, not Merkel) has *lenfero*. Madvig objects to 'letifero' on the ground that '[Eveni] fluminis pestiferam aut omnino insalubrem naturam neque in hac re, neque alioquin quisquam commemoravit.' Of 'lentifero' he says: 'appellatio sumpta a lentium palustrium supra aquam natantium (τῶν ἐπὶ τῶν τελμάτων φακῶν) copia.' Madvig says of this somewhat audacious conjecture, 'confirmatione non eget,' but I hardly think he will find many to agree with him. The river may be very well called 'deadly,' not as a general epithet, but as fatal in this instance to Nessus.

x. 31. Here Madvig notices the difficulty which must strike every one, and reads,

Aut vidi aut *tantum quia* me vidisse putavi.

This deserts P, which gives 'putarem' and does not offer a good sense. The passage still wants emendation. Probably *ut* should be substituted for the first *aut*, as the whole line ought to form the protasis to the pentameter. Cf. xiii. 89.

xiii. 110. Madvig reads,

Cur venit *ah!* verbis multa querela tuis.

Venere. I am glad to find him objecting to 'querela a verbis venit' as I have done. He has not, however, discovered the chief corruption in the line.

xiv. 14. Madvig reads,

> Non est, quam piget esse, *pia*.

This does not sound well to my ear.
On xiv. 86,

> Scilicet ex illo Junonia permanet ira
> Quo bos ex homine est, ex bove facta dea,

he writes, Non sic omittur *tempore* (*quo*). Scribendum *quom* bos cet.

'Reliquas epistolas, quia ab Ovidio abiudicantibus plane assentior, non attingo,' says Madvig, thus giving his sanction to my concluding with Ep. xiv. As I wrote notes on these 'nequitiae sordes' for some time before I was glad to be convinced that they were not by Ovid, I may as well mention that I believe *cunctatas* should be read for 'coniunctas' (MS. *cunctas*) in xvi. [xvii.] 260: *sapiam* for 'faciam' (MS. *sautiam*) ibid. 259: and perhaps *excidit?* = 'Have you forgotten?' for 'exit et,' MS., *esset et*, in xv. [xvi.] 301.

> *Excidit?* 'Idaei mando tibi' dixit 'iturus.'

Editions. I have had before me the notes of Heinsius, Burmann, Van Lennep, Jahn, Loers, and Merkel. The first and last of these are distinguished from the rest, by the fact that they alone allowed a great pre-eminence to the Codex Puteaneus among the MSS. The editions of Jahn and Loers, which would otherwise be extremely valuable, are thus rendered comparatively useless. It is painful indeed to read a note of Loers where he gives the preference to a false reading, *propter auctoritatem librorum*, because, forsooth, there are more copies in favour of it than on the opposite side. For, if ever there was a case where votes should be weighed, not counted, it is in that of the election between contending readings. Jahn and Loers are alike also in superstitious willingness to accept as genuine whatever it placed before them with Ovid's name on it. Thus they both accept the spurious verses in the Epistle of Paris, xvii. 39–142, and of Cydippe, xxi. 13, ad fin., and enter into an elaborate defence even of the Epistle of Sappho, which Jahn has the hardihood to call *omnium praestantissima*.

Editions.

I know of no complete English edition of the Heroides; but I have occasionally made use of the useful notes in Ramsay's selections, and the Eton edition. To these I should add Ruhnken's Dictata on the Heroides, an excellent book for illustration and reference, but deficient in critical faculty, and hasty in interpretation.

I have also looked at an edition, with a metrical German translation by H. Lindemann, (Leipsic, 1867), a work of merit not generally known.

December 10, 1873.

ADDENDA ET CORRIGENDA.

v. 21, note, *for* 203 *read* xvii. 203.
vi. 54. I now perceive that the true reading of this verse is:

Milite tam forti, nauta, tuenda fui.

Everything in P is accounted for by *nauta*: the corrupt *fortuna*, the reading *vita* of a second hand, the loss of *-ta* before *tu-* in tuenda. Note that *tuenda fui* suits the context better than *vita tuenda fuit*. It marks a distinction between Hypsipyle and the other Lemnian women. *They* were able to conquer men, as they had shewn by murdering their husbands: but Hypsipyle did not share their crime. Therefore it is better to say, 'I might well have been defended by such brave soldiers,' than 'our lives might have been defended by such brave soldiers as we are.' 'Milite' and 'nauta' are intentionally contrasted, a sailor being always slightingly spoken of by the ancients, as compared with a soldier. Ovid is rather fond of the vocative of 'navita': so, six lines previously, 'navita Tiphy.'

vii. 54, note, *for* tam *read* quam.
 ,, 172 (Latin note), *for* scilleuissectam *read* scilleuisseicctam.
ix. 10 (in Latin note), *for* 6 *read* 10.
 ,, 27, note, last line but one, *for* 'nominor' *read* 'nominer.'
x. 31 (Latin note), *for* 27 *read* 31.
xii. 149 (Latin note), *for* i. 27 *read* I. ix. 27.
 ,, ,, note, *for* as *read* was.

ABBREVIATIONS.

P = Codex Puteaneus.
G = Codex Guelferbytanus I.
M = The Edition of Rudolph Merkel (1871).

HEROIDES.

EPISTOLA I.

ADDITIONAL ERRATA.

Pref. p. xxi, line 21, *for* iii. 100 *read* ii. 100.
,,   p. xli, line 12, *for* it *read* is.
Ep. ii. 143, note, *for* easy *read* early.
Ep. iii., line 33, *for* his *read* bis.
Ep. x. 186, note, *for* even *read* ever.
Ep. xiii., line 9, *for* ea *read* es.
Ep. xiii. 122, note, *for* (referre in P.) *read* (refere in P.)
Ep. xiii. 144, note, *sic* cet., transpose to end of note on line 137.

well agrees with the staid character of the περίφρων Πηνελόπεια of the Greek epic. This fidelity of Ovid to the conceptions of the authors he followed is very marked, and will be easily recognised in the delineation of Phaedra, Dido, and Medea.

1. *Haec.*] 'These lines.' 'Hanc,' with 'epistolam' omitted, is not sufficiently defended by a solitary instance said to be found in Cicero. It cannot be defended from Ovid.

2. 'Not, however, in order to draw an *answer* from you: come back *yourself.*' I read 'ut tamen,' the suggestion of Gro-

given in the text, *prints* (as Lennep remarked) with a full stop at 'Ulixe,' and a comma at 'tamen;' 'but that you may not have to write anything in reply, come back.' This punctuation might be defended by xviii. 70, 'Neve meis credas vocibus, ipse vide:' 'See for yourself, that you may not have to trust my words.'

4. *Tanti.*] 'Worth the price it cost' (especially, your long absence). 'Tanti' is a favourite expression of Ovid's. It is generally followed by 'ut' with subj., vid. ad. vii. 45, but often used absolutely, as

B

ADDENDA ET CORRIGENDA.

p. 21, note, for 203 read xvii 203.

M = The Edition of Rudolph Merkel (1871).

HEROIDES.

EPISTOLA I.

PENELOPE ULIXI.

HAEC tua Penelope lento tibi mittit, Ulixe:
Nil mihi rescribas ut tamen: ipse veni.
Troia iacet certe, Danais invisa puellis:
Vix Priamus tanti totaque Troia fuit.

1. *Hanc* libri (P nondum exstante), quod miror editoribus satisfecisse. Sic x. 3 libri recentiores dant *quam* pro *quae*.
2. *At tamen* G M, *attamen* rell. codd. Heins. post *attamen* interpunxit. *ut tamen* Gronovius, quam lectionem distinctio verborum *at tamen* in G respicere videtur. *fac tamen* coni. Allenus noster.

I. Whatever materials Ovid wanted for this Epistle he drew directly from the Odyssey, although his perusal of that poem had evidently not been very recent. This is evident from some slight discrepancies between him and Homer, noticed on vs. 15. The style of the epistle is the most severe and classical of the series, and well agrees with the staid character of the περίφρων Πηνελόπεια of the Greek epic. This fidelity of Ovid to the conceptions of the authors he followed is very marked, and will be easily recognised in the delineation of Phaedra, Dido, and Medea.

1. *Haec.*] 'These lines.' '*Hanc*,' with '*epistolam*' omitted, is not sufficiently defended by a solitary instance said to be found in Cicero. It cannot be defended from Ovid.

2. 'Not, however, in order to draw an *answer* from you: come back *yourself*.' I read '*ut tamen*,' the suggestion of Gronovius, adopted by Burmann, and connect it with the previous line. '*Attamen ipse veni*' would not be so Ovidian in form as '*ipse veni*;' cf. viii. 23, 'Nec tu ullo rates sinuosaque vela pararis Nec numeros Danai militis: ipse veni;' and Heinsius' punctuation, which makes '*attamen*' the last word of the sentence, cannot be right. Burmann, while defending the reading given in the text, *prints* (as Lennep remarked) with a full stop at '*Ulixe*,' and a comma at '*tamen*;' 'but that you may not have to write anything in reply, come back.' This punctuation might be defended by xviii. 70, 'Neve meis credas vocibus, ipse vide:' 'See for yourself, that you may not have to trust my words.'

4. *Tanti.*] 'Worth the price it cost' (especially, your long absence). '*Tanti*' is a favourite expression of Ovid's. It is generally followed by '*ut*' with subj., vid. ad. vii. 45, but often used absolutely, as

O utinam tum, cum Lacedaemona classe petebat, 5
 Obrutus insanis esset adulter aquis!
Non ego deserto iacuissem frigida lecto,
 Non quererer tardos ire relicta dies:
Nec mihi quaerenti spatiosam fallere noctem
 Lassasset viduas pendula tela manus. 10
Quando ego non timui graviora pericula veris?
 Res est sollicit plena timoris amor.
In te fingebam violentos Troas ituros:
 Nomine in Hectoreo pallida semper eram.
Sive quis Antilochum narrabat ab Hectore victum, 15
 Antilochus nostri causa timoris erat:
Sive Menoetiaden falsis cecidisse sub armis,
 Flebam successu posse carere dolos.
Sanguine Tlepolemus Lyciam tepefecerat hastam;
 Tlepolemi leto cura novata mea est. 20
Denique, quisquis erat castris ingulatus Achivis,
 Frigidius glacie pectus amantis erat.

8. *Non* G *nec* vulg.
10. *Lassasset* G *lassaret* vulg.
15. Propter Homer. Od. v. 187 correxerunt *Amphimachum, Archilochum* vel *Anchialum* pro *Antilochum*.

here. Cf. Met. ii. 424: 'hoc certe coniunx furtum mea nesciet, inquit: Aut si rescierit: sunt O, sunt iurgia tanti.'
6. *Insanis.*] 'Raging.' Cf. xviii. 28. A good example of Bentley's worst style of emendation is furnished by this line. He proposed 'incanis,' because the waters that might have swallowed up Paris ought to be called 'sanae,' rather than 'insanae.'
8. *Ire dies.*] Hor. Od. IV. v. 7, 'Populo gratior it dies.' Plaut. Ps. I. iii. 10, 'It dies: ego mihi cesso.'
9. *Spatiosam.*] 'Spatiosa vetustas,' Met. xv. 623, 's. aevum,' Met. viii. 529, 'bellum,' Met. viii. 206. Long wearisome duration is here expressed by this epithet. It is rather a favourite of Ovid's, and appears to have been made fashionable by him, as we seldom meet with it before his time, and very frequently afterwards.
15. Antilochus, son of Nestor, was slain by Memnon, not by Hector. Od. iv. 157. Ovid wanders from the Homeric story in other points. He seems to say Penelope sent Telemachus to Pylos, vss. 37, 63; according to Homer he went without her knowledge. The epithet 'dirus' is applied, vs. 91, to Medon, who appears in the Odyssey as a faithful ally of Penelope, and there are other minor discrepancies. Whether these are intentional variations or not, it is useless to inquire: it is absurd to make them the ground of destructive criticism, and on their account, as Lehrs does, to reject some, and remodel the rest of the Epistle.
11. *In.*] 'At the mention of.'
17. 'Or if I heard Patroclus was slain wearing the arms of another, I wept to think stratagem could fail.' Because stratagem, she knew, was her husband's forte.
19. Tlepolemus, son of Hercules and Astyoche, leader of the Rhodians, was slain by Sarpedon, King of Lycia, son of Jove. Il. v. 626, sqq.

Sed bene consuluit casto deus aequus amori :
  Versa est in cineres sospite Troia viro.
Argolici rediere duces: altaria fumant :   25
  Ponitur ad patrios barbara praeda deos.
Grata ferunt nymphae pro salvis dona maritis :
  Illi victa suis Troica fata canunt.
Mirantur iustique senes trepidaeque puellae :
  Narrantis coniux pendet ab ore viri.   30
Atque aliquis posita monstrat fera praelia mensa,
  Pingit et exiguo Pergama tota mero.
'Hac ibat Simois, haec est Sigeïa tellus,
  Hic steterat Priami regia celsa senis :
Illic Aeacides, illic tendebat Ulixes :   35
  Hic lacer admissos terruit Hector equos.'

29. Pro *iusti* mire coni. Riesius *lassi*.
33. *Hac est* G *hic* al. *hos* al. *haec* al. quod reposui Heins. et Werferum secutus.
35. *Illuc* libri quidam voce *tendebat* parum intellecta.
36. *Alacer missos* G M libri plurimi. Veram scripturam olim restituit Egnatius.

———

27. *Nymphae.*] 'Aliquoties apud nostrum dicuntur heroici temporis puellae eaeque nobiliores, cum nuptae tum innuptae. Sic ix. 50. ' Nec referam partus, Ormeni nympha, tuas.' Ibid. 103. ' Se quoque nympha tuis ornavit Iardanis armis.' xvi. 126. ' Applicor in terras, Oebali nympha, tuas.' Lennep. Here, as Heinsius observed, there may be an imitation of the Homeric use of νύμφη for 'a youthful bride.' Cf. Il. i. 130, etc. The student should be warned that the use of 'nympha,' merely for any young girl, common in modern verse-books, is not classical.

28. ' They tell how the destinies of Troy were conquered by their own.' There is no need, as some do, to understand ' fata Troica' as referring to the so-called Fates of Troy, the life of Troïlus, the safety of the Palladium, the horses of Rhesus : and ' fata Graeca' to the arrows Hercules, etc. Vid. Serv. ad Virg. A. i. 14, iii. 402.

29. *Iusti.*] 'Severe,' 'reverend,' 'grave.'
32. Cf. Tibullus, i. x. 31. ' Ut mihi potanti possit sua dicere facta Miles et in mensa pingere castra mero.' Cf. also xvii. 88; Amor. I. iv. 20.

33. I do not think ' hac est' can well mean 'hac decurrit,' as Heusinger explains it. ' It ' I think would be required for ' est,' or ' hic' for ' hac.' ' Hac,' 'this way,' requires a verb of motion. In support of ' haec' Werfer adduced Art. Amat. ii. 133. ' Haec, inquit, Troia est : (muros in litore fecit): Hic tibi sit Simois : haec mea castra puta.'

35. *Tendebat.*] ' Pitched his tent.' ' Illuc,' the reading of some MSS., arose from the transcriber understanding ' tendebat' as meaning ' used to go.' Cf. Virg. Aen. ii. 29, ' hic saevus tendebat Achilles.'

36. ' Here mangled Hector terrified the runaway steeds' (when tied to the chariot of Achilles). Cf. El. in Mort. Drus. vs. 819 : ' Hoc fuit Andromache, cum vir religatus ad axem Terruit admissos sanguinolentus equos.'—' Admissus,' ' Let go at full speed,' is a favourite expression of Ovid. It is applied to horses frequently, e. g. Am. III. ii. 78 ; Art. ii. 434 : its opposite in this application is

Omnia namque tuo senior, te quaerere misso,
  Rettulerat gnato Nestor, at ille mihi.
Rettulit et ferro Rhesumque Dolonaque caesos,
  Utque sit hic somno proditus, ille vigil.   40
Ausus es, o nimium nimiumque oblite tuorum,
  Thracia nocturno tangere castra dolo,
Totque simul mactare viros, adiutus ab uno !
  At bene cautus eras et memor ante mei.
Usque metu micuere sinus, dum victor amicum   45
  Dictus es Ismariis isse per agmen equis.

40. *Ille dolo* G M libri omnes. *dolo* qui eiecerunt recte, me iudice, fecerunt : sed latuit versui fraudi fuisse glossema *Dolon* ad v. *ille* appositum. Varie correxerunt docti : *vigil* ab Auctore Elect. Eton. olim propositum Burmanno improbatum mihi verum videtur. *lucro* coni. Tyrrellus noster.
42. *Frangere* pro *tangere* libri quatuor.

'adductus,' 'tight-held,' vid. F. vi. 586. Also to rivers: ii. 114: 'Qua sacer admissas exigit Hebrus aquas.'—'Lacer': mangled by the weapons of the Greeks. Cf. Il. xxii. 371, Οὐδ᾽ ἄρα οἵ τις ἀνουτητί γε παρίστη. How Merkel and Riese can defend the reading 'alacer missos' I cannot imagine.

37. *Te quaerere misso.*] This and similar constructions are commonly called Graecisms, the expression of a purpose by the infinitive being more common in Greek than in Latin. 'Mitto' with an infinitive, however, is not uncommon in Latin poetry.

39. Rhesus, the Thracian ally of the Trojans, who was slain at night by Ulysses and Diomede, and his horses carried off before they fed on Trojan pastures. Dolon, the Trojan spy slain by the same. Il. x.

40. *Vigil.*] 'While acting the spy.' 'Dolo' is plainly wrong. It has been objected to on account of 'dolo' occurring again immediately, vs. 42. But it has not been noticed that 'dolo' in vs. 40 is perhaps the remains of a gloss on 'ille,' viz., *Dolon*, which may have crept into the text. This would be mistaken for 'dolo,' and the real reading would be lost. An explanatory gloss on 'illo' was likely to be written in the margin, as the ordinary rule is here violated, according to which 'ille' should refer to Rhesus, 'hic' to Dolon. If this theory be correct, the true reading may have been a word quite unlike 'dolo,' and therefore difficult to restore with certainty. Mr. Tyrrell suggested to me 'lucro,' 'the desire of gain,' as Ovid, Met. xiii. 253, brings forward the fact mentioned by Homer, that Dolon was induced by Hector to undertake his expedition by the promise of the possession of the horses of Achilles. This is a good suggestion: but on the whole I prefer 'vigil,' the conjecture of an Eton editor, which I have introduced into the text. It gives a better antithesis : Rhesus was betrayed by sleep, Dolon by being 'too wide awake.' There was no ablative by which this idea could be expressed, and therefore the nominative 'vigil' is employed, rather awkwardly, it is true, but this is also the case in the passage in Art. ii. 135, 136, by which this correction may be defended. Ulysses narrating his adventures to Calypso says, 'Campus erat' (campumque facit) ' quem caede Dolonis Sparsimus Haemonios dum *vigil* optat equos.' The participial use of 'vigil' is exactly the same in both passages.

41. *Tangere.*] 'Penetrate to.' Cf. Met. iv. 778, ' Gorgoneas tetigisse domos.'

45. ' My bosom throbbed with fear until I heard.' Cf. Fast. iii. 36, 'Terreor admonitu : corda dolore micant.' This is the primary meaning of ' mico.' Cf. Cic. N. D. ii. 9, ' Venae et arteriae micare non desinunt quasi igneo quodam motu.'

46. *Ismariis.*] i.e. the horses of Rhesus. Ismarus was a mountain and city of

Sed mihi quid prodest vestris disiecta lacertis
  Ilios, et, murus quod fuit, esse solum,
Si maneo qualis Troia durante manebam,
  Virque mihi dempto fine carendus abest? 50
Diruta sunt aliis, uni mihi Pergama restant,
  Incola captivo quae bove victor arat.
Iam seges est, ubi Troia fuit, resecandaque falce
  Luxuriat Phrygio sanguine pinguis humus:
Semisepulta virum curvis feriuntur aratris 55
  Ossa: ruinosas occulit herba domos.
Victor abes, nec scire mihi, quae causa morandi,
  Aut in quo lateas ferreus orbe, licet.
Quisquis ad haec vertit peregrinam litora puppim,
  Ille mihi de te multa rogatus abit: 60
Quamque tibi reddat, si te modo viderit usquam,
  Traditur huic digitis charta notata meis.
Nos Pylon, antiqui Neleïa Nestoris arva,
  Misimus: incerta est fama remissa Pylo.
Misimus et Sparten: Sparte quoque nescia veri. 65
  Quas habitas terras, aut ubi lentus abes?
Utilius starent etiam nunc moenia Phoebi.
  —Irascor votis heu levis ipsa meis!—

48. *Ilios* G, *Ilion* al., *esse solum* G, *ante* libri plurimi. *quo fuit* codd. nonnulli, *qui fuit* al.
62. *Norata* M, operarum vitio ut videtur. *Notare* enim pro *scribere* sexcenties usurpat noster: *novare* hoc sensu nusquam occurrit.
66. Unus liber *habites*: unus *lentus agas.*

Thrace. The mountain is mentioned by Homer as famous for its vines, Od. ix. 198.
  52. *Incola.*] 'Settled on the spot.' Ovid was thinking of the old Roman colonisation of conquered towns.
  53. Cf. Art. i., 960, 'Mens erit apta capi tunc cum, laetissima rerum, Ut seges in pingui luxuriabit humo.' 'Luxuriare' is often used of rank vegetation. Vss. 53 and 54 together make up one idea: if they did not, I should have put a stop at 'falce,' because the following clauses down to 'victor abes,' in vs. 57, are not connected by a copula.
  67. *Moenia Phoebi.*] The walls of Troy said to have been built for Laomedon by Apollo and Neptune. The stones were said to have been moved into their places by Apollo's lyre. Cf. xvi. 180, 'Moenia Phoebeae structa canore lyrae.'
  68. This line is parenthetical, ''Twere better that the walls of Troy were still standing (I am angry at uttering such a prayer, fickle one that I am!)' Lennep and others wrongly take 'votis' as referring to former prayers supposed to have been offered up by her during the siege of Troy that it might fall, which prayers they understand her to say she now repents of.

Scirem ubi pugnares, et tantum bella timerem,
 Et mea cum multis iuncta querella foret. 70
Quid timeam, ignoro: timeo tamen omnia demens,
 Et patet in curas area lata meas.
Quaecumque aequor habet, quaecumque pericula tellus,
 Tam longae causas suspicor esse morae.
Haec ego dum stulte meditor, quae vestra libido est, 75
 Esse peregrino captus amore potes.
Forsitan et narres, quam sit tibi rustica coniux,
 Quae tantum lanas non sinat esse rudes.
Fallar, et hoc crimen tenues vanescat in auras,
 Neve, revertendi liber, abesse velis! 80
Me pater Icarius viduo discedere lecto
 Cogit, et immensas increpat usque moras.
Increpet usque licet, tua sum, tua dicar oportet:
 Penelope coniux semper Ulixis ero.
Ille tamen pietate mea precibusque pudicis 85
 Frangitur, et vires temperat ipse suas.
Dulichii Samiique et quos tulit alta Zacynthos,

86. Heins. coni: *temperat ira suas.* Burm: *inde suas.* Pessime uterque.

---

75. *Vestra.*] 'Such is the lust of *you men.*' xvi. 40, 'Verbaque dicuntur vestra carere fide.' See note on iii. 12.

77. *Rustica.*] 'Homely' seems to be the best word to translate 'rustica,' applied to women. So Herrick: 'you set too high a rate upon A shepherdess so homely.' The word is often used in this contemptuous sense. In iv. 102, 'Si Venerem tollas rustica silva tua est,' its use is remarkable; xvi. 220, 'Rusticus iste,' 'That *lout.*' Cf. ix. 162.

80. *Revertendi liber.*] 'Free to return.' A very rare construction, not to be confounded with such Graecisms as 'liber, laborum,' 'operum solutus,' &c. It may perhaps be explained in accordance with the rule whereby 'many adjectives were used with the genitive to express a certain reference to a thing which is otherwise expressed by the ablative, or by a preposition.' Madvig, § 200, g. So 'certus eundi,' 'felices operum,' 'fessi rerum,' in Virgil. Thus 'revertendi liber' would be 'free in the matter of returning.' But, I think, the genitive rather depends on the idea of power, or possession, implied in 'liber,' as if it were equivalent to 'compos,' 'potitus.' In Stat. Silv. IV. iii. 24, we have, according to the best reading, 'liberior campi,' of a building possessing a wider extent of ground, to which passage the second explanation seems tho more applicable. The vulgarism 'free of' in such expressions as ' free of the cellar,' is not unlike 'revertendi liber.'

86. *Vires temperat ipse suas.*] 'Refrains from using his full authority.' Ovid is fond of such collocations as 'ipse suas.' Vid. supra, 68, ii. 20, and passim.

87. Od. xvi. v. 123, Δουλιχίῳ τε Σάμῳ τε καὶ ὑλήεντι Ζακύνθῳ where Zacynthus is irregularly masculine, as the old grammarians remarked.

Turba ruunt in mo luxuriosa proci:
Inque tua regnant, nullis prohibentibus, aula:
Viscera nostra, tuae dilacerantur opes. 90
Quid tibi Pisandrum Polybumque Medontaque dirum,
Eurymachique avidas Antinoique manus,
Atque alios referam, quos omnes turpiter absens
Ipse tuo partis sanguine rebus alis?
Irus egens pecorisque Melanthius actor edendi 95
Ultimus accedunt in tua damna pudor.
Tres sumus imbelles numero, sine viribus uxor,
Laërtesque senex, Telemachusque puer.
Ille per insidias paene est mihi nuper ademptus,
Dum parat invitis omnibus ire Pylon. 100
Di, precor, hoc iubeant, ut euntibus ordine fatis
Ille meos oculos comprimat, ille tuos.
Hae faciunt custosque boum longaevaque nutrix,
Tertius immundae cura fidelis harae.
Sed neque Laërtes, ut qui sit inutilis armis, 105
Hostibus in mediis regna tenere potest.
Telemacho veniet, vivat modo, fortior aetas:

95. *Actor* G, *auctor* codd. plurimi et edd. ante Heins. qui correxit.
103. *Hae faciunt* G *hoc faciunt* vulg. Lennep. coni: *huc faciunt* (has partes sequuntur), Merkel. *hinc* eodem sensu, qui sensus procul dubio verus est. *Hae* tamen quod Tyrrelli mei e coniectura scripsi rectius est quam aut *huc* aut *hinc*.

---

90. 'My heart is rent, your wealth is squandered.' An evident zeugma.—'Dilacerantur:' Cf. κτήματα δαρδάπτουσιν, Od. xvi. 315. The line is often wrongly and most unpoetically rendered, 'Your possessions which are my means of support' (viscera). Ruhnken renders 'viscera' by 'patrimonium,' which it certainly does not mean here.
95. 'The beggar Irus, and Melanthius driver of the herd destined to be eaten.' Melanthius was goat-herd to Ulysses' flocks. The old reading 'auctor' was first corrected by Heinsius, who drily remarks that he never read of any proposition being made to the suitors by Melanthius to devour the flocks.

102. *Hae faciunt.*] 'On our side are the ox-herd and the nurse and the swine-herd, (Philoetius, Euryclea, and Eumaeus). The old reading was 'hoc faciunt,' which was interpreted 'hoc precantur:' 'offer up the same prayer,' referring to the preceding lines. Lennep was the first to see the true meaning: he defended his conjecture 'huc faciunt' from Cicero ad Att. vii. 3, 5. But the true reading there is 'illac,' not 'illuc,' as he quoted it; and from this very passage Professor Tyrrell suggested 'hac' to me. The passage is 'vide . . . omnes damnatione ignominiaque affectos illac facere.' Merkel reads 'hinc' in the same sense: but I have no doubt 'hae' is the true reading.

Nunc erat auxiliis illa tuenda patris.
Nec mihi sunt vires inimicos pellere tectis.
Tu citius venias, portus et ara tuis.   110
Est tibi, sitque, precor, natus, qui mollibus annis
In patrias artes erudiendus erat.
Respice Laërten: ut iam sua lumina condas,
Extremum fati sustinet ille diem.
Certo ego, quae fueram te discedente puella,   115
Protinus ut venias, facta videbor anus.

EPISTOLA II.

PHYLLIS DEMOPHOONTI.

Hospita, Demophoon, tua te Rhodopeïa Phyllis
Ultra promissum tempus abesse queror.

---

110. *Portus et aura* G M, *ara* codd. nonnulli : et ita corr. Heins.

---

108. *Erat.*] The imperfect expresses that what ought to have been has not been done. Cf. 'Tempus erat,' Hor. Od. i. 37, 4. Propert. ii. 8, 16. It resembles the use of the indicative mood in Greek after ἵνα, ὅπως, &c.
110. 'Portus' and 'ara' are joined together more than once by Ovid. 'Portus' and 'aura' are not. Pont II. viii. 68, 'Vos critis nostrae portus et ara fugae.' Cf. Trist. IV. v. 2, 5; Cic. Verr. v. 48.
114. 'Laërtes prolongs his latest hours that his eyes may be closed by you.' For this use of 'sustinet,' Burmann quotes Met. x. 188, 'Nunc animam admotis fugientem sustinet herbis.' Senec. Contr. i. 12, 'Deficientis adolescentis spiritus in adventum meum sustinebatur.' Quint. Decl. xii. 2, 'Non ut invisam animam sustineremus.' Others translate: 'Laërtes puts off the day of his death.' In support of this meaning of 'sustinet' Ruhnken quotes El. in Mort. Drus. 372, 'Illa rapit iuvenes, sustinet illa senes.' Liv. ii. 65, 'Plebem sustinendo rem ab seditionibus continere.'

The other translation is, however, strongly supported by iii. 142, 'Sustinet hoc animi spes tamen una tui.'
116. 'Even supposing you return immediately.' This is a very common use of 'ut' with the present subjunctive in Ovid. In these Epistles the student will often meet it. See note on vii. 15.

II.—Demophoon, son of Theseus, on his way home from Troy was received by Phyllis, Queen of Thrace, daughter of Sithon. After remaining with her some time, he sailed to Athens on the plea of settling his affairs, with a promise to return and marry her as soon as possible. As he did not return, Phyllis put an end to her life. I consider this to be one of the finest of the Epistles of Ovid. Although revealing no great depth of passion, there is, especially in the latter part from vs. 63, a loftiness of diction, and correctness of sentiment, which one cannot help wishing Ovid had more frequently attained.

EP. II. PHYLLIS DEMOPHOONTI.

Cornua cum lunae pleno semel orbe coissent,
 Litoribus nostris anchora pacta tua est.
Luna quater latuit, toto quater orbe recrevit,
 Nec vehit Actaeas Sithonis unda rates.
Tempora si numeres bene quae numeramus amantes,
 Non venit ante suam nostra querella diem.
Spes quoque lenta fuit. Tarde, quae credita laedunt,
 Credimus. Invito nunc et amore noces.
Saepe fui mendax pro te mihi, saepe putavi
 Alba procellosos vela referre notos.
Thesea devovi, quia te dimittere nollet :
 Nec tenuit cursus forsitan ille tuos.
Interdum timui, ne, dum vada tendis ad Hebri,
 Mersa foret cana naufraga puppis aqua.

3. *Pleno quater* Burm. e codd. duobus. Sed sequentia non confirmant, ut ait, *quater :* valde quidem repugnant 9 et sqq.
7. *Quae nos numeramus* G, *bene quae* libri plurimi.
10. Ita G *invita nunc et amante nocent* codd. plurimi. *invito nunc es amore nocens* M. *invita nunc et amante noces* Heusinger. *invita nunc et amante iacet* nuper edidit Lindemann.
12. *Notavi* G M *putavi* vulg.
14. Ab hoc v. incipit P.

---

3. 'Pleno orbe,' 'so as to fill out her orb.' Ablative of the manner. It is exactly like Lucr. ii. 98, 'intervallis magnis confulta resultant;' 'rebound, leaving great spaces between.' Burmann prefers 'quater' to 'semel,' first, because one month was too short a time to allow Demophoon to go to Athens to arrange his affairs and return; secondly, because it would be more true to nature to represent Phyllis as exacting the fulfilment of her lover's promise at the precise time agreed on than as waiting for three mouths afterwards before she wrote. But vss. 9-22 support the reading of the best MS.
4. *Pacta est.*] 'Was due.' 'Pacta' from 'pango.' Cf. xvi. 36, 'Te peto quam lecto pepigit Venus aurea nostro.' Forcellini, as Lennep has noticed, makes the curious mistake of supposing 'pacta' here to come from 'pango' in its other sense of 'fastening;' he quotes this passage on 'pactus,' and renders it 'impactus, infixus.'

6. *Actaeas.*] 'Attic,' 'Athenian.' Cf. xviii. 42, 'Actaei ignes;' Virg. Georg. iv. 463, 'Actias Orithyia.' 'Ακτη, 'coast-land,' the ancient name of Attica. 'Sithonis,' 'Thracian.' Sithonia was the central of the three peninsulas of Chalcidice, said to be called from Sithon, father of Phyllis.
9, 10. 'My hopes were long enduring : we are slow to believe what pains us on believing : but now you wound me even in spite of my love' (which is slow to believe, &c.). I cannot see what reason Merkel had for departing from G here.
11. I prefer 'putavi' to 'notavi,' because 'noto' with inf. is rare, and 'notos' in vs. 12 may easily have caused the corruption : besides, it is untrue that she marked Demophoon's sails returning.
13. *Devovi.*] This refers to the magical arts resorted to in ancient times by women when in love. Cf. vi. 91, 'Devovet absentes,' etc.

Saepe deos supplex, ut tu, scelerate, valeres,
  Sum prece turicremis devenerata focis.
Saepe, videns ventos caelo pelagoque faventes,
  Ipsa mihi dixi, 'si valet ille, venit.'   20
Denique fidus amor quidquid properantibus obstat
  Finxit, et ad causas ingeniosa fui.
At tu lentus abes, nec te iurata reducunt
  Numina, nec nostro motus amore redis.
Demophoon, ventis et verba et vela dedisti: 25
  Vela queror reditu, verba carere fide.
Dic mihi, quid feci, nisi non sapienter amavi?
  Crimine te potui demeruisse meo.
Unum in me scelus est, quod te, scelerate, recepi.
  Sed scelus hoc meriti pondus et instar habet.   30
Iura, fides ubi nunc, commissaque dextera dextrae,
  Quique erat in falso plurimus ore deus?
Promissus socios ubi nunc Hymenaeus in annos,
  Qui mihi coniugii sponsor et obses erat?
Per mare, quod totum ventis agitatur et undis,   35
  Per quod saepe ieras, per quod iturus eras,
Perque tuum mihi iurasti, (nisi fictus et ille est),
  Concita qui ventis aequora mulcet, avum,
Per Venerem nimiumque mihi facientia tela,

37. *Fictus* P G *falsus* codd. multi eodem sensu.

---

19. *Caelo pelagoque faventes.*] If 'caelo,' 'pelago' are datives, as I think they are, the meaning of the winds 'favouring both sky and sea,' is that they do not overcast the sky with clouds, nor roughen the sea with tempests. If they are ablatives, 'caelo' might refer to the direction of the winds, the point of the compass, as we say, 'pelago' to the gentleness of their blowing.

23. *Iurata numina.*] 'The deities by whom you swore.' Cf. Met. ii. 46, 'Dis iuranda palus.' Sen. Agam. 'Iurata superis unda.' This passive use of 'iuratus' is rather rare, though 'iurare,' to swear by, without ' per,' is common. Cf. xvi. 319; xxi. 2.

30. 'This fault has the weight and proportions of a virtue.' 'Instar' is the noun, as in xvi. 366, 'Unus is innumeri militis instar habet;' Virg. Aen. vi. 365, 'Quantum instar in ipso est?'

31. *Commissaque d. d.*] As the pledge of fidelity.

32. 'Where is now that God (i. e. Love) who was then always on your tongue?' 'Plurimus:' Cf. Fast. ii. 72, 'Arcadiis plurimus ille iugis' (of Pan); iv. 167, 'Venerem, quae plurima mecum est.'

33. *Socios annos.*] 'Our wedded years.' 'Socius' and 'socialis' frequently have this meaning. Cf. v. 126; iv. 62; xii. 139.

38. *Avum.*] 'Poseidon, father of Theseus·

EP. II. PHYLLIS DEMOPHOONTI. 11

Altera tela arcus, altera tela faces, 40
Iunonemque, toris quae praesidet alma maritis,
Et per taediferae mystica sacra deae.
Si de tot laesis sua numina quisque deorum
Vindicet, in poenas non satis unus eris.
At laceras etiam puppes furiosa refeci, 45
Ut, qua desererer, firma carina foret:
Remigiumque dedi, quo me fugiturus abires.
Heu, patior telis vulnera facta meis!
Credidimus blandis, quorum tibi copia, verbis:
Credidimus generi nominibusque tuis: 50
Credidimus lacrimis: an et hae simulare docentur?
Hae quoque habent artes, quaque iubentur, eunt?
Dis quoque credidimus. Quo iam tot pignora nobis?

45. *At* P. *Ha* (*ah*) G.
47. *Quod me f. haberes* G *quo me f. haberes* P. Hoc nostram respicere videtur.
50. *Nominibusque tuis* P G M. Libenter Heinsio assentior qui praeeuntibus Hubertino et Gronovio mouuit *nominibus* vel invitis libris restituendum, ne bis idem diceretur.

---

39. 'By Venus, and those weapons which tell too well on me.' Ruhnken rightly explains 'facientia:' '*nimis mihi convenientia*, ut ostendat, se proclivem esse ad amorem.' This use of 'facio,' meaning 'to suit,' or as we say, to 'do for,' is found with the dative, cf. Propert. III. i. 20, 'Non faciet capiti dura corona meo.' But far more frequently with 'ad' with the accusative. Cf. vi. 428, 'Medeae faciunt ad scelus omne manus,' xvi. 189, 'Ad talem formam non facit iste locus.' It is also occasionally used absolutely: so Ovid, complaining in his exile, says Trist., 'Nec coelum nec aquae faciunt nec terra nec imber:' 'do not agree with me.' It is thus used especially in medicine. Cf. Colum. viii. 17, 'Facit etiam ex pomis viridibus adaperta ficus:' 'is serviceable.'

41. *Maritis.*] Used here as an adj., as in xii. 87; Prop. iii. 19, 16.

42. Demophoon, as an Athenian, would swear by the Eleusinian mysteries. Ceres is called 'taedifera,' ἐᾳδοῦχος, from the legend of her looking for Proserpine with lighted torches, whence the torchlight procession at Eleusis.

48. This sentiment is well known: under the simile of the eagle struck by a shaft winged with its own feather, it occurs in the poems of Waller, Byron, and perhaps others, the fountain whence it originally came being Aeschylus, Myrmidones, Frag. 123, ταῦτ' οὐχ ὑπ' ἄλλων ἀλλὰ τοῖς αὑτῶν πτέροις.

50. 'Genus' and 'nomen' are so commonly joined together, as sufficiently to support the change from 'numinibus' to 'nominibus,' did not the repetition of 'dis' in 53 make it certain. xvii. 51, 'Quod genus et proavos et regia nomina iactas.' Cf. Mart. v. xvii. 1; Hor. Od. i. xiv. 13, 'Iactes et genus et nomen inutile.' Besides, as Loers well remarks, the poet here uses the word 'credidimus' each time a new idea is introduced, and it would, therefore, be wanted before 'numinibus.' If 'numinibus' is retained it must refer, as Jahn says, to the ancestral gods of Demophoon's race: as distinguished from the gods by whom he swore.

Parte satis potui qualibet inde capi.
Nec moveor, quod te iuvi portuque locoque. 55
Debuit haec meriti summa fuisse mei.
Turpiter hospitium lecto cumulasse iugali
Poenitet, et lateri couseruisse latus.
Quae fuit ante illam, mallem suprema fuisset
Nox mihi, dum potui Phyllis honesta mori. 60
Speravi melius, quia me meruisse putavi.
Quaecumque ex merito spes venit, aequa venit.
Fallere credentem non est operosa puellam
Gloria: simplicitas digna favore fuit.
Sum decepta tuis et amans et femina verbis. 65
Di faciant, laudis summa sit ista tuae.
Inter et Aegidas media statuaris in urbe:
Magnificus titulis stet pater ante suis:
Cum fuerit Sciron lectus torvusque Procrustes

61. *Temeruisse* P *me meruisse* G *te meruisse* vulg. Casaubon corr. *demeruisse* et ita edidit M.

---

61. 'I hoped for better treatment, because I thought I had deserved it: that hope is a reasonable one, which is founded on desert.' 'Demeruisse,' the reading of Merkel, cannot be the true one. For 'demereo' in classical Latinity only means to 'win over by good treatment,' 'to oblige a person,' and always takes an accusative of the person. Thus in vs. 28, supra, 'Crimine te potui demeruisse meo,' 'I might have gained your affections by my very crime.' If Merkel takes 'demeruisse' in its real sense, an accusative is wanting, and 'ex merito' in vs. 62 loses its force. Among other instances of the meaning of 'demereo' are the following: Art. Am. ii. 252, 'nec tibi sit servos demeruisse pudor.' El. in Mort. Drus. 133, 'culta Quos ego non potui demeruisse deos.' It is used more frequently in the deponent form: cf. Tac. Ann. xv. 21, where it is used absolutely: 'plura saepe peccantur dum demeremur quam dum offendimus:' 'when seeking to oblige.' The reading 'te meruisse' is refuted by vs. 62, which shows Phyllis was speaking of her own deserts.

66. 'God grant that that may be the sum total of your fame.'

67. *Statuaris.*] 'May your statue be set up.' Cf. the Greek χαλκοῦν, χρυσοῦν (τινα) ἱστάναι. Aegidae, the posterity of Aegeus, father of Theseus, according to one account.

69. 'When men shall read Sciron's name.' Sciron was a robber, who dwelt in the cliffs of Megara, called after him the Scironian rocks. He used to compel passers by to wash his feet, and kick them into the sea while so employed. He was himself thrown down by Theseus. Procrustes' bed is well known. See Class. Dict. Sinis used to bind men to the summits of two pine trees, which he used to bend down for the purpose (hence called Πιτυοκάμπτης), and then let them spring back. Theseus put him to death by the same method. 'Bimembres,' the Centaurs, defeated by Theseus, at the marriage of Pirithous.

EP. II. PHYLLIS DEMOPHOONTI.

Et Sinis, et tauri mixtaque forma viri, 70
Et domitae bello Thebae, fusique bimembres
  Et pulsata nigri regia caeca dei,
Hoc tua post illos titulo signetur imago,
  ' Hic est, cuius amans hospita capta dolo est.'
De tanta rerum turba factisque parentis 75
  Sedit in ingenio Cressa relicta tuo.
Quod solum excusat, solum miraris in illo.
  Haeredem patriae, perfide, fraudis agis.
Illa, (nec invideo), fruitur meliore marito,
  Inque capistratis tigribus alta sedet: 80
At mea despecti fugiunt conuubia Thraces,
  Quod ferar externum praeposuisse meis.
Atque aliquis 'Iam nunc doctas eat' inquit ' Athenas:
  Armiferam Thracen qui regat, alter erit.
Exitus acta probat.' Careat successibus, opto, 85
  Quisquis ab eventu facta notanda putat.
Ad si nostra tuo spumescant aequora remo,
  Iam mihi, iam dicar consuluisse meis.
Sed neque consului, nec te mea regia tanget,
  Fessaque Bistonia membra lavabis aqua. 90

73. *Post illos* P G *post illum* Heins.
84. *Armiferam* P, *armigeram* G M.
89. *Tanget* P G *tangit* codd. plurimi.
90. Coni. Micyllus *Fessare*.

72. 'And the palace of the gloomy God, at whose door he knocked.' When he went down to Hades to aid Pirithous to carry off Proserpine.

74. Burmann takes 'cuius' with 'hospita:' Loers with 'dolo.' I think it refers equally to both.

75. 'Out of such a number of exploits of Theseus, the only thing which made an impression on you was his desertion of Ariadne.'

77. *Quod solum excusat.*] 'The only thing he has to be ashamed of is the only thing you admire in him.' Ruhnken well compares Stat. Silv. iv. 6, 70, 'Magnoque ex agmine laudum Fertur Thebanos tantum excusasse triumphos.' The ordinary sense of 'excuso,' ' to urge as an excuse,' as ' excusare valetudinem,' is widely different.

78. ' You act the heir to your father's treachery,' i. e. you inherit his treachery, without inheriting his virtues.

80. 'And sits high on a car drawn by harnessed tigers,' i. e. the car of Bacchus.

83. *Doctas Athenas.*] Athens is often called 'doctae': Cf. Prop. i. vi. 13 ; iii. 20, 1.

85. 'The result pronounces judgment on her conduct.' These are supposed to be the words of the Thracians, to which Phyllis replies, ' Careat successibus,' &c.

89. *Nec te mea regia tangit.*] ' Nor will you ever trouble yourself about my palace.' Cf. v. 81, 'Non ego miror opes nec me tua regia tangit.' viii. ii. 'Nec nova Carthago, nec te crescentia tangunt Moenia.' A very common use of 'tango' in Ovid.

90. 'Fessavo' was proposed by Micyllus for ' fessaque.' But negative sentences

Illa meis oculis species abeuntis inhaeret,
  Cum premeret portus classis itura meos.
Ausus es amplecti, colloquo infusus amantis
  Oscula per longas iungere pressa moras,
Cumque tuis lacrimis lacrimas confundere nostras, 95
  Quodque foret velis aura secunda, queri,
Et mihi discedens suprema dicere voce
  ' Phylli, face expectes Demophoonta tuum.'
Expectem, qui me numquam visurus abisti?
Expectem pelago vela negante data? 100
Et tamen expecto. Redens modo serus amanti,
  Ut tua sit solo tempore lapsa fides.
Quid precor infelix? te iam tenet altera coniux
  Forsitan et, nobis qui male favit, amor:
Utque tibi excidimus, nullam, puto, Phyllida nosti: 105
  Ei mihi, si, quae sim Phyllis et unde, rogas.

98. *Face* P *fae* G.
100. *Negateta* P, *negata meo* M G, libri reliqui. Optimi codicis et iam mihi paene carissimi auxilio Ovidio venustatem suam diu deperditam reddidi. *Negate* pro *negante* corrupte scriptum, tum syllaba *da* propter *ta* sequentem omissa erat. Vide quam pulchre iam procedat sententia : " Questus es (v. 96) ventum secundum fuisse : pollicitus es (v. 98) te rediturum. Utrumque mentitus es : hoc, quia fixum tibi erat nunquam redire : illud, quia vero ventus adversus erat, immo vero pelagus ipsum, tempestate motum, negabat te vera praedicare."
102. *Ut* P *Et* G.

---

are occasionally coupled by ' que' or ' et.' Cf. vii. 81, ' nec enim tua fallere lingua Incipit a nobis primaque plectar ego.' The Bistones were a Thracian tribe in the neighbourhood of M. Rhodope.

98. *Face expectes.*] 'Mind you expect your Demophoon back.' The MSS. vary here, as often, between ' fac,' and the older form ' face.' ' Fac' is always short, and whenever it is used before a vowel, ' face' may be substituted for it. Ramsay's Lat. Pros., p. 34. ' Fac' is often, incorrectly, looked upon as long, and those who so regard it always substitute ' face' for it before a vowel.

99, 100. *Expectem.*] ' Expect you, who departed with the fixed resolve of never returning! Expect the return of your sails, that were spread while a storm forbade it!' The subjunctive present is regularly used in astonished repetitions of a previous command or question; ' iubes?' ' rogas?' being properly understood. So to ' quid facis?' the answer is 'quid faciam?' ' what am I doing?' as in Greek to τί ποιεῖς the answer is ὅτι ποιῶ; ' rogas?' ἐρωτᾷς; respectively being understood. Phyllis says that Demophoon lied when he said (vs. 96) that the wind was fair for his voyage to Athens, and also when he pretended that he would return to her. In support of my emendation cf. xiii. 128, ' A patria pelago vela vetante datis.' vii. 55, ' Ut pelago suadente etiam retinacula solvas.' ' Negante' is here used, not ' vetante,' because ' negante' implies that the sea gavo Demophoon the lie, when he hypocritically pretended that the winds were fair.

105. ' And since I have been forgotten by you, you remember, I suppose, no such person as Phyllis.'

Quae tibi, Demophoon, longis erroribus acto
  Threïcios portus hospitiumque dedi,
Cuius opes auxere meae, cui dives egenti
  Munera multa dedi, multa datura fui: 110
Quae tibi subieci latissima regna Lycurgi,
  Nomine femineo vix satis apta regi,
Qua patet umbrosum Rhodope glacialis ad Haemum,
  Et sacer admissas exigit Hebrus aquas:
Cui mea virginitas avibus libata sinistris, 115
  Castaque fallaci zona recincta manu.
Pronuba Tisiphone thalamis ululavit in illis,
  Et cecinit maestum devia carmen avis.
Adfuit Alecto brevibus torquata colubris,
  Suntque sepulchrali lumina mota face. 120

109, 110. Hoc distichon post v. 114 collocari voluit Suringar.
111. *Latissima* G *letissima* P.
114. *Exit* P *exiit* G *exigit* codd. plurimi. *exserit* unus liber. Num *excitat* ?

---

109. *Cuius.*] The impassioned nature of Phyllis' address must excuse the irregular transition here, and in 115.

111. Cf. Virg. Aen. iii. 14. 'Thraces arant, acri quondam regnata Lycurgo.' Lycurgus, son of Dymas, an ancient King of Thrace, famous for his opposition to the worship of Dionysus. Hom. Il. vi. 130.

114. 'And sacred Hebrus urges on his rapid floods.' 'Admissas,' see note on i. 36. 'Sacer,' because of the rites of Bacchus celebrated near it. I have suggested 'excitat,' as it is more easily deduced from P than 'exigit,' and suits 'admissas' better, which properly is applied to horses. 'Exigit,' 'pours along,' not merely 'empties into the sea,' which is the meaning of the Greek ἐξίησι. Cf. Prop. iii. xix. 3. 'Tu quoque qui aestivos spatiosius exigis ignes, Phoebe, moraturae contrahe lucis iter.'

115. *Libata.*] The primary meaning of 'libare' was probably the same as the Greek λείβειν, (1) to offer a libation to the gods: (2) to take the first fruits of anything: thence esp. 'to taste,' which is the meaning here: thence (3) 'to diminish,' 'impair,' 'lessen,' in which sense Ruhnken takes 'libata' here: wrongly, as iv. 27 proves. 'Tu nova servatae capies libamina famae;' where 'libamina' is correctly rendered 'gustamenta' by many commentators. Both meanings may, however, be included in the word.

117. 'Tisiphone usurped Juno's place, and shrieked in my marriage chambers.' Juno was 'pronuba,' or patroness of auspicious marriages. Here a Fury took her office. So Seneca, Oed. 644, 'Et mecum Erinnys pronubas thalami traham.'

118. *Devia avis.*] The lonely bird, i. e. the screech-owl, 'strix' or 'bubo.' Cf. Met. l. c. infra.

119. *Brevibus torquata colubris.*] 'Encircled with a collar of short adders.' The Furies were often represented with serpents instead of hair, or entwined with it. 'Torquata' means that the snakes fell around her neck and shoulders. So Met. iv. 492: . . . 'motae sonuere colubrae, Parsque iacent humeris, pars circum pectora lapsae Sibila dant sanicmque vomunt linguaque coruscant.'

120. It was considered a very bad omen if the torch with which the bride was lighted to her husband's house had been kindled at a funeral pile. For the whole passage cf. Met. vi. 428 : ' Non

Maesta tamen scopulos fruticosaque litora calco,
Quaque patent oculis aequora lata meis.
Sive die laxatur humus, seu frigida lucent
Sidera, prospicio, quis freta ventus agat.
Et quaecumque procul venientia lintea vidi, 125
Protinus illa meos auguror esse deos.
In freta procurro, vix me retinentibus undis,
Mobile qua primas porrigit aequor aquas.
Quo magis accedunt, minus et minus utilis adsto:
Linquor, et ancillis excipienda cado. 130
Est sinus, adductos modice falcatus in arcus:
Ultima praerupta cornua mole rigent.
Hinc mihi suppositas immittere corpus in undas

121. *Litora* P G libri omnes. Burm. parum probabiliter coni. *culmina* quod recepit M.
122. Pro *aequora litora* exhibent P G libri fere omnes, casu repetitum ut videtur a priori v. Corr. Aldus, Iahn, cum vett. edd. plerisque *litora* in utroque versu tuetur.

pronuba Iuno Non Hymenaeus adest, non illi Gratia lecto: Eumenides tenuere faces de funere raptas Eumenides stravere torum, tectoque profanus Incubuit bubo, thalamique in culmine sedit.'

121. *Fruticosaque litora*.] 'The bushy shores.' We read 'amantes litora myrtos,' Virg. Georg. iv. 124: and 'litorea myrto,' Amor. i. ii. 9. I think this is enough to defend 'litora.' Burmann's 'culmina,' which it is surprising Merkel has adopted, has no merit. For, as Ruhnken remarks, 'litora' could scarcely have been written by mistake for 'culmina,' and I doubt if 'culmen' be ever used absolutely for a hill or mountain. In the next line it is extremely probable that 'aequora' was the reading. The preceding 'litora,' and the following 'lata' would cause the change to 'litora.'

123. *Laxatur*.] 'Thawed,' loosened from the frosts of the night. So 'solvo' is frequently used. Cf. Hor. L. iv. 10, 'flore, terrae quem ferunt solutae.'

126. 'I instantly guess them to be my ship.' A part here is put for the whole. 'Deos,' the painted image of the god or gods under whose protection the ship sailed. These images were placed in the stern of the ship. Trist. I. iv. 7, 'Puppique recurvae insilit, et pictos verberat unda deos.' Persius, Sat. vi. 29, 'Ingentes de puppe dei.' The meaning of the passage has generally been mis-stated. Loers explains ' deos' thus: *illa esse quae me servent, mihi Demophoonta meum advehant.'* He quotes Amor. I. xi. 44, 'Et dicam nostros advehit illa (puppis) deos.' Certainly the meaning of 'deos' must be the same in both passages: but it is, I think, that which I have given. 'Meos' may, perhaps, be best explained, if it wants explanation, by the following passage from Martin Chuzzlewit: 'Tom's ship, however; or, at least, the packetboat in which Tom took *the greatest interest* was not off yet.'

129. 'The nearer they (the sails) approach, the more and more powerless I stand; I faint away, and fall into the arms of my maidens.' An extremely elegant use of 'utilis.' 'Linquor' in the sense of 'fainting' generally has 'animo.' Suet. Caes. 45, 'Nisi quod repente animo linqui solebat.'

131. 'There is a bay which slopes gently into the shape of a drawn bow: its extremities are rugged with a massy precipice.' Cf. 'Moles nativa,' v. 61. The plural of 'arcus' is often used for the singular.

EP. II. PHYLLIS DEMOPHOONTI.

Mens fuit, et, quoniam fallere pergis, erit.
Ad tua me fluctus proiectam litora portent, 135
  Occurramque oculis intumulata tuis.
Duritia ferrum ut superes, adamantaque, teque,
  'Non tibi sic' dices 'Phylli, sequendus eram.'
Saepe venenorum sitis est mihi, saepe cruenta
  Traiectam gladio morte perire iuvat. 140
Colla quoque, infidis quia se nectenda lacertis
  Praebuerunt, laqueis implicuisse lubet.
Stat nece matura tenerum pensare pudorem.
In necis electu parva futura mora est.
Inscribere meo causa invidiosa sepulchro. 145
  Aut hoc, aut simili carmine notus eris :
'Phyllida Demophoon leto dedit, hospes amantem :
  Ille necis causam praebuit, ipsa manum.'

EPISTOLA III.

BRISEIS ACHILLI.

QUAM legis, a rapta Briseïde littera venit,
  Vix bene barbarica Graeca notata manu.

142. *Iuvat* P G corr. Heins. e codd. nonnullis.
148. *Ipsam manum* P, *illa manum* G P var. lect. ma. pri.

---

135. 'Proicio' is especially used of bodies cast out unburied. Cf. Ib. 166, 'Indeploratum proiicere caput.'
137. *Teque.*] A very elegant climax. Cf. x. 110, 'Ille qui silices, Thesea, vincat habes.'
143. 'I am determined to atone for my frail modesty by an easy death.'
144. *In necis electu.*] Phyllis is said to have ended her life by hanging, and to have been changed into an almond-tree. According to others she was changed into an almond-tree when about to throw herself into the sea.
145. *Invidiosa.*] 'Which will excite the indignation of men.' Cf. viii. 49, 'arma invidiosa tulisti,' said of Orestes,

who slew his mother. See the note there.
III.—The story of Briseïs is sufficiently well-known. The following epistle is supposed to have been written by her after the failure of the deputation, consisting of Ulysses, Ajax, and Phoenix, sent by Agamemnon to endeavour to appease the wrath of Achilles. Vid. Il. ix. From vs. 45 the poem is a fine specimen of masculine and vigorous composition, with considerable pathos, and not devoid even of sublimity.
2. 'Badly written in Greek by a barbaric hand.' Briseïs was a native of the Mysian town of Lyrnessus, destroyed by Achilles.

Quascumque aspicies, lacrimae fecere lituras.
  Sed tamen et lacrimae pondera vocis habent.
Si mihi pauca queri de te dominoque viroque   5
  Fas est, de domino pauca viroque querar.
Non, ego poscenti quod sum cito tradita regi,
  Culpa tua est : quamvis hace quoque culpa tua est.
Nam simul Eurybates me Talthybiusque vocarunt,
  Eurybati data sum Talthybioque comes.   10
Alter in alterius iactantes lumina vultum
  Quaerebant taciti, noster ubi esset amor.
Differri potui : poenae mora grata fuisset.
  Ei mihi, discedens oscula nulla dedi.
At lacrimas sine fine dedi, rupique capillos :   15
  Infelix iterum sum mihi visa capi.
Saepe ego decepto volui custode reverti :
  Sed me qui timidam prenderet, hostis erat.
Si progressa forem, caperer ne nocte timebam,
  Quamlibet ad Priami munus itura nurum.   20

4. *Et lacrimae* P, *hae lacrimae* G, vulg.
6. *Viroqua queri* P, unde coniecit Heins. aut *si mihi—fas sit*, aut *sit mihi—fas si*.
12. *Vester* invitis libris scribendum censebat Heins.
17. *Progressa* G, *nocte* P G, codd. plurimi : in nonnullis erat *forte* quod ediderunt Heins. et Burm.
20. *Nurum* G, *nurus* sive *nuris* P.

3, 4. Lachmann objected to the repeated epanalepsis in the second line of this, and the following distichs. Merkel proposed the omission of vss. 3, 4, 7, 8. I hardly think a change necessary. Ovid has not yet warmed to his work, and the blemishes in these opening lines appear to me to resemble the weak and uncertain notes of a minstrel which are often the prelude to a full and strong burst of music.

12. *Noster amor.*] ' The love that was between us.' Heinsius proposed 'vester.' But 'vester' is never used simply for 'tuus.' In ix. 1, 'nostris' is the true reading, and in i. 75, xvi. 40, 'vestra' is used in its proper plural sense : 'vestra libido,' 'vestra verba,' ' the caprice,' 'the words,' ' of you men.' So Prop. III. xxvi. 30, 'vester senex,' ' the old favourite of you philosophers.'

13. *Differri potui.*] ' My giving up might have been deferred : the reprieve of my misery would have been welcome.' 'Differo' is often used in a peculiarly pregnant sense, as it is here : and must be translated with regard to the context. So Met. 518, ' Quid di crudeles nisi quo nova vulnera cernam, Vivacem differtis anum?' ' why do you put off the death of an old woman?' Rem. Am. 93, ' nec te venturas differ in horas.' Cic. Div. v. 12, 'Sin autem differs me in aliud tempus. For 'poena' compare xiii. 6, ' Quidquid ab illo Produxi vitae tempore poena fuit.'

19. *Nocte.*] Heinsius wished to restore 'forte,' but 'nocte' is doubtless the true reading. I do not think 'hostis' in the previous line refers to the Trojans, as is generally supposed, but to the Greeks.

Sed data sim, quia danda fui. Tot noctibus absum,
  Nec repetor : cessas, iraque lenta tua est.
? Ipse Monoetiades tum, cum tradebar, in aurem
  'Quid fles ? hic parvo tempore' dixit 'eris.'
Non repetisse, parum : pugnas, ne reddar, Achille. 25
  I nunc, et cupidi nomen amantis habe.
Venerunt ad te Telamone et Amyntore nati,
  Ille gradu propior sanguinis, ille comes,
Laërtaque satus, per quos comitata redirem :
  Auxerunt blandae grandia dona preces, 30
Viginti fulvos operoso ex aere lebetas,
  Et tripodas septem pondere et arte pares :
Addita sunt illis auri bis quinque talenta,
  Bis sex adsueti vincere semper equi,
Quodque supervacuum est, forma praestante puellae 35
  Lesbides, eversa corpora capta domo :

21. *Data sim* P, *data sum* G vulg. Egregii codicis scripturam verissimam recepit Heins. secuto Burm. et edd. omnibus recentibus exceptis Iahno et Loersio.
30. *Blandas* P G cum reliquis plerisque. Correxit Heins. *lebetas-tripodas* in v. 31, *dona* accusativum esse demonstrant. Paulum hoc loco paene titubavit vir doctissimus affirmans *blandas* retineri posse si *lebetes—tripodes* quoque legamus ut multi codd.! habent. *Fulvos* enim (ut ipse quoque post vidit) codd. isti nec mutant nec mutare possunt ad hanc normam—et *tripodes, lebetes*, more Latino pro accusativis scripsisse librarios certum est. *blanda prece* codd. nonnulli.
31. e G *operosos ex.* P.

Briseïs did not identify herself with the side of her captors so thoroughly that 'hostis' cannot refer to them. All she means to say is, if she *turned back* she would fall into the hands of the Greeks: if, on the other hand, she went *forward*, she might be captured at night by some roving Trojans, who would give her as a present to some one of the daughters-in-law of Priam.
21. *Sed data sim.*] 'Grant that I was given up, because I had to be: I have been away so many nights, and you do not try to regain me.'
25. 'It is a small thing for you to refrain from recovering me : you actually try to prevent my being restored to you.' 'Parum' is like the Homeric ἢ ὀνόσαι;
26. *I nunc.*] A very common formula, denoting mockery or reproach. iv. 127, 'I nunc sic meriti lectum reverere parentis.' Mart. ii. 6, 1, ' I nunc edere me iube libellos.'
27. Telamon, father of Ajax, and brother of Peleus. Phoenix was son of Amyntor, and tutor of Achilles. See Il. ix. 438, sqq.
30. *Auxerunt.*] 'Aided,' 'added to the effect of.'
31. The accusatives are in apposition with 'dona,' v. 30. The passage is borrowed at length from Il. ix. 264, sqq. ἑπτ' ἀπύρους τρίποδας, δέκα δὲ χρυσοῖο τάλαντα κ.τ.λ.
32. *Pondere et arte pares.*] 'Equal in weight, and alike in beauty of workmanship.'
36. *Lesbidas.*] Il. l. c.
δώσει δ' ἑπτὰ γυναῖκας ἀμύμονα ἔργ' εἰδυίας Λεσβίδας κ.τ.λ. 'Corpora,' used with propriety of slaves. So σώματα is sometimes used.

Cumque tot his—sed non opus est tibi coniuge—coniux
Ex Agamemnoniis una puella tribus.
Si tibi ab Atride pretio redimenda fuissem,
    Quae dare debueras, accipere illa negas?   40
Qua merui culpa fieri tibi vilis, Achille?
Quo levis a nobis tam cito fugit amor?
An miseros tristis fortuna tenaciter urguet,
    Nec venit inceptis mollior hora meis?
Diruta marte tuo Lyrnesia moenia vidi,   45
    Et fueram patriae pars ego magna meae:
Vidi consortes pariter generisque necisque
    Tres cecidisse—tribus, quae mea mater erat—:
Vidi quantus erat, fusum tellure cruenta,
    Pectora iactantem sanguinolenta virum.   50
Tot tamen amissis te compensavimus unum:
    Tu dominus, tu vir, tu mihi frater eras.

44. *Hora* P G, *aura* codd. plurimi.
48. *Quae mihi* G, *quae mea* P, elegantius.
51. *Heinsius* coni. *amissos te c. uno.*

---

38. The three daughters of Agamemnon are mentioned by Homer, l. c.

τρεῖς δέ οἵ εἰσι θύγατρες ἐνὶ μεγάρῳ εὐπήκτῳ
Χρυσόθεμις καὶ Λαοδίκη καὶ Ἰφιάνασσα,
τάων ἥν κ' ἐθέλῃσθα φίλην ἀνάεδνον ἀγέσθαι.

44. The best MSS. have 'hora,' which is supported by Pont. iii. 3, 84, 'Et veniet votis mollior hora meis.' Prop. ii. 27, 'Extremo veniet mollior hora die.' 'Aura' is, however, excellent. Trist. v. 20, 'Dum veniat placido mollior aura deo;' and, as Loers remarks, the distich may be a nautical metaphor, 'urguet' being used of stormy winds, Aen. i. 113, 'tres Eurus ab alto In brevia et Syrtes urguet.'

46. *Et fueram patriae pars ego magna meae.*] This merely means, I think, that Briseis was a great person in her native town. Cf. Met. v. 577, 'Pars ego nympharum quae sunt in Achaide 'dixit' Una fui.' 'Pars,' applied to a single individual, is common in Propertius and Juvenal as well as in Ovid. Cf. Prop. I. vi. 33,

'Ibis et accepti pars eris imperii,' where apparently from want of appreciation of this usage, L. Müller and others change 'pars' to 'sors.' Id. II. i. 73, 'Maecenas nostrae pars invidiosa iuventae.' Juv. i. 26, 'Cum pars Niliacae plebis cum verna Canopi.' Ruhnken's note is 'ipsa quoque sensi magnam partem calamitatis quae patriam adflixit,' which is scarcely to be got out of the original.

49. 'I saw my husband stretched at full length' (quantus erat), &c. Cf. xii. 58, 'Acta est per lacrimas nox mihi quanta fuit' (the live-long night). Cf. the Homeric κεῖτο μέγας μεγαλωστί. Il. xvi. 776. Loers seems to mistake the meaning: his note is,—' *Quantus erat: sc. Mynes, Ciliciae rex,* ejus coniux fuisse dicitur:' ('great man as he was.')

51. Heinsius prefers to read 'amissos-uno,' but the change is not necessary. 'Against the loss of so many dear ones, I set the gain of you.' Verbs denoting exchange take either construction. Thus 'muto,' as is well known, means either to take an exchange, or to exchange for. Cf. Hor. Od. I. xvii. 2, and I. xxix. 15.

Tu mihi, iuratus per numina matris aquosae,
  Utile dicebas ipse fuisse capi.
Scilicet ut, quamvis veniam dotata, repellas,   55
  Et mecum fugias quae tibi dantur, opes.
Quin etiam fama est, cum crastina fulserit eos,
  Te dare nubiferis lintea velle notis.
Quod scelus ut pavidas miserae mihi contigit aures,
  Sanguinis atque animi pectus inane fuit.   60
Ibis, et—o miseram—cui me, violente, relinquis?
  Quis mihi desertae mite levamen erit?
Devorer ante, precor, subito telluris hiatu,
  Aut rutilo missi fulminis igne cremer,
Quam sine me Phthiis canescant aequora remis,   65
  Et videam puppes ire relicta tuas.
Si tibi iam reditusque placent patriique penates,
  Non ego sum classi sarcina magna tuae.
Victorem captiva sequar, non nupta maritum:
  Est mihi, quae lanas molliat, apta manus.   70
Inter Achaeiadas longe pulcherrima matres
  In thalamos coniux ibit eatque tuos,
Digna nurus socero, Iovis Aeginaeque nepote,
  Cuique senex Nereus prosocer esse velit.

55. *Repellas* P, *repellar*. vulg.
57. *Eos* l' ap. Heins. hodie quidem scriptura evanuit. *hora*. G et vulg.
58. *Lintea vela* P G, *lintea plena* codd. nonnulli. *vella* in quibusdam legebatur unde Micyllus *velle* correxit. Nam *lintea* ut adiectivum nusquam cum *vela* reperitur.

52. The sentiment is Homeric. Andromache says to Hector, Il. vi. 429, "Ἕκτορ ἀτὰρ σύ μοί ἐσσι πατὴρ καὶ πότνια μήτηρ ἠδὲ κασίγνητος σὺ δέ μοι θαλερὸς παρακοίτης.
58. 'That you intend to spread your sails to the cloud-collecting south winds.' 'Lintea vela' never occurs; but 'lintea,' 'sails,' is common. There can, I think, be little doubt of the truth of the emendation of Micyllus. Cf. Am. i. 12, 3: 'Modo cum discedere vellet, ad limen digitos restitit icta Nape.' 'Nubiferi' is a proper epithet of 'Noti,' like 'procellosi,' ii. 12. Cf. Met. i. 264, 265. 'Protinus Aeoliis aquilonem claudit in antris Et quaecumque fugant inductas flamina nubes Emittitque notum: madidis Notus evolat alis.' Cf. Herod. ii. 24.
70. The delicate touch of the hand in drawing the wool from the distaff (colus), and in forming it into thread, was of great importance. If the wool was roughly or carelessly drawn out into thread, it was said to be 'rudis,' or 'raw,' 'unworked,' Cf. i. 73, Art. Am. ii. 217. 'Mollire' was used regularly of working the wool softly and delicately. Fast. iii. 807, ' Pallade placata lanam mollite puellae.'
71. *Socero.*] Peleus, son of Aeacus, who was son of Jupiter and Aegina.

Nos humiles famulaeque tuae data pensa trahemus, 75
  Et minuent plenas stamina nostra colos.
Exagitet ne me tantum tua, deprecor, uxor,
  Quae mihi nescio quo non erit aequa modo,
Neve meos coram scindi patiare capillos,
  Et leviter dicas ' haec quoque nostra fuit.' 80
Vel patiare licet, dum ne contempta relinquar:
  Hic mihi vae miserae concutit ossa metus.
Quid tamen expectas? Agamemnona paenitet irae,
  Et iacet ante tuos Graecia maesta pedes.
Vince animos iramque tuam, qui cetera vincis. 85
  Quid lacerat Danaas impiger Hector opes?
Arma cape, Aeacide, sed me tamen ante recepta,
  Et preme turbatos Marte favente viros.
Propter me mota est, propter me desinat ira:
  Simque ego tristitiae causa modusque tuae. 90
Nec tibi turpe puta precibus succumbere nostris.
  Coniugis Oenides versus in arma prece est.

76. *Plenas* P G sub rasura.
86. Pro *impiger* Hoeeftius coni. *integer.*

75. *Nos humiles.*] I cannot forbear reminding the reader of the ballad of the Nut-Browne Maid, which these Epistles so often recall: 'Tho' in the wode, I undyrstode ye had a paramour, All this may nought remove my thought, but that I wyll be your: And she shall fynde me soft and kynde, and courteys every hour: Glad to fulfil all that she wyll commande me to my power.' 'Pensum' (pendo), the portion of wool weighed out to the spinsters to be spun into thread.
76. *Minuent—colos.*] The 'glomus' or ball of unworked wool was wrapped round the distaff, and as it was drawn off in threads became smaller and smaller. Dict. Ant. s. v. Colus.
77. 'Only let not your wife persecute me, I implore, for I feel sure somehow that she will not look favourably on me.'—'Exagitet' Prop. iii. 7, 81, 'Exagitet nostros manes sectetur et umbras.'
80. *Leviter.*] 'Gently,' 'in a low voice.' Amor. I. iii. 30, 'Tu leviter puerum posce

quid ipse velis.'
83. 'What more do you want? Agamemnon is sorry for his ill-temper.'
85. *Animos.*] ' Anger, resentment.' The plural 'animi,' generally of the more vigorous qualities: courage, anger. Plaut. Men. ii. 7, 43, 'Ego meos animos violentos meamque iram ex pectore jam promam.'
88. *Preme.*] ' Drive pell-mell.' 'Premere' in this sense = the Homeric ἐλάειν, ἰλάσαι, to drive in a thick disordered mass.
90. *Oenides.*] Meleager, son of Oeneus, who, at the entreaty of his wife, Cleopatra, took up arms, after long obstinacy, to aid the Calydonians against the Curetes. He had slain the brethren of his mother, Althaea, in the quarrel about the head of the Calydonian boar, and she pronounced a curse upon him. Enraged with her, he refused to go to war until persuaded by his wife. See Homer. Il. ix. 525. The legend of the burning brand is later. See Class. Dict. Ovid follows it elsewhere. See ix. 156, and Met. vii. 17.

EP. III. BRISEIS ACHILLI. 23

Res audita mihi, nota est tibi : fratribus orba
  Devovit nati spemque caputque parens.
Bellum erat : ille ferox positis secessit ab armis, 95
  Et patriae rigida mente negavit opem.
Sola virum coniux flexit : felicior illa !
  At mea pro nullo pondere verba cadunt.
Nec tamen indignor : nec me pro coniuge gessi
  Saepius in domini serva vocata torum. 100
Me quaedam, memini, dominam captiva vocabat :
  'Servitio' dixi ' nominis addis onus.'
Per tamen ossa viri subito male tecta sepulchro,
  Semper iudiciis ossa verenda meis,
Perque trium fortes animas, mea numina, fratrum, 105
  Qui bene pro patria cum patriaque iacent,
Perque tuum nostrumque caput, quae iunximus una,
  Perque tuos enses, cognita tela meis,
Nulla Mycenaeum sociasse cubilia mecum
  Iuro : fallentem deseruisse velis. 110
Si tibi nunc dicam 'fortissime, tu quoque iura
  Nulla tibi sine me gaudia facta,' neges.
At Danai maerere putant. Tibi plectra moventur,
  Te tenet in tepido mollis amica sinu.

---

94. 'Devoted her darling son to death' expresses the meaning, though not quite literal. 'Spes' is often used in a pregnant sense to denote the person of whom hope is entertained. Cf. 'spes surgentis Iuli,' Virg. Aen. vi. 364. Tac. Ann. xiv. 53, 'quartus decimus annus Caesar est ex quo spei tuae admotus sum.'

98. *Pro nullo pondere.*] i. e. sine pondere, nullius ponderis. Prop. El. i. 10, 'Neu tibi pro vano verba benigna cadant.'

99. 'And yet I cannot complain, for I never conducted myself as a *wife*' (as Cleopatra was).

102. 'By calling me mistress, you add the burden of a title to my position as a slave, and make it worse instead of better.'

103. 'Subito' is here the adjective. 'A hastily formed grave.' Fast. vi. 532, 'Liba sua properata manu Tegeaca sacerdos Traditur in subito cocta dedisse foco,' where 'subitus focus' means 'a hastily made fire.' So Tac. Hist. iv. 76, 'Subitus miles,' 'recruits hastily collected.'

105. *Mea numina.*] 'Who are as gods to me,' i. e. she venerated their shades as divinities, and, especially, called upon their names in swearing, a sense to which the word 'numina' is especially applied. xiii. 150, 'Per reditus corpusque tuum mea numina iuro.' v. 53. xvi. 379, 'Tunc ego iurabo quaevis tibi numina.' vs. 54, supra, 'Tu mihi iuratus per numina matris aquosae.' Sil. Ital. vi. 113, 'Testor mea numina manes.'

106. This is a line of conspicuous grandeur. So Gray—'Ye died amid your dying country's cries.'

109. *Mycenaeum.*] 'The man of Mycenae,' i. e. Agamemnon. Cf. Il. ix. 12.

Si quis iam quaerat, quare pugnare recuses :   115
  Pugna nocet : citharae noxque Venusque iuvant.
Tutius est iacuisse toro, tenuisse puellam,
  Throïciam digitis increpuisse lyram,
Quam manibus clipeos et acutae cuspidis hastam,
  Et galeam pressa sustinuisse coma.   120
Sed tibi pro tutis insignia facta placebant,
  Partaque bellando gloria dulcis erat.
An tantum, dum me caperes, fera bella probabas,
  Cumque mea patria laus tua victa iacet ?
Di melius! validoque, precor, vibrata lacerto   125
  Transeat Hectoreum Pelias hasta latus !
Mittite me Danai! dominum legata rogabo,
  Multaque mandatis oscula mixta feram.
Plus ego quam Phoenix, plus ego quam facundus Ulixes,
  Plus ego quam Teucri—credite!—frater agam.   130
Est aliquid, collum solitis tetigisse lacertis,
  Praesentisque oculos admonuisse sinu.

115. *Si quis quem quaerat* P, pleraque ma. sec. in ras. Ita M: ap. Iahnum P habet *si quis nunc quaerat, et quisquam quaerit* G. Meam coniecturam edidi.
132 *Praesentisque* P G, *praesentique*, quinque libri. *sinum* P, et pro var. lect. *suis. sinu* G et vulg. *sinus* duo libri, *sui* Slichtenhorst. Heins. M locum obelo notavit.

116. *Noxque Venusque.*] The use of the copula is irregular. This may, perhaps, be got over by taking 'nox Venusque' as one idea, coupled by 'que' after 'nox' to 'citharae.' This is, at any rate, better than Jahn's edition, which puts the stop at 'citharae:' 'the battle is bad for playing on the lyre.'
118. *Throïciam.*] The lyre is so called, having been presented to the Thracian Orpheus by Apollo. 'Increpuisse,' ψάλλειν.
121. 'But glorious deeds *used* to please you instead of safe ones.' So Penelope reproaches Ulysses, I. 44, 'At bene cautus eras et memor ante mei.' 'You *once* were cautious, and used to remember me!'
125. *Di melius !*] 'Heaven forbid !' 'Sollennis abominandi formula.' Ruhnken.
126. *Pelias hasta.*] The ashen spear of Achilles, cut on Mount Pelion by Chiron.
127. *Legata.*] 'As an envoy.' 'Mandata,' the regular word for the instructions given to an ambassador.
131. Literally : 'It is of great influence to touch the neck with familiar arms, and with the bosom to remind the eyes of a lover face to face.' There is certainly no cause for Merkel to obelise v. 132 as he does. There is no difficulty in the line, whether we adopt 'sinum,' the reading of P, or 'sinu,' that of G, which I have given in the text. The meaning is the same in either case. In the former case 'sinum' would probably be a second accusative after 'admonuisse,' although it might be taken as the subject to it: 'that one's bosom should remind the eyes of a present lover.' The sentiment is true to nature, and we meet with a passage not unlike it in Coleridge's Genevieve: 'and partly 'twas a bashful art, That I might rather feel than see the swelling of her heart.' 'Ad-

EP. III. BRISEIS ACHILLI.

Sis licet immitis, matrisque ferocior undis,
    Ut taceam, lacrimis comminuere meis.
Nunc quoque—sic omnes Peleus pater impleat annos,   135
    Sic eat auspiciis Pyrrhus ad arma tuis!—
Respice sollicitam Briseida, fortis Achille,
    Nec miseram lenta ferreus ure mora.
Aut, si versus amor tuus est in taedia nostri,
    Quam sine te cogis vivere, coge mori.   140
Utque facis, coges. Abiit corpusque colorque :
    Sustinet hoc animae spes tamen una tui.
Qua si destituor, repetam fratresque virumque :
    Nec tibi magnificum femina iussa mori.
Cur autem iubeas? Stricto pete corpora ferro :   145
    Est mihi, qui fosso pectore sanguis eat.
Me petat ille tuus, qui, si dea passa fuisset,
    Ensis in Atridae pectus iturus erat.
Ah! potius serves nostram, tua munera, vitam.
    Quod dederas hosti victor, amica rogo.   150

136. e G *hospiciis* P *ad arma tuus patris* P.
139. *Aut* P G *at* vulg.
143. *Destituor* P G *destituar* libr. plurimi.
149. *Ah* P *at* G.
150. *Domini iure* P *more* libr. plurimi.

monuisso sui,' the reading proposed by Heinsius, ' to remind of one's self,' is very feeble, and has little or no manuscript authority.
134. 'Though I keep silence, you will be made to falter by my tears.' For 'comminuere,' cf. Met. xii. 471, ' Nec te natalis origo Comminuit?' ' does not the knowledge of your origin weaken your courage?' (addressed to Caeneus, who had previously been a woman). The simple verb ' minuo' is sometimes used in a sense akin to this. Liv. xxi. 52, 'Consul vulnere suo *minutus*,' '*dispirited* by his wound.'
141. *Utque facis*.] 'And as you are going on' (i. e. if you go on as you are doing) ' you *will* compel me,' &c. Cf. vii.
147, ' Utque latet, vitatque tuas abstrusa carinas :' 'And if the land keeps hid as it has done, &c.' ' Corpus,' ' flesh,' as we say, not indeed in poetry : Cf. Met. vii. 291, ' Adiecto corpore.'
142. *Sustinet hoc animae*.] 'The little life I have is supported by the hope of you alone.' For 'sustinet,' cf. i. 114, note.
143. *Repetam*.] ' I will rejoin my brothers and my husband' (i. e. kill myself) v. supra, 103, 115. Ruhnken seems to have forgotten that the husband and brothers of Briseis were dead, or I do not understand his note. ' Repetam, *i. e. petam vel abibo ;* nam compositum repetere hic ponitur pro simplici petere, abeundi significatione.'
147. *Si dea passa fuisset*.] Pallas, Il. i.
154. *Domini iure*.] 'Summon me by the right of an owner.' Cf. viii. 8, and ix. 109, note.

Perdere quos melius possis, Neptunia praebent
Pergama: materiam caedis ab hoste pete.
Me modo, sive paras impellere remige classem,
Sive manes, domini iure venire iube.

EPISTOLA IV.

PHAEDRA HIPPOLYTO.

Qua, nisi tu dederis, caritura est ipsa salute,
Mittit Amazonio Cressa puella viro.
Perlege quodcumque est. Quid epistola lecta nocebit?
Te quoque in hac aliquid quod iuvet, esse potest.
His arcana notis terra pelagoque feruntur. 5
Inspicit acceptas hostis ab hoste notas.
Ter tecum conata loqui ter inutilis haesit
Lingua, ter in primo destitit ore sonus.
Qua licet et sequitur, pudor est miscendus amori.

1. *Quam* P sub ras. *salutem* P sub ras. G. *salute* M.
5. Pro *notis* propter *notas* in sequenti Burm. coni. *modis.*

The chief source from whence Ovid derived the materials for this Epistle was the Hippolytus of Euripides, the spirit of which he has wonderfully caught: in fact, the way in which Ovid, without being a plagiarist, seizes on and enlarges the exact conceptions of the authors from whom he takes his characters forms one of the most striking attributes of his genius. This is well exemplified in his Dido, drawn from Virgil's. This Epistle is supposed to be written to Hippolytus at Troezen by his step-mother Phaedra, during the absence of Theseus. Vide Class. Dict. s. n. Hippolytus.

2. *Puella.*] Though 'puella' is generally used of unmarried girls, and sometimes as equivalent to 'virgo' ('prosit mihi vos dixisse puellas,' Juv. iv. 36), instances are not wanting where it is used of young married women, as here. Juv. ii. 59, 'dederit vivus cur multa puellae.' Hor. Od. III. xxii. 2, 'laborantes utero puellas.' Id. Od. III. xiv. 10, 'puellae iam virum expertae.' 'Amazonio:' Hippolytus was son of the Amazon Hippolyte, or Antiope, according to another account.

4. 'Notas' and 'notis' coming so close together displease some. But Ovid often purposely repeats the same phrase for the sake of emphasis. He never does so accidentally however, and therefore this passage cannot be cited in defence of the repetition of 'dolo' in i. 40, 42, where there is no emphasis whatever. See note on xiv. 62.

9. 'Shame should be joined to love as far as possible, and wherever it will accompany it.' 'Sequitur' is rather hard. I have taken it personally, supplying

Dicere quae puduit, scribere iussit amor. 10
Quidquid Amor iussit, non est contemnere tutum :
Regnat et in dominos ius habet ille deos.
Ille mihi primo dubitanti scribere dixit
'Scribe! dabit victas ferreus ille manus.'
Adsit, et ut nostras avido fovet igne medullas, 15
Figat sic animos in mea vota tuos.
Non ego nequitia socialia foedera rumpam.
Fama—velim quaeras—crimine nostra vacat.
Venit amor gravius, quo serius. Urimur intus :

16. *Figat* P G, *fingat* codd. nonnulli. Vix operae pretium est enumerare coniecturas quales sunt *frangat* Burmanni, *stringat* Handi, et in v. 15 pro *fovet*, Francii *vorat* Oudendorpii *coquit*.
19. *Venit* P G *urit* codd. nonnulli.

'pudor' as nominative, and 'amorem' as object. This construction is supported by line 155, where Phaedra says shame had ceased to accompany her love : 'Depuduit profugusque pudor sua signa reliquit.' Others take 'sequitur' impersonally : 'wherever it is easy.' Thus Gronovius renders it 'facile est,' and Burmann 'utile, conveniens est.' But no instances have been cited where 'sequitur' is used impersonally in these senses. Its only impersonal use is, I think, that used in argument : 'it follows.' Ruhnken follows Gesner in giving the construction I have adopted. Phaedra's meaning is : 'I was ashamed to *speak ;* and I was right not to speak: for shame should, if possible, attend on love: so I *write.*'

11. *Quidquid amor iussit non est contemnere tutum.*] This is the sum of the doctrine of Hippolytus : Σφάλλω δ' ὅσοι φρονοῦσιν εἰς ἡμᾶς μέγα, vs. 6.

12. *Dominos deos.*] Cf. Hor. Od. i. 6, 'Terrarum dominos evehit ad deos.' Am. III. x. 18, 'Haec decet ad dominos munera ferre deos.' For 'ius habere in aliquid,' Cf. Am. I. i. 5, '(Quis tibi, saevo puer, dedit hoc in carmina iuris?'

14. *Dare manus.*] = 'to yield:' a well-known metaphor from the arena, where a conquered gladiator confessed his defeat by extending his hands towards his conqueror. Ovid generally joins some participle with 'manus' in this phrase, as 'victas' here, 'cunctatas' in xvii. 260.

'These epithets, however, import no new idea into the metaphor: to read 'coniunctas,' in the passage just quoted, would introduce an idea which would cause the metaphor to be lost sight of altogether. Vid. not. ad loc.

15. 'As he burns my heart, so may he transfix yours so as to listen to my prayers.' There is a full commentary on these lines in Art. i. 21 :—

Et mihi cedit Amor, quamvis mea vulneret arcu
Pectora iactatas excutiatque faces.
Quo me *fixit* Amor, quo me violentius *ussit,*
Hoc melior facti vulneris ultor ero.

The bow and torch of love are alluded to in ii. 40 ; 'altera tela arcus, altera tela faces,' and so frequently. 'In mea vota :' this is an idiom Ovid is very fond of. Cf. v. 58, 'Scilicet ut venias in mea damna color;' and Met. vii. 738, 'in mea pugno vulnera.' The accusative with 'in' in these passages denotes the end aimed at, or the object arrived at.

17. 'I will not break the marriage tie by mere wanton lewdness.' The emphatic word is 'nequitia,' mere unchastity, such as that of a woman like Messalina, for instance, which Phaedra repudiates and contrasts with her own passion, which she regards as pure, being the first she ever felt.

Urimur, et caecum pectora vulnus habent. 20
Scilicet ut teneros laedunt iuga prima iuvencos,
Frenaque vix patitur de grege captus equus,
Sic male vixquo subit primos rude pectus amores,
Sarcinaque haec animo non sedet apta meo.
Ars fit, ubi a teneris crimen condiscitur annis: 25
Quae venit exacto tempore, peius amat.
Tu nova servatae capies libamina famae:
Et pariter nostrum fiet uterque nocens.
Est aliquid, plenis pomaria carpere ramis
Et tenui primam deligere ungue rosam. 30
Si tamen ille prior, quo me sine crimine gessi,
Candor ab insolita labe notandus erat,
At bene successit, digno quod adurimur igni.

20. *Caecum* P G *tacitum* unus cod. Heins.
26. *Quae venit* P G libri omnes. Heins. coni. *cui venit* sc. amor. Werferus coni. *calet*. Sed nihil mutandum. Obelo locum notavit M.
27. *Carpis* P G M *carpes* vulg. *capies* codd. nonnulli. Hanc lect. praetuli, quia *carpere* mox occurrit v. 29, unde huc quoque redundavit.
31. *Sic tamen* P *si tamen* codd. nonnulli. *Si et sic* in codd. saepius inter se confunduntur. *Et tamen* G *sed tamen* vulg.
33. *Igni* P G *igne* vulg.
34. *Obest* P G *abest* Heins. e cod. Scriv.

---

23. *Rude.*] 'Raw,' 'unpractised.' The word 'raw' translates 'rudis' in most of its senses. Thus, 'lana rudis' is wool in its raw, undressed state, i. 78. 'Rudis indigestaque moles,' Met. i. 6, is the raw material of chaos. 'Rudis tiro,' is a raw recruit.

25. 'When intriguing is practised from early life, it becomes a mere trade: but she who comes to love in later years loves more distractedly.' The strong word 'crimen' is intentionally used by Phaedra to show her condemnation of flirtation or inconstancy: otherwise she might have used the more euphemious term 'furtum.' Verse 26 is obelised by Merkel without cause, as I think. 'Venit,' sc. 'ad amandum,' to be supplied out of the meaning of the previous line, no very harsh ellipse. 'Cui venit,' the suggestion of Heinsius, demands the ellipse of 'amor,' which is at least equally harsh. 'Exacto tempore,' 'when her time is spent.' Cf. Hor. Sat. i. 118. 'Peius amat:' cf. vii. 30, 'peius amo.' vi. 157, 'peiusque relinquat.'

27. I prefer 'capies' to 'carpes,' because I do not think any examples can be found of 'carpo' joined with a word like 'libamina.'

31-33. 'Well, if it *was* fated that my former spotless purity should be marked with an unwonted stain, it has at any rate turned out well that I am consumed by a worthy flame.' 'Si tamen' resembles the Greek use of the particles εἰ δ' οὖν, see Aesch. Ag. 1009, where its force is explained by Paley. A mental ellipse is always implied. '("Twere better indeed not to have sinned,' but if it *was* fated,' etc. With 'digno quod adurimur igni,' cf. Hor. Od. I. xxvii. 15, 'non erubescendis adurit Ignibus, ingenuoque semporeAmoro peccas.'

Peius adulterio turpis adulter obest.
Si mihi concedat Iuno fratremque virumque, 35
Hippolytum videor praepositura Iovi.
Iam quoque—vix credes—ignotas mittor in artes:
Est mihi per saevas impetus ire feras.
Iam mihi prima dea est arcu praesignis adunco
Delia: iudicium subsequor ipsa tuum. 40
In nemus ire libet; pressisque in retia cervis
Hortari celeres per iuga summa canes,
Aut tremulum excusso iaculum vibrare lacerto,
Aut in graminea ponere corpus humo.
Saepe iuvat versare leves in pulvere currus, 45
Torquentem frenis ora fugacis equi.

37. *Credes* P G *credas* codd. nonnulli. *Mutor in artes* P G M *mittor* multi codd. et edd. vett. Heius. coni. *nitor* et id exhibent duo scripti. Perplacet *mittor* propter Met. vii. 188.
46. *Fugacis* G et fortassis P sub. ras. *sequacis* al.

34. 'A base adulterer is worse than adultery itself.' 'Obest' is certainly better than 'abest.' Ruhnken and others translate 'turpis' by 'deformis,' but they do wrong to limit the meaning of the word to physical ugliness. It includes the idea of 'baseborn,' and mental baseness as well. Cf. Hor. l. c., 'Ingenuoque semper Amore peccas.' The sentiment is frequently found in Ovid. Cf. vii. 105, 'Da veniam culpae: decepit idoneus auctor.' So our own ballad of Clerk Saunders: 'I wot 'twas neither knave nor loon Was in the bower last night wi' me.'
37. *Mittor in artes.*] 'I let myself loose into pursuits hitherto unknown.' 'Mutor,' 'nitor,' and 'mittor,' are readings which at first sight it is difficult to decide between. Lennep thought 'mittor' was rendered probable by a comparison with Eur. Hipp. 233, Νῦν δὴ μὲν ὄρος βᾶσ' ἐπὶ θήρας πόθον ἐστίλλου which Ovid may have had in his mind, and used 'mittor,' thinking of ἐστίλλου. This is possible; but I do not think the meaning of the word 'mittor' here is that assigned to it by Lennep: 'quasi invita, contra naturam mei sexus agor, abripior, ire iubeor.' Nearly the opposite sense, that of 'letting loose,' 'giving free play,' is the meaning both of ἐστίλλου, and of 'mittor;' and in this sense 'mittor' is supported by the following passage from Met. vii. 188, which I think is decisive in its favour, 'Dixit et *ignotas animum dimittit in artes*,' said of Daedalus, when about to construct wings. 'Nitor in artes' would resemble 'nitimur in vetitum,' Am. III. iv. 17, 'nitor in adversum,' Met. ii. 72. 'Mutor in artes' would be rather a compendious mode of expression, the nearest parallel to which in Ovid I find in Pont. 1. i. 79, 'Inque locum Scythico vacuum mutabor ab arcu.'
41-44. Cf. Eur. Hipp. 215 sqq.,
πέμπετε μ' εἰς ὄρος, εἶμι πρὸς ὕλαν
καὶ παρὰ πεύκας ἵνα θηροφόνοι
στείβουσι κύνες
βαλιαῖς ἐλάφοις ἐγχριμπτομένα. κ. τ. λ.
43. *Excusso lacerto.*] 'With arm shot forth.' 'Excusso' refers to the vigorous jerk with which the arm is, as it were, shaken out in throwing a spear. On the other hand 'adductus' is used of the first part of the action where the forearm is drawn back to the shoulder; 'Torserat adductis hastilia lenta lacertis,' Met. viii. 28. For 'excussus,' cf. Sen. de Benef. ii. 6, 'infinitum interest, utrum tela excusso lacerto torqueantur, an remissa manu effluant.' Cf. Petronius 95, 'excussissima palma.'

Nunc feror, ut Bacchi furiis Eleleïdes actae,
Quaeque sub Idaeo tympana collo movent,
Aut quas semideae dryades Faunique bicornes
Numine contactas attonuere suo.   50
Namque mihi referunt, cum se furor ille remisit,
Omnia: me tacitam conscius urit amor.
Forsitan hunc generis fato reddamus amorem,
Et Venus ex tota gente tributa petat.
Iupiter Europen—prima est ea gentis origo—   55
Dilexit, tauro dissimulante deum.
Pasiphae mater, decepto subdita tauro,
Enixa est utero crimen onusque suo.
Perfidus Aegides, ducentia fila secutus,
Curva meae fugit tecta sororis ope.   60
En ego nunc, ne forte parum Minoia credar,

47 ad 103 P exciderunt.
54. Schroderus coni.: *Ut Venus*.
56. Pro *dilexit* Marklandus coni. *delusit* vel *elusit*.

---

47. *Feror*.] 'I am going mad.' Cf. xv. 140, 'Illuc mentis inops feror.' Virg. Aen. iv. 371, 'Heu Furiis incensa feror.' Cf. Hipp. 142, σὺ γάρ' ἔνθεος ὦ κούρα, εἴτ' ἐκ Πανὸς εἴθ' Ἑκάτας, ἢ σεμνῶν Κορυβάντων φοιτᾷς ἢ ματρὸς ὀρείας. Ib. 549, δρομάδα τὰν Ἄιδος ὥστε βάκχαν. 'Eleleïdes,' the Bacchae, from the cry ἐλελεῦ, like 'Euiades' from εὐοῖ. Bacchus is called 'Eleleus' in Met. iv. 15.

48. *Quaeque*.] The Galli or emasculated priests of Cybele are here alluded to. The feminine is used as it is by Catullus throughout the 'Atys.'

50. 'Contactus' and 'attonuere' express the same idea of supernatural frenzied inspiration. The compound 'contingere,' is rare in this sense, though 'tangere de caelo' in the literal sense is common. On the other hand, the Greeks used ἐμβροντηθῆναι more frequently in the metaphorical sense. We may compare with 'contactus' Am. iii. 161, 'Iam nunc contacto magnus in ore sonor': where 'contacto' is rendered by Heinsius 'adflato' = 'inspired.' The Greeks and Romans both regarded certain forms of madness as inflicted by the Nymphs: and called the sufferers νυμφόληπτοι, and 'lymphati' 'lymphatici' respectively. Varro. L. L. vii. 87.

51. 'They tell me all about it when my frenzy has abated its violence.' Ruhnken's note is rather careless: 'Remisit: cessavit: saepe enim remittere in hac forma sine casu ponitur:' forgetting 'se;' and he quotes in support of his note xix. 93, 'Ergo ubi saevitiae paullum gravis unda remisit,' where 'remisit' *does* govern a case.

53. *Generis fato*.] It is this 'Curse of Race' which gives the principal interest to most of the tragedies of Aeschylus: and Phaedra seems here to catch something of the sullen 'laissez-aller' of Eteocles. Sept. Cont. Theb. 686,

Ἀλλ' εἰ τὸ πρᾶγμα κάρτ' ἐπισπέρχει
θεός
ἴτω κατ' οὖρον κῦμα Κωκυτοῦ λαχὸν
Φοίβῳ στυγηθὲν πᾶν τὸ Λαΐου γένος.

Cf. viii. 65.

60. *Fugit*.] i. q. 'effugit,' 'escaped from.'

61. 'Now I, lest I should be thought

EP. IV. PHAEDRA HIPPOLYTO.

In socias leges ultima gentis eo.
Hoc quoque fatale est : placuit domus una duabus.
Me tua forma capit : capta parente soror.
Theseïdes Theseusque duas rapuere sorores.   65
Ponite de nostra biua tropaea domo.
Tempore quo nobis inita est Cerealis Eleusin,
Gnosia me vellem detinuisset humus.
Tunc mihi praecipue, nec non tamen ante placebas :
Acer in extremis ossibus haesit amor.   70
Candida vestis erat, praecincti flore capilli,
Flava verecundus tinxerat ora rubor :
Quemque vocant aliae vultum rigidumque trucemque,
Pro rigido, Phaedra iudice, fortis erat.
Sint procul a nobis iuvenes ut femina compti :   75
Fine coli modico forma virilis amat.
Te tuus iste rigor, positique sine arte capilli,
Et levis egregio pulvis in ore decet.
Sive ferocis equi luctantia colla recurvas,
Exiguo flexos miror in orbe pedes :   80
Seu lentum valido torques hastile lacerto.

62. *In solitas* unus liber.
79. *Ferocis* G, *fugacis* libri duo. *Recurvas*, G, libri omnes : *retorques* olim legebatur. Corr. Heins.

---

unconnected with the family of Minos, last of my race, come under the influence of its marriage laws.' I take 'gentis' both with 'ultima' and with 'leges :' and I think 'socias' has the meaning here which it so often has in Ovid. Thus 'socii anni,' ii. 33, are 'wedded years :' 'socii ignes,' Met. ix. 795, are 'marriage torches :' 'socii dei,' v. 126, are 'marriage gods.' This is the only meaning of 'socialis' in Ovid. Loers renders 'leges quae mihi et illis sunt communes,' and there is a variant 'solitas' which gives much the same meaning, but not, I think, the true one.
67. *Tempore quo nobis inita est Cerealis Eleusin.*] Cf. Schol. on Eur. Hipp. 25, ἐν τῇ Ἀττικῇ ἔτι οὖσα ἡ Φαίδρα πρὶν μετοικῆσαι εἰς Τροιζῆνα ἰδοῦσα τὸν

Ἱππόλυτον ἐλθόντα ἐπὶ μύησιν τῶν Ἐλευσινίων ἤρα καί πρίν εἰς Τροιζῆνα ἐλθεῖν.
80. *Exiguo flexos miror in orbe pedes.*] The allusion is to riding in the ring, 'gyrus :' 'pedes' therefore belong to the horse, to turn which in a small circle exhibited the greatest skill. Cf. Met. vi. 225, sqq., 'Conscendunt in equos . . . . . E quibus Ismenos dum certum flectit in orbem Quadrupedis cursus spumantiaque ora coercet,' and Virg. Georg. iii. 115, where see Conington's note. These passages show that the student should beware of referring 'pedes' to Hippolytus, and of understanding the line to refer to 'ringing' horses by a rope held in the hand by a person standing in the centre.

Ora ferox in se versa lacertus habet :
Sive tenes lato venabula cornea ferro,
Denique nostra iuvas lumina quidquid agas.
Tu modo duritiam silvis depone iugosis.   85
Non sum militia digna perire tua.
Quid iuvat incinctae studia exercere Dianae,
Et Veneri numeros eripuisse suos?
Quod caret alterna requie, durabile non est :
Haec reparat vires fessaque membra novat.   90
Arcus—et arma tuae tibi sunt imitanda Dianae—
Si numquam cesses tendere, mollis erit.
Clarus erat silvis Cephalus, multaeque per herbas

84. *Iuvas* G, *iuvat* reliqui omnes.
86. *Materia* G M, quod aegre explicari potest. Mihi temperare nequivi quin admitterem *militia*, quod optimum sensum praebet, suadente, ne dicam imperante, Am II. xiv. 62. Notandum plus licere emendatori si quando lacuna in optimo libro existat ut est h. l.

82. 'Your stubborn arm attracts all eyes.' The application of 'ferox' to 'lacertus' is uncommon.

86. *Non sum militia digna perire tua.*] 'I am not a fitting victim for your prowess.' When we reflect how often Ovid repeats himself, and find in Am. II. xiv. 62, 'Militia fuerat digna perire sua,' it is difficult to resist the introduction of *militia* here, thereby completely restoring sense, instead of *materia*, a reading which caused Ruhnken to say of the verse that it was 'foede corruptus in quo restituendo frustra ingenium experti sunt interpretes eruditi.' Heinsius tried to explain it thus: 'te materiam praebente mortis.' But 'materia' properly denotes the matter out of which anything is composed; hence, fuel for fire, the subject of a poem, the occasion of a war, are all properly denoted by the word 'materia.' The physical notion is present in all these cases : and I doubt whether any instance can be found where that notion is so much lost sight of as here. Accordingly Gesner (Thes. s. v. 'Materia') tries to explain it more in accordance with its general meaning : 'Comparet Phaedra amorem suum cum igne cui materiam et alimenta praebet Hippolytus : 'Non merui ut peream amore quem incendunt et alunt tuae dotes corporis atque animi.'' Burmann understood 'materia' as meaning much the same thing as 'duritia,' in the previous line : 'your hard, rude nature, quoting Cic. Verr. v. 68, 'Fac enim fuisse in illo aut C. Laelii aut M. Catonis materiam atque indolem.' This passage, however, does not support such a very strong use of 'materia:' Cicero uses it in little more than a neutral sense, as its being joined with 'indolem' shows: = 'the stuff,' as we say.

87. *Incinctae.*] i. q. 'succinctae,' for agility in hunting.

88. 'And to rob Venus of her dues.' 'Numeri' are the component parts of anything : hence the well known idioms 'omnibus numeris absolutum esse,' 'omnium numerorum esse,' to be perfect in anything. Cf. Met. i. 427, 'quaedam imperfecta suisque Trunca vident numeris.'

93. Phaedra proceeds to hold up the example of three mighty hunters to Hippolytus : Cephalus, Adonis, and Meleager, who were not averse to love. Cf. Eur. Hipp. 455.

——ἴσασι δ ὡς ἀνήρπασέν ποτε
ἡ καλλιφεγγὴς Κέφαλον ἐς θεοὺς Ἕως
κ. τ. λ.

Conciderant illo percutiente ferae :
Nec tamen Aurorae male se praebebat amandum : 95
Ibat ad hunc sapiens a sene diva viro.
Saepe sub ilicibus Venerem Cinyraque creatum
Sustinuit positos quaelibet herba duos.
Arsit et Oenides in Maenalia Atalanta :
Illa ferae spolium pignus amoris habet. 100
Nos quoque iam primum turba numeremur in ista.
Si Venerem tollas, rustica silva tua est.
Ipsa comos veniam, nec me latebrosa movebunt
Saxa, neque obliquo dente timendus aper.
Aequora bina suis oppugnant fluctibus Isthmon, 105
Et tenuis tellus audit utrumque mare.
Hic tecum Troezena colam, Pittheïa regna :
Iam nunc est patria gratior illa mea.
Tempore abest, aberitque diu Neptunius heros :
Illum Pirithoi detinet ora sui. 110
Praeposuit Theseus—nisi si manifesta negemus—
Pirithoum Phaedrae, Pirithoumque tibi.
Sola nec haec ad nos iniuria venit ab illo.

103. *Salebrosa* codd. unus et alter.
111. *Nisi nos manifesta negemus*, G M. *nos* non habet P. Librarius ut videtur alterum *si* in *nisi si* omiserat, quod vidit Heins. qui correxit. *Negamus* al.

---

100. *Ferae spolium.*] The head and skin of the Calydonian boar, given by Meleager to Atalanta. Cf. 'spolium pecudis'; vi. 13.
102. 'Take away Venus, your woods lose their romance.' Cf. i. 77, note.
103. *Latebrosa*] refers to the dens of wild beasts, 'latebrae.'
104. *Obliquo dente.*] Cf. λικριφὶς ἀΐξας, Hom. Od. xix. 451. 'Verris obliquum meditantis ictum,' Hor. Od. III. xxii. 7. The sidelong thrust of the boar is rendered necessary by the position of his 'terrible tusks' at the sides of his mouth.
106. *Audit.*] 'The narrow land hears both seas :' a highly poetical line, and yet 'claudit' was proposed by Schlichtenhorst. Heinsius compared Sen. Thyest.

113 : 'Vicina gracili dividens terra vada Longe remotos latus exaudit sonos,' and Stat. Theb. i. 335, 'In mediis audit duo litora campis.' The Isthmus is, as Lennep rightly says, the Corinthian, and the two seas are the Saronic and Corinthian gulfs. Troezen is rather vaguely placed near the Isthmus by Phaedra.
111. *Nisi si.*] This idiom is frequent in Ovid, and I have no doubt it is the true reading here: the omission of 'si' in P after the syllable 'si' in 'nisi' was natural: but 'nos' could not possibly have been omitted. Cf. xvii. 151, 'At tu dissimula nisi si desistere mavis.' Heinsius in his note has collected a large number of instances where 'nisi si' is used.

F

In magnis laesi rebus uterque sumus.
Ossa mei fratris clava perfracta trinodi 115
  Sparsit humi: soror est praeda relicta feris.
Prima securigeras inter virtute puellas
  Te peperit, nati digna vigore parens.
Si quaeras, ubi sit—Theseus latus ense peregit:
  Nec tanto mater pignore tuta fuit. 120
At ne nupta quidem, taedaque accepta iugali.
  Cur, nisi ne caperes regna paterna nothus?
Addidit et fratres ex me tibi: quos tamen omnes
  Non ego tollendi causa, sed ille fuit.
O utinam nocitura tibi, pulcherrime rerum, 125
' In medio nisu viscera rupta forent!
I nunc, sic meriti lectum reverere parentis:
  Quem fugit et factis abdicat ille suis.
Nec, quia privigno videar coitura noverca,
  Terruerint animos nomina vana tuos. 130
Ista vetus pietas, aevo moritura futuro,
  Rustica Saturno regna tenente fuit.
Iuppiter esse pium statuit, quodcumque iuvaret:
  Et fas omne facit fratre marita soror.
Illa coit firma generis iunctura catena, 135
  Imposuit nodos cui Venus ipsa suos.
Nec labor est, celare licet: pete munus ab illa. —

127. *Si meriti* P G *si* pro *sic* sollenni errore. Heins. pro *si* in P *ii* legens dedit *I nunc, i meriti*.
128. *Ille* P *ipse* G.
137. Nescio quod mendum h. v. credo contraxisse. Vid. Comm.

115. *Fratris.*] i. e. the Minotaur. This is perhaps the most flagrant instance of bad taste in the Heroides. It is repeated, x. 77.
132. *Rustica.*] 'Old-fashioned,' 'out of date.'
134. 'The fact that Juno married her brother sanctions everything.' 'Omne' = 'everything' is very rare except perhaps in the phrase 'omne quod.' But cf. xii. 28. 'Fratre' is a sort of instrumental ablative: 'marita' is used adjectively.
137. The Commentators get over this line without making any difficulty about it, though two very different explanations of it are given. Loers refers 'illa' to 'noverca' so far back as 129: his note is: 'celare licet: exempli causa sic: pete munus ab illa, sc. noverca.' In other words, he considers that Hippolytus would be furnished

Cognato poterit nomine culpa tegi.
Viderit amplexus aliquis, laudabimur ambo :
  Dicar privigno fida noverca meo. 140
Non tibi per tenebras duri reseranda mariti
  Ianua, non custos decipiendus erit.
Ut tenuit domus una duos, domus una tenebit.
  Oscula aperta dabas, oscula aperta dabis.
Tutus eris mecum laudemque merebere culpa, 145
  Tu licet in lecto conspiciare meo.
Tolle moras tantum, properataque foedera iunge!
  Qui mihi nunc saevit, sic tibi parcat Amor.
Non ego dedignor supplex humilisque precari.
  Heu! ubi nunc fastus altaque verba iacent? 150
Et pugnare diu, nec me summittere culpae
  Certa fui : certi siquid haberet amor.
Victa precor, genibusque tuis regalia tendo
  Brachia: quid deceat, non videt ullus amans.

139. Ita G *amplexos* P.
150. Drakenborchius distinxit : *Heu ubi nunc fastus altaque verba? iacent.*

---

with a good excuse for being often with his step-mother by the pretext of asking her for a present. This is quite absurd. However Loers mentions no other interpretation. All other editors who say anything about the line refer 'illa' to 'Venus' in 136, and so, if the text is sound, we must understand it. 'Ask a gift from 'Venus,' viz.: that she will aid us to conceal our loves. But in the first place, this meaning is not sufficiently clearly expressed : secondly, it was no part of Venus' office to aid in concealing love ; she was not able to hide her own intrigue with Mars: thirdly, line 140 takes up a mode of concealment quite independent of the help of Venus. I believe the line to be corrupt. Every member of it is faulty: for what is 'nec labor est:'? 'Nec labor est celare amorem' would be intelligible. Then 'celare' is never used in Ovid without an accusative expressed : and 'pete munus ab illa' is, as I have tried to show, barely defensible. I believe, though I do not expect to carry conviction, that the original line ran thus : Nec labor est celare, licet peccemus, amorem. The copyist having connected 'celare' with 'licet' in his mind, would be willing enough to extract PETE MVNVS out of PECCEMVS which gave no sense, and 'amorem' he rejected altogether as unintelligible. 'Peccemus' occurs exactly in this sense in xvi. 395, 'Nunc ea peccemus quae corriget hora iugalis,' and passim. The 'cognatum nomen' in 138 is not to be referred to the relationship between a 'noverca' and 'privignus,' as is done by the commentators, but it means their love would be called by the kindred name of affection. Cf. Art. i., 720, 'Intret amicitiae nomine tectus amor.' This meaning agrees perfectly with what follows, and makes better Latin.

Depuduit, profugusque pudor sua signa reliquit. 155
　Da veniam fassae, duraque corda doma!
Quod mihi sit genitor, qui possidet aequora, Minos,
　Quod veniant proavi fulmina torta manu,
Quod sit avus radiis frontem vallatus acutis,
　Purpureo tepidum qui movet axe diem— 160
Nobilitas sub amore iacet. Miserere priorum.
　Et mihi si non vis parcere, parce meis!
Est mihi dotalis tellus Iovis insula, Crete.
　Serviat Hippolyto regia tota meo.
Flecte feros animos : potuit corrumpere taurum 165
　Mater : oris tauro saevior ipse truci ?
Per Venerem, parcas, oro, quae plurima mecum est.
　Sic numquam quae te spernere possit, ames :
Sic tibi secretis agilis dea saltibus adsit,
　Silvaque perdendas praebeat alta feras : 170
Sic faveant satyri, montanaque numina Panes,
　Et cadat adversa cuspide fossus aper.
Sic tibi dent nymphae—quamvis odisse puellas
　Diceris—arentem quae levet unda sitim.
Addimus his precibus lacrimas quoque. Verba precantis 175
　Perlegis, et lacrimas finge videre meas.

155. *Reliquit* P *relinquit* G.
157. Ita P G (nisi quod G fortassis *quid*) edd. vett. ante Heins. qui Micylli *Quo mihi quod* edidit. Antiquam lectionem iure restituit M. Iahnus dedit : *Quid mihi quod*. Latuit locus simillimus Met. vii. 705 sqq.
176. *Perlegis et* P codd. plurimi. *Perlege sed* cod. Linc. *Perlege et* G. *Perlegis at* Burm.

---

155. *Depuduit.*] 'I have ceased to blush, and shame has deserted his ensign.' vid. note on vs. 9.
157. *Quod mihi sit genitor.*] ' Though I have Minos who rules the waves for my father.' Of all authors, Ovid can be most readily emended and explained from himself. The passage before us affords a striking instance of this. For plausible though the reading of Micyllus, 'Quo mihi quod,' appears, 'quod mihi sit,' the reading of the best MSS., is established by a comparison with an exactly similar passage in Met. vii. 705, which I have not seen referred to by editors, where several successive clauses are introduced by 'quod sit,' the apodosis not coming till after four such clauses, just as here it does not come till after three.

―――― Quod sit roseo spectabilis ore,
Quod teneat lucis, teneat confinia noctis,
Nectareis quod alatur aquis—ego Procrin
　amabam.

Cf. also xviii. 41.

167. *Quae plurima mecum est.*] 'Who is with me in all her power.' Cf. Eur. Hipp. 1. Πολλὴ μὲν ἐν βροτοῖσι κοὐκ ἀνώνυμος. Ib. 444. Κύπρις γὰρ οὐ φορητὸς ἦν πολλὴ ῥυῇ.

EPISTOLA V.

OENONE PARIDI.

Perlegis, an coniux prohibet nova? perlege! non est
   Ista Mycenaea littera facta manu.
Pegasis Oenone, Phrygiis celeberrima silvis,
   Laesa queror de te, si sinis, ipsa meo.
Quis deus opposuit nostris sua numina votis?   5

3. *Pegasis* P G libri omnes. Micyllus coni. *Pedasis.* Egregie ille quidem sed nihil muto.
4. *Ipsa* P *ipse* G.

V.—The story of Oenone and Paris, so favourite a subject with modern poets, is treated with great taste in this epistle, which contains some passages of exceeding beauty. Thus verses 9-35 are an admirable description of the happy shepherd life of the pair: the ravings of the wild Cassandra are dramatically drawn in verses 113-122, and the concluding lines are gently pathetic. Ovid followed the account given by Apollodorus in his treatment of the legend, which was unknown to Homer.

1, 2. *Perlegis an coniux prohibet nova.*] Ovid seems to have become sensible of the bad effect produced by this sort of epistolary mannerism, and strove to avoid it by beginning abruptly and without introduction. This is done with excellent effect in vii. and xii. This abruptness displeased some copyists of the 12th or 13th century, who added in many instances a prefatory distich, a practice which extended itself to epistles where no abruptness can be alleged, as here. In this case the spurious lines are,

Nympha suo Paridi quamvis meus esse recuses
Mittit ab Idaeis verba legenda iugis.

I had rather reject vv. 1, 2, than accept these, as the poem begins much more simply at v. 3.

3. *Pegasis.*] 'The fountain-nymph' (πηγή). Micyllus objected to 'Pegasis,' because as a patronymic it ought to be formed from 'Pegasus,' not from πηγή, and the word occurs elsewhere only as applied to the Muses. He proposed 'Pedasis' from the town Pedasus in Mt. Ida near the Cebren (the river from which Oenone sprung). See Hom. Il. xxi. 87. It is not indeed anywhere stated that Oenone was born at Pedasus. Nevertheless the correction of Micyllus would be a good one if one was wanted: but it is not necessary. 'Pegasis' may be formed from πηγή, incorrectly, it is true, but on the analogy of 'Pegasus' which the Greeks at all events supposed to be formed from πηγή. Hesiod, Theog. 282, says the horse was so called because he was born near the sources of Ocean. The fact that the fountain Hippocrene was produced by Pegasus led to the Muses being called 'Pegasides' in the first instance: then 'Pegasides' was applied to them without reference to Pegasus, but rather to the fountain: lastly, the name was extended to all fountain-nymphs.

4. *Ipsa meo.*] As I have already observed, see note on i. 86, Ovid is particularly fond of such collocations. The reading 'si sinis ipse' is refuted by this consideration. Cf. vi. 3.

Ne tua permaneam, quod mihi crimen obest?
Leniter, ex merito quicquid patiare, ferendum est.
 Quae venit indigno poena, dolenda venit.
Nondum tantus eras, cum te contenta marito
 Edita de magno flumine nympha fui. 10
Qui nunc Priamides,—absit reverentia vero—
 Servus eras : servo nubere nympha tuli.
Saepe greges inter requievimus arbore tecti,
 Mixtaque cum foliis praebuit herba torum.
Saepe super stramen fenoque iacentibus alto 15
 Defensa est humili cana pruina casa.
Quis tibi monstrabat saltus venatibus aptos,
 Et tegeret catulos qua fera rupe suos?
Retia saepe comes maculis distincta tetendi :
 Saepe citos egi per iuga longa canes. 20
Incisae servant a te mea nomina fagi,
 Et legor Oenone falce notata tua:
Et quantum trunci, tantum mea nomina crescunt:

8. *Indigno* P G *indigne* codd. plurimi. *indignae* Heins. e cod. uno.
11. *Absit* P G *adsit* multi libri.
16. *Depressa* P *deprensa* G. Corr. Parrhasius.

6. Loers remarks on this line with just severity : ' Bentleius, quo nullus unquam infelicior Ovidii emendator fuit, pro ' crimen' legendum existimans 'sidus,' non legisse videtur versus 7 et 8.'
7, 8. 'One can easily endure what one deserves to suffer: the punishment which comes to one not deserving it is painful.'
10. So Tennyson . 'I am the daughter of a river-god.'
11, 12. ' You, who are now a prince, were then—let not respect for persons stand in the way of truth—a slave.' ' Adsit,' a reading of weak authority, would mean, ' let all respect be paid to the truth.'
15. The change of construction is remarked by Ramsay. It is probably to be explained by the difference between straw and hay : the former being harder, a person lying upon it does not sink into it, as into hay : hence 'alto feno,' 'in the deep hay.'
19. *Maculis.*] These were probably knots in the hunting net at the corners of the meshes, for the purpose of giving greater strength. They were certainly not meshes, as the following passages quoted by Ramsay and Ruhnken prove : Varro de R. R. iii. 11, speaking of the construction of a νησσοτροφεῖον, or duck yard, says : ' id que totum rete grandibus maculis integitur, ne eo involare aquila possit, neque ex eo evolare anas :' and Columella de R. R. viii. 15. ' locus clathris superpositis vel grandi macula retibus contegitur, ne aut evolandi sit potestas domesticis avibus aut aquilis vel accipitribus involandi.' These knots probably derived the name of 'maculae' from the fact that they were of a different colour from the net itself.

Crescite, et in titulos surgito rite meos.
Populo, vivo, precor, quae consita margine ripae 27
  Hoc in rugoso cortice carmen habes,
'Cum Paris Oenone poterit spirare relicta,
  Ad fontem Xanthi versa recurret aqua.' 30
Xanthe, retro propera, versaeque recurrite lymphae!
  Sustinet Oenonen deseruisse Paris.
Illa dies fatum miserae mihi dixit, ab illa
  Pessima mutati coepit amoris hiems,
Qua Venus et Iuno, sumptisque decentior armis 35
  Venit in arbitrium nuda Minerva tuum.
Attoniti micuere sinus, gelidusque cucurrit,
  Ut mihi narrasti, dura per ossa tremor.
Consului, neque enim modice terrebar, anusque
  Longaevosque senes. Constitit esse nefas. 40

24. *Recta* P G M *rite* unus et alter et edd. ante Heins. Hoc reposui secutus Heusingerum cui *recta* ortum esse videbatur a glossemate *recte* ad *rite* adscripto. Post h. v. in codd. rec. sequebatur distichon, *Populus est memini fluviali consita ripa, Est in qua nostri littera scripta memor.* Sed in aliis ante v. 23, in aliis post v. 28, positum erat.
28. *Carmen* P G *nomen* codd. nonnulli.
30. *Ita* G *Xanthum* P.
31. *Lymphae* P G. Heins. maluit *nymphae* quod P et septem alios habere ille quidem scribit.
33. *Dixit* P G *duxit* multi libri.
40. e G. *Longaevusque senex* P.

---

24. 'Grow on, and duly rise to form an inscription in my honour.' I prefer 'rite' to 'recta' for the reasons mentioned above: besides 'surgite' is more naturally referred to 'trunci' than to 'nomina,' to which it must refer if 'recta' is the true reading. For 'in' with acc. denoting the object, see note on iv. 16.
28. *Carmen.*] 'Inscription.' Cf. ii. 146, and so, frequently. A reading of inferior authority, which I would otherwise prefer, is 'nomen:' 'this entry' an expression derived from bookkeeping, which would add one to the many legal metaphors in Ovid.
34. *Pessima mutati coepit amoris hiems.*] 'Hiems' is not winter but 'tempest' here, as Ruhnken rightly takes it. The metaphor is from a fine sunshiny day becoming overcast with clouds. 'O Lord what is this worldys blysse That changeth as the mone? *My somer's day in lusty May Is derked before the none.*' Ballad of the Nut-Browne Mayd.
35. *Decentior.*] 'Who would be more comely with her armour on' (than nude). ' Decentior,' sc. futura. Cf. Hor. III. xxiii. 18, 'Non sumtuosa blandior hostia Mollivit aversos Penates Farre pio et saliente mica:' where 'blandior' is in the same construction as 'decentior' here.
37. *Micuere sinus.*] Cf. i. 45.
40. *Constitit esse nefas.*] 'It was agreed on all hands that an ill-omened deed was done.'

Caesa abies, sectaeque trabes, et classe parata
  Caerula ceratas accipit unda rates.
Flesti discedens—hoc saltim parce negare:
  Praeterito magis est iste pudendus amor:—
Et flesti, et nostros vidisti flentis ocellos: 45
  Miscuimus lacrimas maestus uterque suas.
Non sic adpositis vincitur vitibus ulmus,
  Ut tua sunt collo brachia nexa meo.
Ah! quoties, cum te vento quererere teneri,
  Riserunt comites! ille secundus erat. 50
Oscula dimissae quoties repetita dedisti!
  Quam vix sustinuit dicere lingua 'vale'!
Aura levis rigido pendentia lintea malo
  Suscitat, et remis eruta canet aqua.
Prosequor infelix oculis abeuntia vela, 55
  Qua licet, et lacrimis humet arena meis.
Utque celer venias, virides Nereïdas oro:
  Scilicet ut venias in mea damna celer.

41. *Parata* P G *peracta* libr. quidam et Burm.
53. *Rigido* P G *Phrygio* cod. Iun. et ita coni. Heins.

41. *Parata.*] 'Parare classem' was the regular phrase for building a fleet. Burmann, in support of the reading 'peracta,' quoted Sueton. Calig. 21, 'Quorum operum a successore eius alterum peractum.' Id. Otho, 6, 'Peragere domum auream.' Ruhnken adds 'peracta aegide' from Valerius Flaccus. 'Peractus' in these passages means 'finished,' which is not the meaning required here, but simply 'built.' 'Ceratas,' 'caulked:' the bottoms of the ancient ships had their chinks stopped with wax.

45. *Nostros vidisti flentis ocellos.*] = 'ocellos mei flentis.' Professor Ramsay has collected a useful list of instances where the possessive pronoun is substituted for the genitive of the personal: indeed, this is the regular idiomatic construction in both Greek and Latin. Vid. Valckenar. ad Eur. Phoen. 1518. There is an exact parallel to the passage before us in Martial, VII. li. 7, where 'nostros' is also used for 'meos,' and a singular genitive of the participle follows: 'Cum tenet absentis nostros cantatque libellos.'

49, 50. The obvious meaning is, that Paris was detained by his love for Oenone, but threw the blame on the wind, which was really favourable for his sailing. Burmann strangely misses the point in supposing the wind to have really been adverse to his sailing, and so 'secundus,' in reference to Oenone. His note is: 'Secundus, sc. mihi amanti, quia te retinebat.'

54. *Eruta.*] 'Eruere' in agriculture is properly to dig up anything out of the ground: hence the metaphor is applied to the sea, which is 'turned up,' as it were, by the oars.

57. *Virides.*] So called apparently from the green colour of the sea. Cf. Trist. I. ii. 59, 'Pro superi viridesque dei quibus aequora curae.'

Votis ergo meis alii rediture redisti?
Ei mihi, pro dira pellice blanda fui! 60
Aspicit immensum moles nativa profundum:
Mons fuit: aequoreis illa resistit aquis:
Hinc ego vela tuae cognovi prima carinae,
Et mihi per fluctus impetus ire fuit.
Dum moror, in summa fulsit mihi purpura prora. 65
Pertimui: cultus non erat ille tuus.
Fit propior, terrasque cita ratis attigit aura:
Femineas vidi corde tremente genas.
Non satis id fuerat—quid enim furiosa morabar?—
Haerebat gremio turpis amica tuo. 70
Tunc vero rupique sinus et pectora planxi,
Et secui madidas ungue rigente genas,
Implevique sacram querulis ululatibus Iden.
Illuc has lacrimas in mea saxa tuli.

59. Pro *ergo* coni. Santenius *ecce*.
74. *Illuc* G *illinc* multi. libr. *Illic* al.

---

59. *Votis ergo meis.*] The quantity of the final syllable in 'ergo' is commonly made short by post-Augustan poets: a few instances will suffice. Lucan ix. 256, 'Ergo pari voto gessisti bella iuventus;' Juv. xiv. 64, 'Ergo miser trepidas ne stercore foeda canino;' Sulpicia 45, 'Ergo Numantinus Libycusque erravit in isto.' As Leunep on this passage well remarks: 'Scilicet Augusti saeculi poëtarum agmen quasi clausit Ovidius, et in bene multis a priorum severitate iam deflexit.' There is no occasion for doubting the correctness of the reading: 'Ergo' occurs with *o* short again in Trist. i. 87, 'Ergo cave, liber, et timida circumspice mente,' which was corrected by Heinsius, 'Ergo, care liber, timida,' etc., but without sufficient authority. Ovid also departed from the Virgilian rule of always lengthening the final syllable of verbs in *o*. See note on xi. 127; but, most remarkable of all, would be his shortening of the final syllable of the gerund in *do*, ix. 126, were 'tegendo' there the true reading. Vid. not. ad loc.

60. *Blanda fui.*] 'I used my persuasions.' 'Blandus' is regularly used of coaxing entreaties. Cf. iii. 30.

61. *Moles nativa.*] 'A crag reared by nature's hand.' This expression occurs again, Fast. v. 149. 'Nativus' is used of the gifts of nature, opposed to anything artificial. Thus 'nativa coma' is opposed to false hair, in a very pretty poem, Am. I. xiv. 56.

71. 'I was not satisfied with that (and yet I ought to have been): for what did I gain by madly lingering? Nothing but the sight of a mistress clinging to your bosom.' 'Quid morabar?' = 'What object was there in my waiting?' 'Enim,' as usual, has an elliptical reference. Professor Ramsay explains the line somewhat differently: 'had that been enough to satisfy me of your infidelity, why did I madly linger? No, I did not believe the worst until,' &c. Heusinger and Jahn make 'Non satis id fuerat' interrogative: but this does not make the passage easier, and 'enim' loses its force.

74. *Illuc.*] 'For thither, to my rocks, I bore these tears.' This line is explanatory of the preceding: Oenone had been on the cliffs by the shore; but, on seeing Helen, had fled to her own Mount Ida. There is another reading, 'illinc,' of less authority, which might seem to imply

Sic Helene doleat, desertaque coniuge ploret, 75
  Quaeque prior nobis intulit, ipsa ferat.
Nunc tibi conveniunt quae te per aperta sequantur
  Aequora, legitimos destituantque viros.
At cum pauper eras armentaque pastor agebas,
  Nulla nisi Oenone pauperis uxor erat. 80
Non ego miror opes, nec me tua regia tangit,
  Nec de tot Priami dicar ut una nurus.
Non tamen ut Priamus nymphae socer esse recuset,
  Aut Hecubae fuerim dissimulanda nurus.
Dignaque sum et cupio fieri matrona potentis: 85
  Sunt mihi, quas possint sceptra decere, manus.
Nec me, faginea quod tecum fronde iacebam,
  Despice: purpureo sum magis apta toro.
Denique tutus amor meus est tibi: nulla parantur
  Bella, nec ultrices advehit unda rates. 90
Tyndaris infestis fugitiva reposcitur armis:
  Hac venit in thalamos dote superba tuos.
Quae si sit Danais reddenda, vel Hectora fratrem,
  Vel cum Deïphobo Polydamanta roga.

75. Ita G. *Sic bene doleat defectaque* P.
77. *Tecum veniunt* codd. nonnulli.
86. *Quas possint* P G *quae* nonnulli.

---

that the 'saxa' in 74 were elsewhere than on Mount Ida. It admits, however, of defence: for it makes a distinction between 'ululatus' and 'lacrimae,' which was, perhaps, intended. She first filled the open mountain with her shrieks; then, when her first transports were over, she retired to the solitude of a rocky cave to weep there. 'Has lacrimas,' = 'the tears I shed as I write.' 'Has lacrimas' is in favour of the reading 'hae lacrimae' against 'et lacrimae' in iii. 4.

75. *Desertaque coniuge.*] The preposition 'a' would be expected. Ruhnken, however, quotes several instances where 'desertus' is used with the ablative alone. Cf. xii. 161; Prop. II. vii. 17; Lucan i. 195. On the other hand, Ovid often uses the preposition where the ablative alone would be expected. See note on x. 138.

77. *Conveniunt.*] 'Please you.' Rem. Am. 312, 'Conveniens animo non erat illa meo.'

82. Supply 'tangit' from preceding line in impersonal sense. 'Nor do I count it a great thing that I should be called one out of so many daughters-in-law of Priam.'

83, 84. 'Not however that Priam should decline to be father-in-law to a Nymph, or that Hecuba should be ashamed of me for a daughter-in-law.'

85. *Matrona.*] = 'uxor.' Cf. Met. ii. 466, 'Magni matrona Tonantis.'

86. *Sunt mihi quas possint sceptra decere manus.*] The Etonian editor quotes Gray's Elegy: 'Hands that the rod of empire might have swayed.'

92. *Dote.*] Cf. Aesch. Agam. 669, τὰν δορίγαμβρον ἀμφινεικῆ θ' Ἑλέναν.

EP. V. OENONE PARIDI.

Quid gravis Antenor, Priamus quid suadeat ipse,   95
    Consule, quis aetas longa magistra fuit.
Turpe rudimentum, patriae praeponere raptam.
    Causa pudenda tua est: iusta vir arma movet.
Nec tibi, si sapias, fidam promitte Lacaenam,
    Quae sit in amplexus tam cito versa tuos.   100
Ut minor Atrides temerati foedera lecti
    Clamat, et externo laesus amore dolet,
Tu quoque clamabis. Nulla reparabilis arte
    Laesa pudicitia est: deperit illa semel.
Ardet amore tui? sic et Menelaon amavit.   105
    Nunc iacet in viduo credulus ille toro.
Felix Andromache, certo bene nupta marito.
    Uxor ad exemplum fratris habenda fui.
Tu levior foliis, tum cum sine pondere succi
    Mobilibus ventis arida facta volant.   110
Et minus est in te, quam summa pondus arista,
    Quae levis assiduis solibus usta riget.

95. *Suadeat* P G. Falso notatur, ut scribit M, *censeat* e G, quod habent quidam libri et recepit Burm.

---

95. *Priamus.*] Professor Madvig, in his Adversaria Graeca (1871), emending Art. iii. 440, 'Praeceptis Priami si foret usa sui,' among other arguments, denies that Priam ever advised the Trojans to restore Helen, and corrects: 'Praeceptis Priamei si foret usa tuis,' so that 'Priamei' should be the vocative of 'Priameïs,' 'daughter of Priam,' i. e. Cassandra. The line in the text disposes of the above argument, it being clear that Ovid, at any rate, looked upon Priam as giving the same advice as Antenor, 'belli praecidere causam.' [The MS. reading 'Priame —— tuis' is easily explicable: 'Priami' being copied down 'Priame' caused the next copyist, forgetful of metre, to look on it as a vocative, and change 'sui' to 'tuis.' Add, that the contraction 'Priamei' for 'Priameï' is unheard of, and that 'praeceptis' is a word far more applicable to the sage advice of Priam than to the ravings of Cassandra: besides, the epic transition to the vocative does not suit the spirit of the poem at all.]

97. *Turpe rudimentum.*] 'It is a base beginning' (of your new life as Prince of Troy). 'Rudimentum' properly denoted the first lesson of the 'rudis tiro' in martial exercises. It occurs only once more in Ovid, Art. l. 193, 'Tale rudimentum tanto sub nomine debes Nunc iuvenum princeps deinde future senum,' supposed to be addressed to one of the young Caesarian princes, Tiberius or Caius Caesar, when preparing to undertake an enterprise against the Parthians.

99. *Fidam promitte.*] Hor. Od. I. xiii. 11, 'Non, si me satis audias, speres perpetuum,' &c.

106. *Credulus.*] Hor. Od. 1. v. 9, 'Qui nunc te fruitur credulus aurea.'

112. *Solibus.*] 'Heat of the sun.' The plural is used for 'rays of the sun,' 'hot, sunny days,' just as in Greek οἱ ἥλιοι.

Hoc tua—nam recolo—quondam germana canebat,
    Sic mihi diffusis vaticinata comis:
'Quid facis, Oenone? Quid arenae semina mandas?   115
    Non profecturis litora bubus aras.
Graia iuvenca venit, quae te patriamque domumque
    Perdat! io prohibe! Graia iuvenca venit!
Dum licet, obscenam ponto demergite puppim!
    Heu, quantum Phrygii sanguinis illa vehit!'   120
Dixerat. In cursu famulae rapuere furentem.
    At mihi flaventes diriguere comae.
Ah! nimium miserae vates mihi vera fuisti.
    Possidet, en, saltus Graia iuvenca meos!
Sit facie quamvis insignis, adultera certe est.   125
    Deseruit socios hospite capta deos.
Illam de patria Theseus,—nisi nomine fallor—
    Nescio quis Theseus abstulit ante sua.
A iuvene et cupido credatur reddita virgo?
    Unde hoc compererim tam bene, quaeris? Amo.   130
Vim licet appelles, et culpam nomine veles:
    Quae toties rapta est, praebuit ipsa rapi.
At manet Oenone fallenti casta marito:
    Et poteras falli legibus ipse tuis.

---

115. Ab hoc v. ad vi. 49 in P desunt.
119. *Demergite* G *demergite* alii *di mergite* al. quod Heinsio placebat, et vulgo legebatur.
121. *In cursu* G. Micyllus scripsit *incursu* pro 'accursu,' 'interventu.' Sed nihil mutandum.
128. *Arte* codd. nonnulli *arce* al.

---

113. *Recolo.*] This verb properly means to till fallow land: hence it is a highly poetical expression for going over a subject in one's thoughts. It is used in its literal sense in the only other place in which it occurs in Ovid, Met. v. 147.

114. 115. Proverbial expressions for wasting labour. Cf. xviii. 139, 'Quid bibulum curvo proscindere litus aratro Spemque sequi coner quem locus ipse neget'? The proverb occurs twice in Juvenal vii. 48, and i. 157, to which latter passage no other meaning can possibly belong. These lines are powerfully dramatic, and produce an effect like the grand passage in the Agamemnon, where Cassandra is introduced, which Ovid must have known and appreciated. There Cassandra applies the simile of a 'juvenca' to Clytemnestra, v. 1004, ἄπεχε τῆς βοὸς τὸν ταῦρον.'

121. *In cursu.*] 'In the midst of her mad career.' Micyllus proposed 'incursu,' 'rushing in upon her.' But cf. 203, 'Cursibus in mediis novitatis plena relinquis Gnidia.'

126. *Socios deos.*] 'The Gods of marriage.' See note on iv. 62. For 'hospite capta,' cf. 75, supra, 'desertaque coniuge.'

131. This line bears out my interpretation of 'cognato nomine' in iv. 138.

EP. V. OENONE PARIDI.

Me satyri celeres—silvis ego tecta latebam— 135
Quaesierant rapido, turba proterva, pede,
Cornigerumque caput pinu praecinctus acuta
Faunus, in immensis qua tumet Idā iugis.
Me fide conspicuus Troiae munitor amavit, 139
Admisitque meas ad sua dona manus. 146
Quaecumque herba potens ad opem radixque medendi
Utilis in toto nascitur orbe, mea est.
Me miseram, quod amor non est medicabilis herbis!
Deficior prudens artis ab arte mea. 150
Quod nec graminibus tellus fecunda creandis,
Nec deus, auxilium tu mihi ferre potes.

139. Post h. v. sex versus ut subditicios obelo sinistro notavit M. quem subsequor: erant autem *Ille meae spolium virginitatis habet, Id quoque luctando. Rupi tamen ungue capillos, Oraque sunt digitis aspera facta meis. Nec pretium stupri gemmas aurumque poposci: Turpiter ingenuum munera corpus emunt. Ipse ratus dignam, medicas mihi tradidit artes,*
147. Coni. Heins. *medenti.*
150. *Deficior* G *Destituor* alii.
151. Hic quoque duo versus iure damnavit M: erant—*Ipse repertor opis vaccas pavisse Pheraeas fertur, et e nostro saucius igne fuit.*

---

137. *Pinu praecinctus acuta.*] 'Wreathed with sharp-pointed pine leaves. Cf. Met. xiv. 638, ' pinu praecincti cornua Panes.'
139. i. e. Fidicen Apollo. Cf. i. 67. Merkel has given the weight of his authority to the rejection of six lines here, and two after 150, all of which disfigure the poem. Accordingly I have omitted them from the text. They were probably an interpolation by somebody who thought ' ad sua dona' in 146 not sufficiently explicit without the explanatory ' medicas artes.' The lines are self-condemned in every possible way: not to speak of the grossness of sentiment which contrasts so strongly with the rest of the poem, the first line directly contradicts 133: the repetition of ' opem' so soon after ' opis' in the same peculiar sense of ' medicine,' is flagrant; and the utter absurdity and needlessness of the last two lines to prove Apollo was subject to love, after 139, is apparent. These last two lines were probably an effort of the same interpolator, who wished to display his acquaintance with Callimachus, where this form of the legend of Apollo's feeding the flocks of Admetus is given: Hymn. in Apoll. 48,

'Ἐξότ' ἐπ' Ἀμφρυσῷ ζευγίτιδας ἔτρεφεν
ἵππους
ἠϊθέου ὑπ' ἔρωτι κεκαυμένος Ἀδμήτοιο.

150. *Deficior.*] This might be translated ' I am abandoned by my own art' (vid. ad x. 138); but such a strongly passive use of ' deficior' hardly occurs. It means ' to fail,' with reference to something, as ' tempore deficior,' ' fail in point of time,' Trist. ii. 407; and as ' defici ab' is also a prose idiom, cf. Caes. B. C. iii. 64, ' Quum aquilifer a viribus deficeretur,' it is better to translate here, ' I am found wanting in respect to my own art.' It was probably the above incorrect interpretation of ' deficior' that led to ' destituor' being adopted by some copyists.

152. *Auxilium.*] According to Ruhnken this word is properly used as a medical term. He quotes Celsus Praef. i. 1, ' herbas aliaque prompta in auxilium vulnerum.' Cf. Rem. Am. 528.

Et potes, et merui: dignae miserere puellae!
Non ego cum Danais arma cruenta fero:
Sed tua sum tecumque fui puerilibus annis,
Et tua, quod superest temporis, esse precor.

155

EPISTOLA VI.

HYPSIPYLE IASONI.

Litora Thessaliae reduci tetigisse carina
    Diceris, auratae vellere dives ovis.
Gratulor incolumi, quantum sinis. Hoc tamen ipsum
    Debueram scripto certior esse tuo.
Nam ne pacta tibi praeter mea regna redires,
    Cum cuperes, ventos non habuisse potes.
Quamlibet adverso signatur epistola vento.

5

1. Lacuna in P manet usque ad v. 49.
3. *Ipso* libri omnes nisi quod *ipse* unus. Heins. corr. *ipsa*. *Ipsum* suasit Douza, quod edidi.
7. *Signetur* G. Corr. M.

---

155. The conclusion is very graceful: 'puerilibus annis' recalls Tennyson's conception, cf. 'Mournful Oenone wandering forlorn Of Paris, once her playmate on the hills.'

VI.—Jason and the Argonauts touched at Lemnos on their outward voyage. They found the island destitute of male inhabitants, the men having all been murdered by the women, with the sole exception of king Thoas, who had been saved by his daughter, now the reigning Queen, Hypsipyle. The Argonauts were hospitably entertained, and, according to Ovid, remained more than two years on the island, although other authors make the time much shorter. This epistle is supposed to be written by Hypsipyle on hearing of Jason's return to Thessaly, in company with Medea. The authorities followed by Ovid here, as well as in the twelfth epistle, were for the most part Apollodorus and Apollonius Rhodius.

3. 'I congratulate you on your safe return, as far as you permit me:' i. e. if you are unwilling to send me a letter, you may be unwilling to accept my congratulations. 'Hoc tamen ipsum' is used as if 'scire' followed, instead of 'certior esse,' to which it is equivalent.

5-7. For you may have been hindered by adverse winds from returning past Lemnos, while desirous of doing so: but a letter can be written no matter how bad the weather is.' 'Pacta:' 'promised you as my marriage portion.' Cf. vs. 117, sqq.

HYPSIPYLE IASONI.

Hypsipyle missa digna salute fui.
Cur mihi fama prior, quam nuntia littera venit?
Isse sacros Martis sub iuga panda boves, 10
Seminibus iactis segetes adolesse virorum,
Inque necem dextra non eguisse tua:
Pervigilem spolium pecudis servasse draconem,
Rapta tamen forti vellera fulva manu.
Haec ego si possem timide credentibus 'ista 15
Ipse mihi scripsit' dicere, quanta forem!
Quid queror officium lenti cessasse mariti?
Obsequium, maneo si tua, grande tuli.
Barbara narratur venisse venefica tecum,
In mihi promissi parte recepta tori. 20
Credula res amor est. Utinam temeraria dicar
Criminibus falsis insimulasse virum.
Nuper ab Haemoniis hospes mihi Thessalus oris
Venerat, et tactum vix bene limen erat,
'Aesonides' dixi 'quid agit meus?' Ille pudore 25
Haesit, in opposita lumina fixus humo.
Protinus exsilui, tunicisque a pectore ruptis
'Vivit, an' exclamo 'me quoque fata vocant?'

10. *Martis* G *Marti* nonnulli.
15. *Hoc* G *haec* multi libri.
28. *Trahunt* libri plurimi.

---

10. *Martis loves.*] The two brazen-hoofed, fire-breathing bulls, which grazed in the plain of Mars, πεδίον Ἀρήϊον, Ap. Rhod. v. 410. 'Mavortis arvum,' Met. vii. 101. 'Pandus,' 'curving,' rather a common word in Ovid.
13. *Spolium pecudis.*] 'The fleece.' So iv. 113, ix. 114.
15. *Timide credentibus.*] 'Timide credere dicuntur qui sic credunt ut tamen timeant ne quod credunt falsum reperiatur:' Ruhnken, who compares 'timide gaudere,' Met. x. 287: 'timide confidere,' Art. ii. 143.
16. *Quanta forem.*] 'What a proud woman I would be!'

17. 'Officium' refers, as it often does, to the outward forms of civility, such as writing a letter, vs. 7. 'Obsequium' means more, = 'kindness,' 'feeling.' The meaning is: 'If you only remain true to me, you indeed treat me with consideration: in that case I need not complain of your being slow in complying with external forms.'
25. *Quid agit.*] = 'ut valet?' Cf. Hor. Sat. I. ix. 4, 'Quid agis, dulcissime rerum'?
26. *Opposita humo.*] 'The ground in front of him.' Cf. Met. xiii. 541. 'Fixus:' cf. Apoll. Rhod. i. 785, ἐπὶ χθονὸς ὄμματ' ἐρείσας.

48   HEROIDES.

'Vivit' ait.   Timidumque mihi iurare coegi.
   Vix mihi teste deo credita vita tua est.   30
[Utque animus rediit, tua facta requirere coepi.
   Narrat aënipedes Martis arasse boves:
Vipereos dentes in humum pro semine iactos,
   Et subito natos arma tulisse viros :
Terrigenas populos civili marte peremtos   35
   Implesse aetatis fata diurna suae :
Devictus serpens. Iterum, si vivat Iason,
   Quaerimus : alternant spesque timorque fidem.]
Singula dum narrat, studio cursuque loquendi
   Detegit ingenio vulnera nostra suo.   40
Heus, ubi pacta fides? ubi connubialia iura,
   Faxque, sub arsuros dignior ire rogos?
Non ego sum furto tibi cognita : pronuba Iuno
   Affuit et sertis tempora vinctus Hymen.
At mihi nec Iuno, nec Hymen, sed tristis Erinys   45
   Praetulit infaustas sanguinolenta faces.
Quid mihi cum Minyis, quid cum Tritonide pinu?

29. *Timidumque mihi* G *timidum s. timide quod ait* alii.
31–38. Hos. v. uncinis inclusi M. secutus.
32. *Aeripedes* G. Corr. Heins.

31–38. These lines are condemned by Merkel on good grounds. They follow too closely after the similar account vs. 10–14: and 'devictus serpens,' vs. 37, is very strange Latin for 'devictum esse serpentem.' Loers and others understood it = 'postquam devictum ab eo audivissem,' but this meaning ought to have been more correctly expressed.

36. *Diurna.*] ἐφήμερα, 'only lasting for the day.'

40. *Ingenio suo.*] 'Naturally,' 'without intending it;' 'sponte natis verbis,' as Ruhnken well explains it. He appositely quotes Petron. 126, 'Crines ingenio suo flexi,' 'Hair curling naturally.' The Schol. on the Trèves MS. renders it 'simplicitate sua,' but it does not mean quite so much. 'Ingenium' is often opposed to 'ars,' e. g. where Ovid says, Am. I. xv. 14, of Callimachus, 'Quamvis ingenio non valet, arte valet.' Cf. also Met. iii. 159, 'simulaverat artem Ingenio Natura suo.'

41. *Connubialia.*] This word must be pronounced as if of only five syllables by synecphonesis, as the *u* in 'connubium,' and all words derived directly from 'nubo,' is long. So also, 'connubio,' in Met. vi. 428. 'Pronubus,' 'innubus,' etc., are derived not from 'nubo,' but its short root. But vid. Munro ad. Lucr. iii. 776.

42. The torch that lighted the bride to the house of the bridegroom, and that which kindled the funeral pile, were often placed in juxta-position by the Roman poets: as in Propertius' superb pentameter, 'Viximus insignes inter utramque facem:' El. V. xi. 46.

43. *Furto.*] 'Furtum' is the regular word for an intrigue. It is contrasted with a lawful marriage under the auspices of Juno Pronuba.

47. *Minyae.*] An ancient appellation of the Argonauts, derived from a race dwelling round Iolcos. The Argo is called

EP. VI. HYPSIPYLE IASONI.

Quid tibi cum patria, navita Tiphy, mea?
Non erat hic aries villo spectabilis aureo,
Nec senis Aeetae regia Lemnos erat.   50
Certa fui primo, sed me mala fata trahebant,
Hospita feminea pellere castra manu.
Lemniadesque viros, nimium quoque, vincere norunt.
Milite tam forti vita tuenda fuit.
Urbe virum iuvi tectoque animoque recepi.   55

---

51. Ita P G *mea fata* plurimi codd.
54. *Milite tam fortuna tuenda* P mendose. *forti vita* G P ma. sec., libri longe plurimi. Pro *vita* unus et alter *ripa* quod Burm. placuit. M edidit *causa*. Sed non agebatur de *vita* Lemniadum, *ripa* pro *litus* displicet, *causa* a libris nimium discrepat, quod cadit etiam in *vita et ripa*.
55. *Urbe virum vidi* P G M libri odd. omnes. Audacter in textum recepi meam coniecturam *iuvi* pro *vidi* quod frigere fatentur omnes, quod Naso scripsisse non potest. Quidnam significat *urbe virum vidi? in urbe*, an *ab urbe?* At illud ridiculum: anne otiose spatiantem in platea Iasonem casu vidit Hypsipyle? Hoc nec Latinum nec Ovidianum est. Nam *ab* non poterat omitti nec Ovidius appropinquationem classis ita breviter solet describere. Certum est in archetypis tale quid exaratum fuisse viuīvivi et librarios viuīvidi negligenter descripsisse. Iam confer locos simillimos nostri poetae quos in comm. contuli. Heins. coni. *ridua* pro *vidi*: sed epitheton vocis *urbe* male congruit cum structura versus nec probabile est *vidi* ex *ridua* fluxisse.

'Tritonis pinus' because it was built at the suggestion of Athene, by Argus: Ἀθηνᾶς ὑποθεμένης, Apollod. Bibl. 16. Tiphys was the helmsman of the Argo. Ibid.

53. See prefatory remarks. Λήμνια ἔργα was a proverb throughout Greece for wicked deeds. Cf. Herod. vi. 38, Aesch. Cho. 623.

54. The true reading here is doubtful. Vid. Adn. Crit. On the whole I have decided to retain 'vita,' the reading of G, and P by a late hand. ' Such brave soldiers as we are might have defended our lives against you.' The difficulty, that the lives of the Lemnian women were not called in question, may be got over by the reflection that they would have been, had the women resisted the landing of the Argonauts, in which case, says Hypsipyle, they were well able to take care of themselves. 'Fortuna,' the corruption in P, may have arisen from the transcriber fusing the beginnings of the words 'forti' and 'tuenda.'

55. *Iuvi*.] ' I aided him with the resources of my city, and received him to my home and heart.' In support of my emendation ' iuvi,' instead of the meaningless ' vidi,' I adduce the following passages:—(1) ii. 55, where Phyllis says to Demophoon: ' Nec moveor quod te ICVI PORTUQUE LOCOQUE,' a passage strikingly similar to that in the text. Still stronger is (2), Met. xi. 281, where 'urbe' is actually used with 'iuvo;' Peleus is wandering in exile, after slaying his brother Phocus, and presents himself before the Trachinian King Ceyx: ' Mentitusque fugae causam, petit URBE vel agro Se IUVET.' We may add a number of passages illustrating this use of 'iuvo,' as (3) Juv. iii. 211,—' nudum ac frusta rogantem, Nemo cibo nemo hospitio tectoque iuvabit.' ' Iuvare urbe,' ' tecto,' etc., were regular phrases for affording shelter to distressed outcasts: hence used with great propriety of allowing the Argonauts the harbour and city to recruit in, lay in provisions, etc.: and in Apollonius we find Hypsipyle's first step was to supply the Argonauts with provisions: Arg. i. 659,

Ὦ φίλαι εἰ δ ̓ ἄγε δὴ μενοεικέα δῶρα
πόρωμεν
Ἀνδράσιν οἷά τ ̓ ἔοικεν ἄγειν ἐπὶ νηὸς
ἔχοντας
Ἠϊά καὶ μέθυ λαρὸν κ.τ.λ.

Hic tibi bisque aestas bisque cucurrit hiems.
Tertia messis erat, cum tu dare vela coactus
  Implesti lacrimis talia verba tuis,
'Abstrahor, Hypsipyle : sed dent modo fata recursus,
  Vir tuus hinc abeo, vir tibi semper ero.   60
Quod tamen e nobis gravida celatur in alvo,
  Vivat, et eiusdem simus uterque parens.'
Hactenus. Et lacrimis in falsa cadentibus ora
  Cetera te memini non potuisse loqui.
Ultimus e sociis sacram conscendis in Argo :   65
  Illa volat : ventus concava vela tenet.
Caerula propulsae subducitur unda carinae :
  Terra tibi, nobis aspiciuntur aquae.
In latus omne patens turris circumspicit undas :
  Huc feror, et lacrimis osque sinusque madent.   70
Per lacrimas specto, cupidaeque faventia menti
  Longius adsueto lumina nostra vident.
Adde preces castas, immixtaque vota timori,

65. <i>Argo</i> P <i>Argon</i> G <i>concedis</i> M.
71. Pro <i>menti</i> coni. Volscus <i>amanti.</i>
73. <i>Adde</i> P G <i>addo</i> multi recentiores.

Valerius Flaccus also, describing the arrival of the Argonauts at Lemnos, makes the Lemnian prophetess Polyxo use the words 'Portum demus,' which is precisely = 'urbe iuvemus.' I believe the passages I have quoted, joined with the reasons mentioned in my critical note, justify me in restoring 'iuvi.' With respect to 'vidi' Heinsius remarked long ago, and every one must agree with him, 'τὸ vidi vehementer friget.' For let no one defend it by comparing it with such phrases as 'et vidi, et perii,' xii. 33. The word 'urbe' makes all the difference, and 'tectoque animoque recepi' is a very different thing from 'perii.'

56. Lennep supposes Ovid to have here followed some authority other than those which have come down to us, as the latter only represent the Argonauts to have stayed a few weeks or months in Lemnos.

58. *Implesti.*] Cf. x. 37, 'Quod voci deerat plangore replebam.' We may translate 'accompanied,' remembering Liv. vii. 2, 'impletas modis saturas' = 'farces accompanied with music :' the idea being that a musical accompaniment supplies something wanting in 'ussa vox.'

62. *Vivat.*] An allusion to the Roman custom, by which a father decided whether a child should live, and be recognised as his. This was done 'tollendo,' by taking the child up from the ground. Cf. iv. 124, and see Apoll. Rhod. i. 884.

67. *Subducitur.*] 'The water flies from beneath the ship.' Cf. Virg. Aen., v. 199, 'subtrahiturque solum,' and for the word Juv. I. i. 15, 'Et nos ergo manum ferulae subduximus.'

73. *Adde.*] 'Think also of my chaste prayers.' 'Addo' is of later authority than 'adde,' and need not, therefore, form an exception to the ordinary rule as to the quantity of o final. See note on xi. 127. 'Castas :' cf. ix. 35, 'votis operata pudicis.'

EP. VI. HYPSIPYLE IASONI.

Nunc quoque te salvo persoluenda mihi.
Vota ego persolvam? votis Medea fruetur? 75
Cor dolet, atque ira mixtus abundat amor.
Dona feram templis, vivum quod Iasona perdo?
Hostia pro damnis concidat icta meis?
Non equidem secura fui, semperque verebar,
Ne pater Argolica sumeret urbe nurum. 80
Argolidas timui : nocuit mihi barbara pellex.
Non expectata vulnus ab hoste tuli.
Nec facie meritisque placet : sed carmina novit,
Diraque cantata pabula falce metit.
Illa reluctantem cursu deducere lunam 85
Nititur, et tenebris abdere solis equos.
Illa refrenat aquas, obliquaque flumina sistit :
Illa loco silvas vivaque saxa movet :
Per tumulos errat passis discincta capillis,
Certaque de tepidis colligit ossa rogis : 90
Devovet absentes, simulacraque cerea fingit,
Et miserum tenues in iecur urget acus :
Et, quae nescierim melius. Male quaeritur herbis

---

82. *Exspectata* P *exspectato* G.
83. *Carmine morit* G vulg. *carmina morit* P *carmina novit* nonnulli, quod verum esse apertum est.
90. *Colligit* G, *colligat* P.
91. *Fingit* G, *figit* P.
93, 94. Hoc distichon iam inde ab Aldina ediderunt : *Et quae nescierim melius. Male quaeritur herbis Moribus et forma conciliandus amor.* Optimo sane sensu. Sed pro *male* P G plerique recentiores *mage :* ex quo paene restitueram *maga*, vocem, ut in comm. docui, huic loco aptissimam.

70-82. ' I never indeed felt quite secure of your fidelity : but I never thought you would marry a barbarian.'
83. *Carmina.*] ' Incantations.' Am. I. viii. 5, ' Illa magas artes Aeaeaque carmina novit.'
84. *Cantata.*] ' Enchanted.' Cf. Am. II. v. 38. ' Aut ubi cantatis luna laborat equis.'
84, 94. A pretty complete enumeration of the arts attributed to witches by the ancients. Their description formed a favourite commonplace with the Roman poets. Loers gives a long list of passages similar to this collected by Gierig and Jahn ad Med. vii. 180, sqq.
88. *Viva.*] Proleptic. ' Calls into life.' So Met. vii. 204. ' Vivum saxum' in the sing. is merely ' the natural rock.'
93, 94. ' And arts which I had rather know nothing of. 'Tis ill to seek to gain by means of herbs the love that ought to be won by beauty and character !' I at one time changed the ordinary reading

Moribus et forma conciliandus amor.
Hanc potes amplecti, thalamoque relictus in uno 95
Impavidus somno nocte silente frui?
Scilicet ut tauros, ita te iuga ferre coegit:
Quaque feros angues, te quoque mulcet ope.
Adde, quod adscribi factis procerumque tuisque
Se cavet, et titulo coniugis uxor obest. 100
Atque aliquis Peliao de partibus acta venenis
Imputat, et populum, qui sibi credat, habet.
'Non haec Aesonides, sed Phasias Acëtine

94. *Me* . . . . P *nobilis* G.

100. *Se favet* P G M, pessime. *facit* plurimi libri, *volet* pauci, *sese aret* coni. Allenus noster. *se cavet ego.* Leguleiorum formulas sapere verba poetae crediderim, et eadem officina procusa qua ista quoque *cede bonis,* ix. 110, *tradet habendam,* vii. 163, et similia.

103. *Filia fasias etc* G P ma. sec. Corr. Heins. ex P vestigiis

---

'male' to 'maga' = 'magical arts,' for two reasons. (1). If the easy 'male' is the true reading, the existence of 'mage' in all good MSS. is difficult to be accounted for; (2). The word 'magus' is peculiarly appropriate, whenever that part of sorcery is mentioned, which consists in the cutting and decoction of herbs. Cf. Med. Fac. 35, 'Sic potius nos urat amor quam fortibus herbis Quas maga terribili subsecat arte manus,' a passage exactly similar to the one before us in sentiment, and where 'maga' is also used as adj. Met. vii. 196, '(Quaeque magas tellus pollentibus instruis herbis,' etc. But inasmuch as the sense is perfect with *male,* and the construction would be difficult with *maga,* the received reading is best allowed to stand. We may suppose the copyist to have been thinking of magical arts, and hence to have changed 'male' to 'mage.' Sometimes the ordinary reading is pointed with a stop after 'et:' 'and, what I had rather know nothing of, she wickedly tries to gain,' etc. This has the fault of mistranslating 'male quaeritur,' which can only be a general reflection.

99, 100. 'Besides, she takes care that her name should be endorsed upon the exploits of yourself and the other chiefs, and so the wife is a bar to the fame of the husband.' The metaphor is clearly a legal one (see notes on ix. 110, viii. 5), as is

shown by the word 'adscribere,' which is the technical word 'for adding a codicil, or saving clause. 'Cavet,' which I have substituted for the corrupt 'favet,' is the regular word for taking many legal steps, esp. entering a 'caveat' as we say. Thus in Cicero de Inv. ii. 41, we find 'cavere' and 'adscribere' joined together: 'Amentiae fuit quum heredi vellet *cavere,* id *adscribere,* quo non adscripto nihilominus heredi caveretur.' The regular construction of 'caveo' in this legal sense is 'ut,' with the subjunctive; but it occasionally takes the accusative and infinitive, even in prose. Cf. Paul. in Pand. xxiv. 3, 49, 'Cavere instrumento se daturum decem.' Ulp. ib. xvii. 18, 'ut caveas to restituturum.' These passages strongly bear out the restoration of 'cavet,' as the accusative of the pronoun is used in both.

101, 102. 'And some one of the faction of Pelias attributes your exploits to the drugs of Medea, and has a following to believe him.' Pelias was Jason's uncle, who opposed his claim to the crown of Iolcos. 'Atque aliquis:' this is a regular phrase = καί τις: it occurs often in Ovid. cf. i. 31. 'Partes' is common in plur. = 'side,' 'faction,' both in poetry and prose. 'Imputat' is used here in its ordinary secondary sense of 'ascribing,' with dat.

103. *Phasias Acëtine.*] 'The Colchian daughter of Acëtes.' Acëtine is a patronymic, like Oceanine, Nonacrine, Eueanine.

EP. VI. HYPSIPYLE IASONI.

Aurea Phrixeae terga revellit ovis.'
Non probat Alcimede mater tua—consule matrem— 105
Non pater, a gelido cui venit axe nurus.
Illa sibi Tanai Scythiaeque paludibus udae
Quaerat et a patria Phasidis usque virum.
Mobilis Aesonide, vernaque incertior aura,
Cur tua polliciti pondere verba carent? 110
Vir meus hinc ieras: vir non meus inde redisti.
Sim reducis coniux, sicut euntis eram!
Si te nobilitas generosaque nomina tangunt,
En ego Minoo nata Thoante feror.
Bacchus avus: Bacchi coniux redimita corona 115
Praeradiat stellis signa minora suis.
Dos tibi Lemnos erit, terra ingeniosa colenti.
Me quoque dotales inter habere potes.
Nunc etiam peperi. Gratare ambobus, Iason.
Dulce mihi gravidae fecerat auctor onus. 120

107. *Tanais* P G *undae* P G. Corr. Heins.
118. *Quoque q.... lis inter* P *quoque quod tales* G. *res tales* M e cod. Erfurt. et sic vulgo legitur. Lindemannus nuper edidit *opes tales*, Sed verum est *dotales* ad quod proxime accedit G. 'Me quoque inter alios Lemni incolas, qui ut dotales servi tibi tribuentur, numerare potes.' Dictum est, ut illud Maronis Aen. iv. 102. 'Dotalesque tuae Tyrios permittere dextrae.' Salmasius olim coni. *dotales* pro *dutatas*, sed *dotalis* nunquam idem valet quod *dotatus*. Heins. coni. *Me quoque, quot tales, inter habere potes.*

---

111. Refers to Jason's words, vi. 60, supra.
114. *Feror.*] κέκλημαι, 'men call me,' in effect = 'sum.' Thoas, father of Hypsipyle, was son of Bacchus and Ariadne, daughter of Minos. 'Corona:' the crown given by Bacchus to Ariadne, or apparently, according to Ovid, Ariadne herself, was translated to the skies. Cf. Art. i. 557, 'Munus habe coelum : coelo spectabere sidus ; Saepe reges dubiam Cressa Corona ratem.'
117, 118. 'Lemnos shall be given you as my dowry, a land kindly to the cultivator: and my person you may reckon among your slaves acquired by dowry.' See Adn. Crit. and the passage from Virg. there quoted. 'Dotales' generally has 'servi' or some noun accompanying it. Here a noun must be supplied out of 'Lemnos' above. 'Inter Lemnios' (or rather 'Lemniadas') 'dotales servos tuos.' It is strange how editors can have hesitated about the true reading. Merkel has gone out of his way, as he confesses, Pref. p. viii. to adopt the worthless 'res tales' from a MS. which he condemns. The fact is, Salmasius led every one astray by suggesting 'dotales,' but translating it as if it were = 'dotatas,' 'richly dowered :' which of course was wrong. 'Ingeniosa :' cf. Stat. Sylv. I. iii. 15, 'Ingenium quam mite solo :' Fast. iv. 684, 'ad segetes ingeniosus ager.'

HEROIDES.

Felix in numero quoque sum, prolemque gemellam,
　Pignora Lucina bina favente dedi.
Si quaeris, cui sint similes? cognosceris illis.
　Fallere non norunt: cetera patris habent.
Legatos quos paene dedi pro matre ferendos.　　　　　125
　Sed tenuit coeptas saeva noverca vias.
Medeam timui: plus est Medea noverca:
　Medeae faciunt ad scelus omne manus.
Spargere quae fratris potuit lacerata per agros
　Corpora, pignoribus parceret illa meis?　　　　　130
Hanc, hanc, o demens, Colchisque ablate venenis,
　Diceris Hypsipyles praeposuisse toro?
Turpiter illa virum cognovit adultera virgo.　κόρη
　Me tibi, teque mihi taeda pudica dedit.
Prodidit illa patrem. Rapui de clade Thoanta.　　　135
　Deseruit Colchos. Me mea Lemnos habet.
Quid refert, scelerata piam si vincet, et ipso
　Crimine dotata est emeruitque virum?
Lemniadum facinus culpo, non miror, Iason.

131. *Hanc tamen* G *tamen* in P deest: alterum *hanc* omiserat librarius, more suo. vid. ad iv. 111, xiii. 137. *Hanc* reponens vim suam sententiae reddere mihi quidem videor: indignantis est: cf. Hor. Epod. iv., 20, ' Hoc, hoc tribuno militum.'

---

123. *Cognosceris illis.*] i. e., 'You are recalled to every one's recollection by them, so closely do they resemble you.'

125, 126. 'Ferendos' is very expressive: ' I was very near sending them to be carried in arms to you, as ambassadors for their mother: but (the thought of) their cruel stepmother stopped the expedition.'

128. *Faciunt ad.*] Cf. ii. 39.

129. *Fratris.*] Absyrtus, who was cut up by Medea, and his limbs scattered about, to delay the pursuit of Aeetes, at the place thence, it was said, called Tomi, (τέμνω) the scene of Ovid's exile.

131. *Ablate.*] 'Captivated,' not 'alienatus' as Burmann rendered it. Cf. 'abstulit,' vi. 150 infra, and xii. 36, note.

137. *Quid refert.*] ' What is the use of it all, if the guilty Medea is to be preferred to the pious Hypsipyle, and is dowered by her very crime, and has won the affections of her husband by it?' 'Emeruit' is used here in the same sense in which 'demereo' is generally used. See note on ii. 28. Cf. Trist. iv. 85, 'At vos admoniti nostris quoque casibus este Aequantem superos emeruisse virum.' 'Emereo' often means simply ' to earn :' and it would not give an inferior meaning if taken in that sense here: ' has earned a husband by her crime.' The commentators generally prefer the former interpretation.

139-150. The connexion appears to be this: 'I am naturally merciful: I blame the cruel Lemnian women: but you must remember that wrongs will drive even the weakest to arms: and even I, merciful as I am, would have slain Medea if you had put in at Lemnos with her: and you would have deserved the same fate.'

EP. VI. HYPSIPYLE IASONI.

Quamlibet infirmis ipse dat arma dolor.   140
Die age, si ventis, ut oportuit, actus iniqui
Intrasses portus tuque comesque meos,
Obviaque exissem fetu comitante gemello,
—Hiscere nempe tibi terra roganda fuit—
Quo vultu natos, quo me, scelerate, videres?   145
Perfidiae pretio quo nece dignus eras?
Ipse quidem per me tutus sospesque fuisses :
Non quia tu dignus, sed quia mitis ego :
Pellicis ipsa meos implessem sanguine vultus,
Quosque veneficiis abstulit illa suis.   150
Medeae Medea forem. Quod siquid ab alto
Iustus adest votis Iuppiter ipse meis,
Quod gemit Hypsipyle, lecti quoque subnuba nostri
Maereat, et leges sentiat ipsa suas.
Utque ego destituor coniux materque duorum,   155
Cum totidem natis orba sit illa viro.

140. *Quamlibet iratis* P ma. sec. *iratis* omissum ma. pr. *quodlibet ad facinus* G *quaelibet* codd. nonnulli et Lennep. *Quamlibet iratis* hic nullum sensum idoneum habet. Desiderabatur tale quale *infirmis* quod olim coni. F. Heusinger, et Lindemannus nuper edidit.

156. *A totidem natis orba sit illa viro* P G codd. plurimi *aque viro* M pauci libri. *atque viro* vulgo edunt. Praeclaram Lindemanni emendationem ut certissimam recepi. Ille scribit *A* initio h. v. ex *cum* breviter scripto derivatum esse, quod verisimile est.

---

140. *Quamlibet infirmis.*] 'Grief supplies weapons to the distressed, no matter how feeble they may be.' ' Quamlibet iratis' was absolute nonsense, and called down the derision of Lennep : ' Nonne hoc idem est ac si dicas, vinum homines titubare facit, quamvis ebrios : hieme algeo, quamvis nudus.' The conjecture 'infirmis' is by far the best made, being so strongly supported by Am. I. vii. 66, 'Quamlibet infirmis adiuvet ira manus.'

144. Cf. iii. 63, 'Devorer ante precor subito telluris hiatu,' and the Homeric τότε μοι χάνοι εὑρεῖα χθών.

147. *Per me.*] ἐμοῦ γε ἕνεκα, 'as far as I am concerned.'

153. *Subnuba.*] This word is ἅπαξ εἰρημένον. It is formed like 'pronubai,' 'innuba.' ' Sub' seems to have something of the force it has in ' sufficio,' ' to elect in the room of another.' Transl. : ' She who has supplanted me in your bed.'

156. Vid. Adn. Crit. The common reading, 'A totidem natis orba sit aque viro,' or ' atque viro,' was objectionable for three reasons. (1). Instead of 'aque' or 'atque' the best MSS. have 'illa;' (2). 'Orbus does not admit of ' a' or ' ab,' but governs the plain abl. In the passage quoted from Cic. Flacc. 23, ' orba ab optimatibus concio,' if the reading is sound, ' ab' means, as it often does, 'in respect of :' 'The assembly, in point of men of note, was empty.' This is a very different thing from being ' bereaved of,' ' deprived

Nec male parta diu teneat, peiusque relinquat:
  Exulet, et toto quaerat in orbe fugam.
Quam fratri germana fuit miseroque parenti
  Filia, tam natis, tam sit acerba viro. 160
Cum mare, cum terras consumpserit, aëra temptet:
  Erret inops, exspes, caede cruenta sua.
Haec ego, coniugio fraudata Thoantias oro.
  Vivite devoto nuptaque virque toro!

EPISTOLA VII.
DIDO AENEAE.

Sic ubi fata vocant, udis abiectus in herbis
Ad vada Maeandri concinit albus olor.

162. *Exspes* G *expers* P.

of;' (3). Hypsipyle prays that Medea may meet the same fate that she herself had. What was that fate? Not, that she was bereft of her children and her husband, but abandoned, with her two children, by her husband. Hence she prays with perfect consistency, 'as I, a wife, and mother of two children, am heartlessly abandoned, so may she, with the same number of children, be deserted by her husband.' This was what actually did happen to Medea. I regard this emendation of Lindemann's as perfectly certain.

157. *Peiusque relinquat.*] The poet, as Lennep remarks, was probably thinking of the proverb quoted by Cicero, Phil. ii. 27. from some old poet, 'male parta male dilabuntur.'

161. *Aëra tentet.*] Alludes to the flight of Medea from Corinth to Athens in a chariot drawn by winged dragons.

VII.—The following epistle is entirely founded on the Fourth Book of the Aeneid. Although Ovid has drawn largely from Virgil, yet there is in the poem so much of the softness and gentleness peculiar to the later poet, as to make us forget it is an imitation. Ovid evidently intended to remind his readers of Virgil's work: this is especially apparent from vs. 95, 'Nymphas ululasso putavi,' which demands a reference to Aen. iv. 168. In many instances the poem vies with its great original in beauty; in one passage, vs. 57, sqq., when developing the appeal of Dido, Aen. iv. 309, 'Quin etiam hiberno moliris sidere classem,' I think Ovid excels Virgil, and approaches the sublime.

1, 2. The opening is excellent. With regard to its abruptness, see note on v. 1. Two prefatory lines are to be found in a few late MSS. These introductory distichs will not be noticed in future in this edition. Ruhnken renders 'abiectus' 'temere iacens;' but 'temere' is rather expressive of the carelessness of luxurious repose, and this suits 'abiectus' in the other passages quoted by Ruhnken, Prop. I. xiv. 1, 'Tu licet abiectus Tiberina molliter unda,' and Phaedr. IV. i. 12: here translate, 'lying helpless.' The song of the swan before death is a well-

Nec quia te nostra sperem prece posse moveri,
 Adloquor : adverso movimus ista deo.
Sed merita et famam corpusque animumque pudicum
 Cum male perdiderim, perdere verba leve est.
Certus es ire tamen miseramque relinquere Dido,
 Atque idem venti vela fidemque ferent?
Certus es, Aenea, cum foedere solvere naves,
 Quaeque ubi sint nescis Itala regna sequi?
Nec nova Carthago, nec te crescentia tangunt
 Moenia, nec sceptro tradita summa tuo?
Facta fugis, facienda petis : quaerenda per orbem
 Altera, quaesita est altera terra tibi.
Ut terram invenias, quis eam tibi tradet habendam?
 Quis sua non notis arva terenda dabit?
Alter amor tibi restat habendus et altera Dido :
 Quamque iterum fallas, altera danda fides.
Quando erit, ut condas instar Carthaginis urbem,
 Et videas populos altus ab arce tuos?

4. *Movimus* G *norimus* P sollenni errore, cf. vi. 83, *vorimus* Heins. e cod. uno.
5. *Merite famam* P *meriti famam* G. Corr. Heins.
13. Pro *facienda* multi codd. *fugienda.*
17. *Tibi est habendus* P *tibi et exstat habenda et* G. Corr. Naugerius.

known tradition. The Lydian rivers Maeander and Caystrus used to abound in swans, and are said to do so still.

3, 4. 'I do not address you in the hope that you can be moved by my prayers : I have taken up my pen with the fates against me.' 'Movimus ista' = 'I write these words.' For 'moveo,' used of writing, cf. xv. 4, 'Hoc breve nescires unde movetur opus,' and Art. Am. i. 29. 'Deo,' perhaps = 'Love,' as Loers says.

5, 6. ' But after vainly throwing away kindly deeds, my fair fame, my charms of person, and purity of soul, it is a trifle to waste words.' 'Leve:' cf. xviI. 2, 'Non rescribendi gloria visa levis.'

7. *Certus es ire*] recalls Virg., who has 'certus iter,' 'certus eundi,' 'certa mori,' close together. Aen. iv. v.

8, 9. Cf. ii. 25. ' Cum foedere solvere navis,' 'to cast off your moorings and your engagement together.'

10. *Sequi.*] Virg. Aen. v. 629, 'Italiam sequimur fugientem.'

12. *Summa.*] 'The supreme authority.' 'Summa' in this sense generally has 'rerum,' as in Cic. Rep. 1. 26, 'Quem penes est omnium summa rerum regem illum unum vocamus.' It is used absolutely, Plaut. Truc. IV. ii. 15, 'Solus summam hic habet apud nos.'

13, 14. Dido means that Aeneas makes life a pursuit. 'You fly from what you have achieved, you seek other things to be achieved : no sooner have you gained one land than you must seek another through the world.' Ruhnken, however, supplies 'moenia' with 'facta' and 'facienda :' he is decidedly wrong, in my opinion.

15. 'Suppose you find the land.' 'Ut' is thus used, vv. 21, 55, 146, infra. 'Tradet habendam' is a legal phrase. See Dict. Ant. s. v. Traditio.

Omnia ut eveniant, nec di tua vota morentur,
  Unde tibi, quae te sic amet, uxor erit?
Uror, ut inducto ceratae sulphure taedae.
  Aeneau animo noxque diesque refert. 25
Ille quidem malo gratus et ad mea munera surdus,
  Et quo, si non sim stulta, carere velim:
Non tamen Aenean, quamvis male cogitat, odi:
  Sed queror infidum, questaque peius amo. 30
Parce, Venus, nurui, durumque amplectere fratrem,
  Frater Amor: castris militet ille tuis.
Aut ego quae coepi—neque enim dedignor—amare,
  Materiam curae praebeat ille meae.

21. *Omnia . . veniant* P *si veniant* G vulg. *Te* P G. Lenncp. coni. *di quod* edidi.
23. Post h. v. in quibusdam sequuntur *Ut pia fumosis addita tura rogis : Aeneas oculis semper vigilantis inhaeret.*
33. Ita P G nisi quod *Aut* non fuit sub ras. G. *quem* pro *quae* libr. plurimi, et ita vulgo legitur. Obelum suum apposuit M. Non tolerabilis tamen est coni. quam in praef. ed. suae protulit ipse: *Haud ego quae coepi plecti dedignor : amarae:* Burm. coni. *Atque ego quae.* Omnia sana esse credo.

---

21. 'Though all things should turn out as you expect, and the gods should not retard your prayers.' It is not necessary to understand 'eveniant' = 'prospere eveniant.' A colloquial phrase gives the exact meaning: 'though everything should come off.' I think Lennep has made out his case for 'di' against 'te:' his note is, 'Ut saepe dicitur aliquis alicuius morari vota quemadmodum,' Ep. xviii. 5, de Diis: 'Sed non sunt faciles: nam cur mea vota morantur?' Ep. xix. 95, 'Non ego tam ventos timeo mea vota morantes,' Met. viii. 71, 'solus mea vota moratur,' id est, 'obstat quominus optata re potiar,' ita prorsus insolens est dictio, 'morantur aliquem sua vota,' ad quam h. l. offensus etiam Heinsius legendum coniiciebat: ' nec te tibi fida morentur.'

27. 'True, he is an ingrate, and deaf to all my kindness, and a man whom I ought to be glad to be rid of, were I not a weak fool.'

31-34. 'Venus spare thy daughter-in-law, and Love, clasp thy hard-hearted brother (Aeneas): let him serve in thy camp: or let me who began to love—and I am not ashamed to do so—let him, I say, afford a subject to my passion.' There is an anacoluthon remarkable in Ovid in tha last two lines. Dido intended to say, 'Let me go on loving him;' but, after the break caused by the parenthesis, the construction is not unnaturally changed. This is better, I think, than making a longer stop at 'amare,' and carrying on 'militem,' 'let *me* serve,' out of the previous line, because it is not usual to carry on the meaning from one distich to another, unless it is continued to the end of the latter. Heinsius first saw the meaning of the couplet by the light of Am. I. iii. 2.: 'Aut amet, aut faciat cur ego semper amem: Ah, nimium volui, tantum patiatur amari.' There is no reason to read 'quem' for ' quae:' it has less authority, and evidently removes the emphasis from ' ego,' where it was intended, to 'ille,' where it is out of place: besides, it makes a very unnatural construction to have the antecedent of 'quem' so very far *after* it. ' Militet,' cf. Am. I. ix. 1, ' Militat omnis amans et habet sua castra Cupido: Attice, crede mihi, militat omnis amans.'

Fallor, et ista mihi falso iactatur imago. 35
Matris ab ingenio dissidet ille suae.
Te lapis et montes innataque rupibus altis
Robora, te saevae progenuere ferae,
Aut mare, quale vides agitari nunc quoque ventis :
Quo tamen adversis fluctibus ire paras. 40
Quo fugis? obstat hiems! Hiemis mihi gratia prosit.
Aspice, ut eversas concitet Eurus aquas.
Quod tibi malueram, sine me debere procellis :
Iustior est animo ventus et unda tuo.
Non ego sum tanti,—quid non censeris inique?— 45
Ut pereas, dum me per freta longa fugis.

45. *Tanti quid non* . . . *eris* (prima syllaba incerta ap. Heins. *terreris*) P, *quod non ceneris ut videtur sub. ras.* G *censeris* G ma. sec. *quod tu censeris* Erf. *quantus censeris* Hafn. *Quamvis mercaris inique* vulg. *quamvis mediteris* quinque libr. probante Iahn. *quod non mediteris* multi libr. M edidit *quod non verearis inique*, quod displicet quia apparet apodosin post *tanti* esse *ut pereas:* tum *ne pereas* postulabatur. Heins. malebat *quamvis censeris inique* quod non longe a veritate abest. *Censeris* enim in archetypis fuisse pro certo habeo. Unde enim rarioris verbi vestigia in tam multis codd. obvia? tum *censeri* aestimandi significationem habere posse in comm. docui. *Quid non* tamen non erat cur immutaret Heins.

35. 'I am wrong : that picture vainly presents itself before my eyes,' i. e. the picture of Aeneas serving in the camp of Love. Ruhnken gives a very far-fetched explanation, if it is an explanation : ' falso gloriaris te Venere natum esse. Imago est nobilitas generis, quod Romani illustrium maiorum imagines, in atrio collocare solebant.' This interpretation seems to have come from translating ' mihi iactatur,' ' is boasted of by you to me,' whereas it is equivalent to ' menti obversatur,' 'ante oculos versatur.'

37. Cf. Virg. Aen. iv. 365 : ' Nec tibi Diva parens,' etc. Hom. Il. xvi. 33 :

Νηλεὶς οὐκ ἄρα σοί γε πατὴρ ἦν ἱππότα Πηλεύς
Οὐδὲ Θέτις μήτηρ γλαυκὴ δί σε τίκτε θάλασσα
Πέτραι τ' ἠλίβατοι, ὅτι τοι νόος ἐστίν ἀπηνής.

Loers gives a list of similar passages, where this favourite common-place was introduced.

39. *Quale.*] 'A stormy sea like that even now before your eyes may have been your parent.'

45. 'It is not such an object to get rid of me—what do you not rate unfairly?—that you should be drowned while avoiding me.' This is one of the most vexed passages in these epistles. I have restored it, as I believe it to have existed in the best MSS. Vid. Adn. Crit. The only remaining question is, can ' censeri' have this meaning : = ' aestimare.' That great scholar Heinsius thought so, and I believe he was right. He read, ' quamvis censeris inique,' remarking, ' censeri pro aestimare veteres aevo optimo dixisse certum est.' ' Quamvis,' however, is too far removed from the best MS. ' Quid non' is the reading of P, and it gives sufficiently good sense to make the sentence interrogative, especially as it is a parenthesis. ' Censeor' was properly passive, meaning ' to be rated by the censors:' hence it came to take a deponent sense ' to give in a return of property.' Vid. Cic. Flacc. xxxii., ' Census es mancipia Amyntae. Neque huic ullam in eo fecisti iniuriam. Possidet enim ea mancipia Amyntas. Ac primo quidem pertinuit quum te audisset servos esse censum :' this is a clear

Exerces pretiosa odia et constantia magno,
  Si, dum me careas, est tibi vile mori.
Iam venti ponent, strataque aequaliter unda
  Caeruleis Triton per mare curret equis.   50
Tu quoque cum ventis utinam mutabilis esses :
  Et nisi duritia robora vincis, eris.
Quid, si nescires, insana quid aequora possunt ?
  Expertae toticns quam male credis aquae !
Ut pelago suadente etiam retinacula solvas,   55
  Multa tamen latus tristia pontus habet.

53. *Nescieris* libr. quidam. Pro *possunt, possint* al. s. *possent.*
54. *Tam* al.
56. Hoeoftius malebat *laetus*, Santenius *stratus.*

---

middle use of 'censeor;' it is used of a man who fraudulently registered another man's property as his own. 'Censeo' was also used = 'censeor' in this sense. Now, we have in Fast. v. 25, according to the reading preferred by Heinsius, and which is evidently the true one : 'Hinc sata Maiestas hos est dea censa parentes;' 'these (Honor and Reverentia) are the parents which Maiestas returns as hers :' but this is still the ordinary use of the word. But in Pont. I. ii. 140, we have a case more in point : 'Hanc probat, et primo dilectam semper ab aevo Est inter comites Marcia censa suas,' where the simple meaning of 'rating' is more nearly approached: this passage, joined with Am. II. xv. 2, 'Anule, formosae digitum vincture puellae, In quo censendum nil nisi dantis amor,' where 'censendum,' clearly = 'aestimandum,' appears to me fully to establish the fact that Ovid, in this passage may have used 'censeris' = 'aestimas.' True, in the passage last quoted, we must take 'censendum' from 'censeo,' not 'censeor;' but it goes to establish the meaning of the word. The deponent form is sufficiently attested without it. The propriety of 'censeris' is further shown from the number of expressions denoting price or value in the context : 'tanti,' 'vile,' 'pretiosa,' etc. My chief reason for restoring 'censeris' is the fact that such a rare word is traceable in so many MSS. perhaps even in P itself. The easy vulgate 'Quamvis merearis, inique,' is open to the objection, complacently overlooked by many editors, that its authority is the weakest possible. Merkel's reading does not seem to me to be Latin : 'tanti' requires 'ut,' not 'quod,' after it: and 'verearis' would require 'ne pereas,' not 'ut pereas.'

49. *Ponent.*] 'The winds will fall.' Cf. Virg. Aen. vii. 27, 'Cum venti posuere.' Ib. x. 103. Conington quotes Lucan iii. 523, 'Posito Borea ;' but this is not to the point.

53. *Quid si nescires.*] 'What greater folly could you commit if you were unacquainted with the effects of the raging seas?'

54. *Tam male credis.*] 'How foolishly do you repose confidence in the water whose fury you have so often experienced ?' Loers, who does not make the line interrogative, gives quite a different sense to 'male' = 'aegre' 'vix' 'non.' 'So little do you believe the sea (what horrors it has), although you have experienced them so often.' The Heusingers joined 'male' with 'expertae,' = 'tanto cum malo tuo expertae.' I think there can be little doubt about the true meaning.

55, 56. 'Even suppose the sea invited you to loose your moorings, yet the wide ocean has many hardships.' 'Latus:' 'etenim quo latius est mare, eo plura illa permeantibus obvenire possunt tristia.' Lennep.

EP. VII. DIDO AENEAE. 61

Nec violasso fidem temptantibus aequora prodest :
Perfidiae poenas exigit ille locus,
Praecipue cum laesus amor : quia mater Amorum
Nuda Cytheriacis edita fertur aquis. 60
Perdita ne perdam, timeo, noceamve nocenti,
Neu bibat aequoreas naufragus hostis aquas.
Vive, precor : sic te melius, quam funere perdam.
Tu potius leti causa ferere mei.
Finge, age, te rapido—nullum sit in omine pondus— 65
Turbine deprendi : quid tibi mentis erit ?
Protinus occurrent falsae periuria linguae,
Et Phrygia Dido fraude coacta mori :
Coniugis ante oculos deceptae stabit imago
Tristis et effusis sanguinolenta comis. 70
Quid tanti est ut tum ' merui : concedite !' dicas *pardon*

71. Ita P G, nisi quod pro *ut tum* habent P *tutum*, G *totum;* pro *dicas* G *dices.* Vulgo codd. et edd. habent ' *Quicquid id est, totum merui ! concedite' dices,* quam lectionem describens disrumpor. M locum obelo damnavit. Paeno nulla mutatione locum desperatum restitui. Scriptum erat ESTVTTVM ex quo librarius cod. P ut qui sententiam nihil moraretur, EST TVTVM descripsit. *Tutum* deinde in *totum* corruptum tenebras sententiae necessario offudit, quum *totum merui* interpretarentur. Nec Ovidianum est *totum merui* sed *merui* absolute positum, quod sollemnem usum in tali re, ut videtur, habet. Vid Comm.

---

57. A noble line. The idea of the sea punishing the guilty, especially the perjured, prevailed among both Greeks and Romans. Cf. a fine couplet, xii. 118. Antiphon, quoted by Paley, on Aesch. Theb. i.99, οἶμαι γὰρ ὑμᾶς ἐπίστασθαι ὅτι πολλοὶ ἤδη ἄνθρωποι μὴ καθαροὶ χεῖρας ἢ ἄλλο τι μίασμα ἔχοντες συνεισβάντες εἰς τὸ πλοῖον συναπώλεσαν μετὰ τῆς αὑτῶν ψυχῆς τοὺς ὁσίως διακειμένους τὰ προς τοὺς θεούς. Cf. Eur. El. 1354.

61, 62. 'Ruined, I fear lest I prove your ruin, and injure him who has injured me, and lest my drowning foe should gulp down the sea water.' Virgil's Dido is much more vengeful. Aen. iv. 382, 600, and so far the Ovidian Dido is the more pleasing conception, though, I fear, a less common character. Burns more beautifully still : ' Ye mustering thunders from above Your willing victim see : But spare and pardon my false love His wrongs to heaven and me !' 'Bibat' here seems to bear out the interpretation rejected by Conington of 'hausurum' in Aen. iv. l. c.

66. *Deprendi.*] This verb is used of being unexpectedly caught in any situation: esp. of being caught by a storm on the high seas. Met. xi. 699, ' Nubilus Aegaeo deprendit in aequore navim Auster.' Virg. Geo. iv. 421, ' Deprensis nautis.'

71. 'What can possibly make up for your then having to exclaim " I am guilty : pardon me !"' and for your thinking every thunderbolt that falls launched at your head ?' The priceless value of the Codex Puteaneus is nowhere more conspicuous than here. Had it not preserved the corrupt 'tutum' the true reading 'ut tum' would probably have been obscured for ever by ' totum,' to which it is changed in G, and the rest of the MSS., which followed this change up, by removing ' tanti,'

HEROIDES.

Quaeque cadent, in te fulmina missa putes?
Da breve saevitiae spatium pelagique tuaeque:
Grande morae pretium tuta futura via est.
Nec mihi tu curae: puero parcatur Iulo: 75
Te satis est titulum mortis habere meae.
Quid puer Ascanius, quid di meruere Penates?
Ignibus ereptos obruet unda deos?
Sed neque fers tecum, nec, quae mihi, perfide, iactas,
Presserunt humeros sacra paterque tuos. 80
Omnia mentiris: nec enim tua fallere lingua
Incipit a nobis, primaque plectar ego. *suffer*
Si quaeras, ubi sit formosi mater Iuli,
Occidit, a duro sola relicta viro.
Haec mihi narraras: at me movere: merentem 85

75. *Curae* P G *parcatur* al. *parcas* al.
82. *Plector* P *plectar* G.
85. *Narras a ... me .... novere* P *at me novere* G Heusinger. coni. *an me movere?* Burm. *nec me movere* quod Lennepio placuit.

---

now meaningless, and supplying its place by 'Quicquid id est,' on which Lennep, as quoted by Loers, most unhappily remarks that it is a formula used 'cum significatur aliquid inepti.' I confess I do not see the application of this remark, unless it be to the reading in question itself, in which case it has much pungency. The phrase 'totum merui' is not Ovidian: but 'merui' by itself is frequent, and is peculiarly used of a person confessing guilt, and acknowledging the justice of punishment that overtakes them. The following instances will suffice to prove this: Fast. iv. 239, 'Voxque fuit 'Merui: meritas do sanguine poenas.' Trist. I. ii. 95, 'Et iubet, et merui.' Pont. I. i. 54, 'alter ob huic similem privatus lumine culpam Clamabat media se meruisse via.' The last passage most clearly explains the use of the word: a man struck blind by the gods for some offence used to call out in the middle of the streets 'merui,' hoping to appease the wrath of the divinities by thus acknowledging his guilt. Madvig, in his Adversaria Graeca (1871) had anticipated me in the restoration of this passage, but I had made the emendation before I had seen his work: in fact it must have occurred to any one reading the collation of P in Merkel's edition, who asked himself where was the 'ut' wanted after 'tanti' and before 'dicas.' With 'concedite,' 'pardon me,' cf. Trist. ii. 31, 'Sed nisi peccassem quid tu concedere posses.' It is translated by others 'avaunt ye!' supposed to be addressed to the thunders, and haunting images; and this meaning it may bear, no doubt.

82. *Primaque plectar ego.*] 'Nor shall I be the first woman to suffer for it.' For 'que' coupling negative sentences, cf. ii. 90, note: and for the full force of 'plectar' see note on xi. 110.

83. For the fate of Creusa, mother of Iulus, cf. Aen. ii. 738.

85, 86. This is another vexed passage. Vid. Adn. Crit. I accept it as sound as it stands, not being able to suggest anything better. 'You told me all this story: it affected me: break my heart (ure), for I deserve it: my punishment will be less

EP. VII. DIDO AENEAE.

Ure: minor culpa poena futura mea est.
Nec mihi mens dubia est, quin te tua numina damnent:
Per mare, per terras septima iactat hiems.
Fluctibus eiectum tuta statione recepi,
Vixque bene audito nomine regna dedi.   90
His tamen officiis utinam contenta fuissem,
Et mihi concubitus fama sepulta foret!
Illa dies nocuit, qua nos declive sub antrum

86. Ita P. *Inde minor culpa poena futura tua est* G. Scilicet librarius G vice editoris h. l. fungitur, et textum mutavit ita ut ad Aeneae non Didus poenam referatur, quod minime verum. *Illa minor* P. ma. sec. libr longe plurimi. *Iure* Franc. *inde* al. *unde* al. Lectionem P' sanam esse iudico.
87. *Quin te te munera damnant* P.

than my guilt.' She looked on herself as guilty for listening to the stories of Aeneas, and believing and being affected by them. Cf. xii. 82, where Medea says of Jason's prayers: 'Haec animum—et quota pars haec sunt?—*movere* puellae,' and afterwards, looking on herself as guilty for being so foolish as to believe Jason's promises, she says, v. 119, 'Meritas subeamus in alto, Tu fraudis poenas, *credulitatis* ego.' 'Haec movere' does not especially refer to the death of Creusa, but generally to the whole tale of Aeneas: perhaps indeed vv. 81-84 were not written by Ovid at first, but added on a revision of the poem. 'Uro' is often used of the pains of love. In iii. 138, we have the imperative 'Nec miseram lenta ferreus uro mora.'

87. I think the manes of Creusa are intended to be at least included among the 'numina' of Aeneas here spoken of. The shades of the dead became 'Numina' to their surviving relatives. Cf. note on iii. 105.

88. *Septima.*] Aen. i. 759, 'Nunc te iam septima portat, Omnibus errantem terris et fluctibus aestas.'

89 With 'eiectum,' cf. vs. 173, and Aen. iv. 373, 'Fluctibus eiectum tuta statione recepi.'

92. 'Would that the scandal of our intercourse had been for ever buried.' 'Concubitus fama' is a very extraordinary expression, and as 'fama' is used in a good sense when joined with 'sepeliri,' in Pont. i. v. 85,—'tunc cum mea fama sepulta est,' the emendation of Werfer 'Nec — concubitu' will naturally occur to every one. But Ovid evidently refers to *the* rumour of Dido's intercourse with Aeneas, described at length in a famous passage Aen. iv. 172, 'Extemplo Libyae magnas it fama per urbes,' etc.

93. *Illa dies nocuit.*] Virg. Aen. iv. 165,

Speluncam Dido dux et Troianus eandem
Deveniunt: prima et tellus et pronuba
  Iuno
Dant signum: fulsere ignes et conscius
  aether
Connubii, summoque ululatunt vertice
  Nymphae.
Ille dies primus leti, primusque malo-
  rum
Causa fuit.

'Illa dies' and 'Nymphas ululasse putavi' show how closely Ovid followed Virgil: and the manner in which the latter words are brought in, Dido correcting Virgil as it were, shows that Ovid intended to remind his readers of his original. The sing. of 'dies' is used in Ovid indifferently of either gender when a particular day is intended. In other respects he conforms to the well-known rules that the fem. is used when length of time is meant: and that the plural is always masc.—'Ululasse:' as Conington remarks ad Aen. l. c., Ovid supposed the 'ululatus' of the nymphs to be a good sign = ὀλολυγμός, which was nearly always joyous. 'Ululare' is used of triumphal or festive cries, such as doubtless greeted the marriage procession.' Dido says, she thought she heard the

Caerulcus subitis compulit imber aquis.
Audieram vocem: Nymphas ululasse putavi. 95
Eumenides fati signa dedere mei.
Exige, laese pudor, poenas, violate Sychaeo
Ad quas—me miseram!—plena pudoris eo.
Est mihi marmorea sacratus in aede Sychaeus:
Oppositae frondes velleraque alba tegunt. 100
Hinc ego me sensi noto quater ore citari:
Ipse sono tenui dixit 'Elissa, veni!'
Nulla mora est, venio, venio tibi debita coniux.
Sum tamen admissi tarda pudore mei.

97. *Poenas viole . . te Syene P penas violate Sychaei G Sichen v. Sichaeu* libr. plurimi. *Sichaeo* Nangerius edidit. Locus corruptus est. Cod. Reg. Heins. habebat: *Exige laese pudor poenas violataque. . . . Iura nec ad cineres fama retenta meos Vosque mei manes animaeque cinisque Sichaei Ad quas,* etc., quod edidit Lennep legens, post *violataque, lecti*, atque *quem pro ad quae.* Nec multum adversatur M. in praef. ed. suae, p. viii. Sed lacuna, quam h. l. existere apertum est, post *violateque* (s. *violentaque?* cf. xi. 97), a quolibet melius explebitur. Verbosa enim et prorsus inepta est ista interpolatio, nec vitiis peioribus caret.
103. *Dedita* G *debita* P.
104. *Amissi* P *amisso* G.

---

marriage chant of the nymphs, but it was really the yells of the Furies. 'Ululatus' is used in good sense in Met. iii. 528, 'Festis ululatibus:' Cf. Caesar B. G. v. 36, vii. 80, Val. Flacc. ii. 537.

96. For the oft-recurring contrast between the auspicious and inauspicious or irregular marriage, cf. ii. 118. The Furies were generally supposed to preside on occasions of the latter sort. Lennep quotes in support of 'fati mei' against 'fatis meis, El. in Mort. Drus. 401, 'Jupiter ante dedit fati mala signa cruenti.' The change is very small, and as I go on the principle of correcting Ovid from his own works, I have admitted 'fati:' and it decidedly improves the sense. I do not think it likely that a Roman poet would talk of the Furies giving a signal to the Fates.

97. Vid. Adn. Crit. It is evident that the text as it stands never came from the pen of Ovid, although it is possible to torture a translation out of it. The recurrence of ' pudoris' so soon after 'pudor' suggests a lacuna: and so does the absence of a fitting antecedent to 'quas:' 'poenas' never could have been the antecedent.

The lacuna was probably caused by the transcriber's eye catching the 'que,' which probably existed in the real verse, before Sychaeo, or Sychaei, and going on from that, instead of from the 'que' after 'violate,' or whatever the reading was. This slip may be easily accounted for: the copyist had marked the 'que' as being in the second line above Sychaeo, and on looking up the page caught the word Sychaeus in 99, instead of going on to look for Sychaeo in 97: the consequence was, that he left out two whole lines. I cannot, however, accept the padding supplied by the Codex Regius of Heinsius. It is mere iteration; and the composer forgot to supply a correct antecedent to 'quas.'

99-103. Cf. Virg. Aen. iv. 457.

'Praeterea fuit in templis de marmore templum
Coniugis antiqui, magno quod honore colebat
Velleribus niveis et festa fronde revinctum.
Hinc exaudiri voces, et verba vocantis
Visa viri, nox quum terras obscura teneret.'

Da veniam culpae: decepit idoneus auctor.   105
   Invidiam noxae detrahit ille meae.
Diva parens seniorque pater pia sarcina nati
   Spem mihi mansuri rite dedere tori.
Si fuit errandum, causas habet error honestas.
   Adde fidem, nulla parte pigendus erit.   110
Durat in extremum, vitaeque novissima nostrae
   Prosequitur fati qui fuit ante, tenor.
Occidit internas coniux mactatus ad aras,
   Et sceleris tanti praemia frater habet.
Exsul agor, cineresque viri patriamque relinquo,   115
   Et feror in dubias hoste sequente vias:
Applicor ignotis, fratrique elapsa fretoque
   Quod tibi donavi, perfide, litus emo.
Urbem constitui, lateque patentia fixi
   Moenia finitimis invidiosa locis.   120
Bella tument: bellis peregrina et femina temptor,
   Vixque rudes portas urbis et arma paro.

106. Ita G *derabit* P.
108. *Tori* G *viri* P.
113. *In terras* P G. Corr. Naugerius. Coni. Micyll. *Herculeas.* Dan. Heins. *infernas.* N. Heins. *Herceas.*
116. *Duras* P G *dubias* al. quod malim.

---

105. *Decepit idoneus auctor.*] Cf. iv. 34, note.
110. *Adde fidem.*] i. e. 'the only quality Aeneas wants to be perfect is fidelity.'
113. *Internas aras.*] = the altars of the Penates situated 'in penetralibus aedium,' where Sychaeus was slain by Pygmalion, Dido's brother. Aen. i. 349. 'Herculeas,' the conjecture of Micyllus, was derived from the fact that Sychaeus is said to have been priest of Hercules. 'Herceas,' the conjecture of Heinsius, means the altars of Jupiter. 'Herceus,' 'the god of the homestead,' an ancient Roman appellation, = Ζεὺς ἑρκεῖος. This is a good conjecture, save that it is too far removed from the MSS. Heinsius quotes in support of it Ibis, 'Cui nihil Hercei profuit ara Iovis,' said of Priam, slain by Pyrrhus. Lucan ix., 'Herceas, monstrator ait, non respicis aras.'

116. I prefer 'dubias,' though of weaker authority, to 'duras,' as the former word is often used by Ovid of the dangers of the sea, of which Dido is evidently speaking, since 'applicor' in 147 is a nautical expression, meaning 'to come to land,' κατάγεσθαι. It is used either with dat. as here, or acc. with prep. cf. xvi. 126, 'Applicor in terras Oebali nympha tuas.' 'Ignotis' is masc. of the inhabitants. For 'dubius' of the dangers of the sea, cf. Trist. I. xi. 13, 'dubius iactabar ab haedis.' Her. xvi. 21, 'dubias a litore feci Longa Phereclea per freta puppe vias.' Art. i. 558, 'Saepe reges dubiam Cressa corona ratem.'
119, 120. Cf. Virg. Aen. iv. 656, 'Urbem praeclaram statui: mea moenia vidi.' 'Invidiosa,' 'looked on with dislike.'
122. Owing to the sudden hostility of the neighbouring tribes, Dido says she

Mille procis placui, qui me coiere querentes
    Nescio quem thalamis praeposuisse suis.
Quid dubitas vinctam Gaetulo tradere Iarbae?   125
    Praebuerim sceleri brachia nostra tuo.
Est etiam frater, cuius manus impia possit
    Respergi nostro, sparsa cruore viri.
Pone deos et quae tangendo sacra profanas:
    Non bene caelestes impia dextra colit.   130
Si tu cultor eras elapsis igne futurus,
    Poenitet elapsos ignibus esse deos.
Forsitan et gravidam Dido, scelerate, relinquas,
    Parsque tui lateat corpore clausa meo.
Accedet fatis matris miserabilis infans,
    Et nondum nati funeris auctor eris:
Cumque parente sua frater morietur Iuli,
    Poenaque connexos auferet una duos.
Sed iubet ire deus. Vellem, vetuisset adire,
    Punica nec Teucris pressa fuisset humus.   140

127. *Possit* P G *poscit* multi et edd. vett.
138. *Auferat* P *auferet* G.

---

was forced hurriedly to put rude gates to her city, before the walls were finished, and make warlike preparations. 'Portas' here is strongly in favour of 'portas' in Aen. iv. 87, where it is rejected by Conington, in favour of 'portus.'

'Non coeptae assurgunt turres, non *arma* iuventus
Exercet, *portasve* aut propugnacula bello
Tuta *parant*.

The coincidence of language is very remarkable, if Ovid was not thinking of the passage.

123. Cf. Vir. Aen. iv. 320, 535. The construction is, 'coiere querentes me praeposuisse,' etc. Lennep reminds us that coëo only takes a cognate acc., 'societatem coire,' and finds fault with Heinsius for thinking it might govern 'me,' like 'convenire.' But Heinsius never said so, nor, I think, implied it: his note on the construction is merely 'Refer autem' 'me' ad 'querentes' non ad 'coire.'

124. *Nescio quem.*] A remarkable instance of the inseparability of the words in this phrase: it is used with contempt of the strange Aeneas: 'nobody knows who.'

133. Virgil apparently avoids using the oblique cases of Dido, but inflects her other name Elissa instead. Conington ad Aen. iv. 383. Ovid here, and in vs. 7 uses the Greek acc., but no other inflection of the word.

136. Heinsius proposed 'nato,' to avoid the ambiguity. But this is sufficiently avoided by the pause natural at the end of the first member of the pentameter.

139. *Sed iubet ire Deus.*] 'But, you say, the gods command your departure.' Cf. Aen. iv. 376. sqq.

EP. VII. DIDO AENEAE.

Hoc duce nempe deo ventis agitaris iniquis,
  Et teris in rapido tempora longa freto?
Pergama vix tanto tibi erant repetenda labore,
  Hectore si vivo quanta fuere forent!
Non patrium Simoënta petis, sed Thybridas undas. 145
  Nempe ut pervenias quo cupis, hospes eris.
Utque latet vitatque tuas abstrusa carinas,
  Vix tibi continget terra petita seni.
Hos potius populos in dotem, ambage remissa,
  Accipe et advectas Pygmalionis opes. 150
Ilion in Tyriam transfer felicius urbem,
  Iamque locum regis sceptraque sacra tene.

152. *Namque*, ut videtur, sub ras. P, unde Salmasius *nomine coregis* ab ipso correctum *cum regis* elicuit, de quo dubitabat Heins. *Inque loco regis regia sceptra tene* G et ita plurimi libr. nisi quod *sceptraque sacra* (ut est etiam in P). Heins. coni. *Nomine et hanc regis.* Burm. *Hanc que locum regni.* Lennep. *nomen et hic regis.* M *Hanc que loco regis* e cod. Leidens. *Hicque* al. et Iahn. Lindemann, revocavit antiquam lect., *Inque loco regis sceptra sacrata tene*, quam exhibent codd. nonnulli. Credo in P fuisse aut *iamque locum* aut *remque loco*. Illud praetuli.

141. *Nempe.*] Ironical. 'You are surely a favourite of heaven: you who are driven a tempest-tost wanderer.'

142. *Rapido.*] Here used, as often, = 'rapaci,' 'devouring' (rapio). It is applied in this sense to the heat of the sun: cf. Met. viii. 225; Am. III. vi. 106: to wild beasts; cf. Her. XI. iii. x. 96, to the sea, as here: cf. Met. vi. 399: Am. II. iv. 8. In fact, it is used more often in this sense in Ovid, than in its ordinary meaning.

146. *Nempe.*] Not ironical. 'In fact, supposing you arrive at your destination, you will be stranger.' Cf. note on 'nempe,' ix. 61.

147. *Utque latet.*] 'And to judge from the way in which the land you seek lies hidden, and avoids your vessels, you will hardly reach it even in your old age.' Cf. 'utque facis, coges,' iii. 141.

149. Virg. Aen. iv. 104, 'liceat Phrygio servire marito Dotalesque tuae Tyrios permittere dextrae.' A similar inducement is offered by Phaedra to Hippolytus,

iv. 163, and by Hypsipyle to Jason, vi. 117. 'Ambage remissa,' 'and wander no more.'

150. *Advectas Pygmalionis opes.*] 'The imported wealth of Pygmalion,' i. e. the treasures which Dido carried with her from Tyre to Carthage, Aen. i. 362, 'naves, quae forte paratae, Corripiunt, onerantque auro: portantur avari Pygmalionis opes pelago.' A difficulty is here raised, as to how the treasures of Sychaeus, which Dido carried away, could be said to be the property of Pygmalion. Heyne ad Virg. l. c. explains ' opes quas Pygmalion animo et spe iam praeceperat:' Conington says, 'Pygmalion may not have actually taken possession of the treasures, but they were his from the time when he slew their owner.'

152. *Iamque locum regis, sceptraque sacra tene.*] 'At once (i. e. without waiting till you arrive at your promised Italy) assume the position of a king, and the sacred sceptre.' I have here adopted a conjecture of my own, as none of the

Si tibi mens avida est belli, si quaerit Iulus,
 Unde suo partus marte triumphus eat,
Quem superet, nequid desit, praebebimus hostem. 155
 Hic pacis leges, hic locus arma capit.
Tu modo—per matrem fraternaque tela, sagittas,
 Perque fugae comites, Dardana sacra, deos!
Sic superent, quoscumque tua de gente reportas,
 Mars ferus et damni sit modus ille tui, 160
Ascaniusque suos feliciter impleat annos,
 Et senis Anchisae molliter ossa cubent!—
Parce, precor, domui, quae se tibi tradit habendam.
 Quod crimen dicis praeter amasse meum?
Non ego sum Phthias magnisque oriunda Mycenis, 165
 Nec steterunt in te virque paterque meus.

155. *Quod superest* P (ap. Heins).
165. *Pthias* P *pytia* (*Pthia*) G.

received readings are satisfactory, and 'iamque,' approaches most nearly to the appearance of the erasure in P. But I doubt whether *Remque loco regis*, &c., is not the true reading. 'Rem.' i.e. 'Rem Tyriam;' cf. 'res Romana,' Met. xiv. 809; 'res Troiana,' Met. xv. 438; and for 'rem tenere,' cf. 'res coeli tenuit,' Fast. v. 125: govern the state as a king (loco regis). Merkel's 'hancque' supplying 'urbem,' is very harsh, and it, as well as 'hicque,' is open to the objection that it violates euphony. In fact, I believe that it may be laid down as a canon that Latin poetry does not admit of the copula 'que' being joined with a word ending in *e*, unless it is separated from it by the sense, as in Fast. iv. 848. The reading 'Inque loco regis sceptra sacrata tena,' changes P in the only place where the reading is certain, substituting 'sacrata' for 'sacra.' Besides, not to dwell on the fact that 'sacrum,' 'holy,' as a general epithet of 'sceptrum,' is more appropriate than 'sacratum,' which is properly 'consecrated,' Ovid never makes the *a* short in 'sacro' or its participle 'sacratus,' though he uses the verb five times, and the partic. fifteen times at least.

154. *Triumphus eat.*] 'Graphice et a more sumtum Romanorum.' Loers.
156 *Capit* = χωρεῖ, 'contains.' 'Hic locus aptus est sive pacem colere velis sive bellum genere.' Ruhnken.
160. 'And may that fierce warfare (the Trojan war) be the last of your disasters.'
162. *Molliter ossa cubent.*] A common wish for the repose of the dead = 'Requiescat in pace.' It forms part of tho epitaph written by Ovid for himself, Trist. III. iii. 76.
165. 'I do not come from the land of Achilles or Agamemnon.' The adj. form Φθιάς occurs in Eur. And. 'If Phthia' is read, it is abl. depending like Mycenis on 'oriunda.' For the sentiment, cf. Aen. iv. 425, 'Non ego cum Danais Troianam exscindere gentem Aulide iuravi, classemve ad Pergama misi.' 'Steterunt: the penult. is shortened by Ovid whenever it suits the metre. Cf. xii. 71 and passim.

EP. VII. DIDO AENEAE.

Si pudet uxoris, non nupta, sed hospita dicar.
   Dum tua sit Dido, quodlibet esse feret.
Nota mihi freta sunt Afrum frangentia litus.
   Temporibus certis dantque negantque viam.   170
Cum dabit aura viam, praebebis carbasa ventis.
   Nunc levis eiectam continet alga ratem.
Tempus ut observem, manda mihi: serius ibis,
   Nec te, si cupies, ipsa manere sinam.
Et socii requiem poscunt, laniataque classis   175
   Postulat exiguas semirefecta moras.
Pro meritis et siqua tibi debebimus ultra,
   Pro spe coniugii tempora parva peto:

172. e G *Scilleuissectam* P.
173. *Serius* G *certius* vulg.
177. *Praebebimus* libr. duo.

---

167. *Non nupta, sed hospita dicar.*] Adapted from Virg. Aen. iv. 323, 'cui me moribundam deseris hospes? Hoc solum nomen quoniam de coniuge restat.'

168. *Dum tua sit Dido quodlibet esse, feret.*] Cf. xii. 110, 'Munus in exilio quolibet esse tuli.' The sentiment is much more beautifully expressed in the Ballad of the Nut-Browne Mayd: 'Yet am I sure of one pleasure And shortely, it is this: That where you be, me seemeth, perdé, I could not fare amiss,' words which never were excelled in any language, by any poet.

169. *Frangentia.*] Heinsius preferred 'plangentia,' 'beating.' He says truly that the ancients generally said 'litus frangit fluctus' rather than 'fluctus frangunt litus,' quoting 'fluctifragum litus' from Lucretius. He might also have quoted Hor. Od. I. xi. 5, (Iliems) 'Quae nunc oppositis debilitat pumicibus mare.' But 'frangere litus' is not only unobjectionable, but used with great propriety by Dido, who wishes to paint the violence of the African storms, not merely to draw a fanciful picture of any sea.

172. *Nunc levis eiectam continet alga ratem.*] The meaning is, that a tempest is raging, as is indicated by the heaps of seaweed thrown on the shore. Aen. vii. 590. 'Eiectam ratem' must mean that the ship is drawn up high and dry on the beach, 'cast out,' as it were by the waves. Loers speaks of 'eiectae algae' as if it were in the text.

177. *Pro meritis, et siqua tibi debebimus ultra.*] The commentators have failed to perceive the force of these words. They have generally been interpreted 'in return for past and future services,' and as 'debebimus' was hard to explain in this meaning, Burmann read 'praebebimus.' 'Debebimus' is however to be explained by a reference to Fast. ii. 825, where Lucretia asks, 'Hoc quoque Tarquinio debebimus?' 'Shall I owe this also to Tarquin?' (i. e. shall Tarquin be the cause of my having to tell the tale of my violation, as well as of the act?) Dido alludes to vs. 5, 'Sed merita et famam corpusque animumque pudicum, Cum male perdiderim perdere verba leve est.' 'Merita' are her kind deeds to Aeneas: but her character and chastity are '*ultra merita*,' *far beyond those.*

There is also an allusion to the thought suggested in vs. 133, that she may become a mother, and I think this helps to explain the use of the future, as well as the vagueness of the second clause, which is a sort of hint: and 'pro spe coniugii' is evidently suggested by that clause. Translate: 'In return for my past kindness to

Dum freta mitescunt et amor, dum tempore et usu
    Fortiter edisco tristia posse pati. 180
Si minus, est animus nobis effundere vitam
    In me crudelis non potes esse diu.
Aspicias utinam, quae sit scribentis imago.
    Scribimus, et gremio Troicus ensis adest:
Perque genas lacrimae strictum labuntur in ensem, 185
    Qui iam pro lacrimis sanguine tinctus erit.
Quam bene conveniunt fato tua munera nostro!
    Instruis impensa nostra sepulchra brevi.
Nec mea nunc primum feriuntur pectora telo:
    Ille locus saevi vulnus amoris habet. 190
Anna soror, soror Anna, meae male conscia culpae,
    Iam dabis in cineres ultima dona meos.
Nec, consumpta rogis, inscribar Elissa Sychaei,
    Hoc tamen in tumuli marmore carmen erit:
'Praebuit Aeneas et causam mortis et ensem. 195
    Ipsa sua Dido concidit usa manu.'

---

179. *Amor dum tempteret* P *usum* P ma. sec. Corr. Salmasius. *amor dum forte tepescat* G, *amor dum temperat usum* vulg.

---

you, for anything surpassing kindness I shall have to lay to your charge, instead of the hope of marriage you have held out to me, all I ask is a little delay.'

179. Virg. Aen. iv. 133, 'Tempus inane peto, requiem spatiumque furori, Dum mea me victam doceat fortuna dolere.'

181. *Troicus ensis.*] Aen. iv. 646. 'Consecdit furibunda rogos, ensemque recludit Dardanium non hos quaesitum munus in usus:' where see Conington's note.

190. 'Impensa,' according to Ruhnken, is properly used of funeral expenses. He quotes Justin ii. 6, 'Impense humati ad ceterorum exemplum.' I doubt if the word is more applicable to funerals than to anything else that is costly. Heinsius denies it means 'expense' here, but is

'res quaelibet ad ornandum sepulchrum idonea:' quoting Juv. iii. 216, 'Conferat impensas' where it means 'materials,' 'ornaments' for restoring a house that had been burnt down. Transl.: 'You adorn my tomb with scanty show,' because the only ornament he had contributed for its decoration was his sword.

191. *Culpae.*] Her intercourse with Aeneas, which her sister Anna was aware of. Aen. iv. 550.

193. In inscriptions on the tombs of married women, it was usual to put their name and the genitive of that of their husband, omitting 'uxor.' Lucan ii. 343, 'Liceat tumulo scripsisse Catonis Marcia.' Dido considered herself unworthy of being called the wife of Sychaeus, even on her tombstone.

EPISTOLA VIII.

HERMIONE ORESTAE.

Pyrrhus Achillides, animosus imagine patris,
    Inclusam contra iusque piumque tenet.
Quod potui, renui, ne non invita tenerer.   5
    Cetera feminae non valuere manus.
'Quid facis, Aeacide? non sum sine vindice' dixi:
    'Haec tibi sub domino est, Pyrrhe, puella suo.'
Surdior ille freto clamantem nomen Orestis
    Traxit inornatis in sua tecta comis.   10

9. *Surdhos ille* P. *Orestes* P, *Orestae* Heins.

VIII.—Hermione, daughter of Menelaus and Helen, was betrothed by her grandfather Tyndareus, to her cousin Orestes, during the absence of Menelaus at the siege of Troy. The latter, ignorant of her engagement, promised her to Pyrrhus, who forcibly carried her off and married her on his return. Vid. Servius ad Virg. Aen. iii. 328. There was a tragedy of Sophocles called 'Hermione,' in which the legend probably appeared in the same shape as it does in the following epistle.

1. *Animosus imagine patris.*] i. e. 'Exemplo patris,' 'hot-headed like his father.' Cf. Virg. Aen. ii., 'Instat vi patria Pyrrhus. Achilles is called 'animosus' by Horace, Sat. I. vii. 12.

2. *Inclusam.*] The ellipse of 'me' seems very harsh, there being no antecedent to which to refer 'inclusam.' I am inclined to think the true reading is 'Hermionem,' and that 'inclusam' was a gloss explaining the meaning of 'tenet,' which made its way into the text before the age of P. Otherwise we have not the name Hermione until vs. 59.

5. *Quod potui, renui.*] 'I refused compliance, which was the only thing I could do,' or, in other words, 'What I could. I did—namely, refused compliance.' Cf. Met. iv. 681, 'Colasset vultus si non religata fuisset, Lumina, *quod potuit*, lacrimis implevit obortis.' Burmann and Ruhnken make a grave error in translating 'quantum potui.'

7. *Non sum sine vindice.*] There is an allusion here to the legal process of 'manus iniectio.' The defendant (in such a case, when seized by the plaintiff) was not permitted to make any resistance, and his only mode of defence was to find some responsible person (*vindex*) who would undertake his defence. If he found no vindex, the plaintiff might carry defendant to his house and keep him in confinement for sixty days.' Dict. Ant. s. v., 'Manus iniectio.' Cf. xii. 158, and for other legal metaphors in Ovid, see note on ix. 109. Pyrrhus had in this instance wrongfully

72   HEROIDES.

Quid gravius capta Lacedaemone serva tulissem,
  Si raperet Graias barbara turba nurus?
Parcius Andromachen vexavit Achaïa victrix,
  Cum Danaus Phrygias ureret ignis opes.
At tu, cura mei si te pia tangit, Oreste,   15
  Inice non timidas in tua iura manus.
An siquis rapiat stabulis armenta reclusis,
  Arma feras, rapta coniuge lentus eris?
Si socer exemplo nuptae repetitor ademptae,
  Nupta foret Paridi mater, ut ante fuit.   20
Nec tu mille rates sinuosaque vela pararis,
  Nec numeros Danai militis: ipse veni!
Sic quoque eram repetenda tamen: nec turpe marito, 25
  Aspera pro caro bella tulisse toro.

17. *Reclusis* libri. Burm. coni. *revulsis*. Male.
19. Pro *si, sit* habent libr. plurimi, et post h. v.; sequebantur in quibusdam libris: *Cui pia militiae causa puella fuit Si socer ignarus vacua stertisset in aula*, sed quum in omnibus antiquioribus desint, et multum offendat *stertisset* pro *stertuisset*, pro quo coni. Burm. *sedisset*, omittere praestat.
24. *Numeros* P *numerum* vulg.

---

resorted to the 'manus iniectio,' and Hermione exhorts Orestes to use the same process with greater right, vs. 16. Cf. iii. 153. 'Domini iure venire iube.' Hermione denies the right of Pyrrhus to take possession of her, as she was not 'sui iuris,' but under the 'dominium' or ownership of Orestes by virtue of her betrothal to him.

16. See last note. The 'iniectio manus' was a favourite illustration of Ovid's. Cf. Am. I. iv. 40, 'Et dicam, mea sunt, iniciamque manus.' Fast. iv. 90, 'Quem Venus iniecta vindicat alma manu.'

17. 'If a thief were to burst open your folds, and steal your herds.' 'Reclusis' was thought weak by Burmann, who proposed 'revulsis.' Lennep however quoted Plautus Capt. IV. iv. 10, 'Cellas refregit omnes, reclusitque armarium.'

19. *Exemplo.*] sc. 'tuo.' 'After your fashion.' It must be admitted that this is an awkward line, as a verb must be supplied, as well as 'tuo.' It is easy enough if we read 'sit' for 'si,' and admit the distich that follows in some MSS. But these lines are open to grave objections: they are found only in a few inferior codices: the repetitions of 'socer' and 'fuit,' and the incorrectness of the form 'stertisset' seem to me decisive against them.

24. *Numeros.*] 'Companies' 'troops.' This use of 'numeri' approaches the meaning the word came to have in later times = 'cohorts.' Heinsius quotes Tertullian Apol. 'Si hostes agere vellemus, deesset nobis vis numerorum et copiarum?' Cassiodorus Hist. Lib. i. 'Romanorum cohortes nunc numeri vocantur.' This meaning is not uncommon in Tacitus. Ernesti Clav. Cic., claims it for the Augustan age also.

25. *Sic quoque.*] 'Even so,' i.e. 'even if you had to bring an armed force, you should have tried to rescue me.'

EP. VIII. HERMIONE ORESTAE.

Quid, quod avus nobis idem Pelopeïus Atreus,
  Et, si non esses vir mihi, frater eras?
Vir, precor, uxori, frater succurre sorori:
  Instant officio nomina bina tuo.   30
Me tibi Tyndareus, vita gravis auctor et annis,
  Tradidit: arbitrium neptis habebat avus.
At pater Aeacidae promiserat, inscius acti.
  Plus quoque, qui prior est ordine, possit avus.
Cum tibi nubebam, nulli mea taeda nocebat: 35
  Si iungar Pyrrho, tu mihi laesus eris.
Et pater ignoscet nostro Menelaus amori:
  Succubuit telis praepetis ipse dei.
Quem sibi permisit, genero concedet amorem.
  Proderit exemplo mater amata suo.   40
Tu mihi, quod matri pater est: quas egerat olim
  Dardanius partes advena, Pyrrhus agit.
Ille licet patriis sine fine superbiat actis.
  Et tu quae referas facta parentis, habes.
Tantalides omnes ipsumque regebat Achillem.   45
  Hic pars militiae, dux erat ille ducum.
Tu quoque habes proavum Pelopem Pelopisque parentem.
  Si medios numeres, a Iove quintus eris.

33. *Posset* P G.
48. *Melius numeres* P G M. Nodellii emendat. recepit Lenn. quem subsequor. Cf. xvi. 174, medios ut taceamus avos.

---

27. *Quid quod.*] This phrase always introduces an additional argument. 'Besides I am your cousin, as well as your wife.' 'Frater' is often used for a first cousin. Cf. xiv. 1, Met. xiii. 31.

31. 'Tyndareus, whose character and age gave his authority weight, betrothed me to you: as grandfather he had the disposal of his grandchild: but my father Menelaus promised me to Pyrrhus through ignorance of that transaction: let my grandfather then, as he is first in order of time, also carry the preference.' 'Prior ordine' is understood by Jahn to mean simply 'older:' as I understand it, it means that the promise of Tyndareus was made before that of Menelaus. I join 'quoque' closely with 'possit,' but it might also be understood to refer to the previous line, and to supply an additional argument: 'besides.'

35. *Mea taeda.*] 'My marriage.' Cf. vi. 184, 'Me tibi teque mihi taeda pudica dedit.'

40. 'The precedent of my father's love to my mother will be of service to us.'

45. *Tantalides.*] Agamemnon, whose great grandfather was Tantalus. 'Dux ducum,' from Agamemnon's titles of ἄναξ ἀνδρῶν, βασιλεύτατος.

48. *Si medios numeres.*] 'If you count the ancestors who intervene, you are fifth

Nec virtute cares   Arma invidiosa tulisti:
   Sed tu quid faceres? induit illa pater.   50
Materia vellem fortis meliore fuisses.
   Non lecta est operi, sed data causa tuo.
Hanc tamen implesti, iuguloque Aegisthus aperto
   Tecta cruentavit, quae pater ante tuus.
Increpat Aeacides, laudemque in crimina vertit: 55
   Et tamen aspectus sustinet ille meos.
Rumpor, et ora mihi pariter cum mente tumescunt,

50. *Induit illa pater* P *patrem* G.

---

in a direct line from Jupiter.' Cf. xvi. 174, 'Pliada si quaeres, in nostra gente *Ioremque*, Invenies *medios* ut taceamus avos,' a passage so like that in the text, that I have accepted the emendation of Nodellius, called 'certissimam' by Lennep. 'Melius' can of course stand, and is in some degree supported, as Loers says, by ii. 7, 'Tempora si numeres, bene quae numeramus amantes,' if ' bene' is the real reading there. The line of descent was—Jupiter, Tantalus, Pelops, Atreus, Agamemnon.

49. *Arma invidiosa tulisti.*] 'You took up arms abhorred by all:' when proceeding to avenge the murder of Agamemnon on Clytaemnestra and Aegisthus. 'Invidiosus' = ἐπίφθονος 'looked on with abhorrence,' on account of the unnatural slaying of a mother. On the other hand the Chorus in the Choephoroe, urging Orestes to the deed, say vs. 811. sqq.:

σὺ δὲ θαρσῶν ὅταν ᾔκῃ μέρος ἔργων,
ἐπαύσας πατρὸς αὐδὰν θροοῦσα τέκνον,
πέραιν' οὐκ ἐπίμομφον ἄταν:

50. *Sed tu quid faceres.*] Excusandi formula. Cf. Virg. Ecl. i. 41, 'Quid facerem?' Ruhnken. '*Induit illa pater.*' 'Your father dressed you in those arms,' an expression which shows how thoroughly Ovid had caught the spirit of the Orestean dramas of Aeschylus and Sophocles,—in which the dead Agamemnon is ever looked upon as an active agent working from Hades to his ultimate revenge on his murderers. This is also apparent from vs. 120, 'Quod se sub tumulo fortiter ulta iacent.' The first passage I open at in the Choephoroe, for instance, vs. 315, sqq., τίκτον, φρόνημα τοῦ θανόντος οὐ δαμάζει πυρὸς μαλερὰ γνάθος φαίνει δ' ὕστερον ὀργάς. ὀτοτύζεται δ' ὁ θνῄσκων ἀναφαίνεται δ' ὁ βλάπτων κ.τ.λ. Ibid. 368, τῶν μὲν ἀρωγοὶ κατὰ γῆς ἤδη. Ibid. 872, τὸν ζῶντα καίνειν τοὺς τεθνηκότας λέγω and passim. For the construction: cf. Art. i. 197, 'Induit arma tibi genitor patriaeque tuusque.' There is a reading in most MSS., 'patrem' from which we have fortunately been preserved by P, as it destroys the sense altogether. It was probably introduced by some copyist who was thinking of the robe spread over Agamemnon by Clytaemnestra in the bath, 'illa' being supposed the nom. sing.

51. 'I wish you had had a better subject to show your bravery on: but you did not' choose your cause: it was assigned to you. I think 'materia' refers exclusively to the cowardly Aegisthus, whom Hermione considered an antagonist unworthy of Orestes. I think this is borne out by the expression 'lecta est' in 52. The force of 'lego' is to pick out an antagonist, especially one's match. So in Plautus Amph. I. i. 163, 'alia forma oportet esse quem tu pugno legeris,' 'He must be a different make of man you would pick out to box with.'

53. *Hanc tamen implesti.*] 'Yet, such as it was, you thoroughly performed it.'

EP. VIII. HERMIONE ORESTAE. 75

Pectoraque inclusis ignibus usta dolent.
Hermione coram quisquamne obiecit Oresti,
  Nec mihi sunt vires, nec ferus ensis adest ?
Flere licet certe ; flendo defundimus iram,
  Perque sinum lacrimae fluminis instar eunt.
Has solas habeo semper, semperque profundo
  Hument incultae fonte perenne genae.
Num generis fato, quod nostros errat in annos,   65
  Tantalides matres apta rapina sumus ?
Non ego fluminei referam mendacia cygni,
  Nec querar in plumis delituisse Iovem.
Qua duo porrectus longe freta distinct Isthmos,
  Vecta peregrinis Hippodamia rotis.   70
[Castori Amyclaeo et Amyclaeo Polluci

61. *Defundimus* P, verissime. *diffundimus* M, *dispargimus* G.
65. *Nam* P, *hoc* vulg. *Fato* P G, *fatum* vulg. *Erat* P, *errat* plurimi codd. Lennepius recepit Heinsii coni. *durat*.
69. *Freta destinat* P G, *hemos* P.
71, 72. Spurii videntur. Vid. Praef. huius ed.

'Hanc,' I think, refers to 'causam' in the previous line, not to 'materiam' in 51, to which Ruhnken refers it. He quotes Trist. IV. iii. 73, 'materiamque tuis tristem virtutibus imple,' but that may be a coincidence : the abl. 'virtutibus' makes all the difference. For 'implere' = to 'exccute,' 'perform,' cf. Cic. Cluent. xviii. 51, 'ne id profiteri videar, quod non possum implere.'

59, 60. ' Does any one dare to speak ill of Orestes in presence of Hermione, and can I not find strength, or a weapon to avenge it ?' 'Obicere' = 'exprobrare' must have an accusative supplied, 'aliquid.'

65, 66. ' Can it be that owing to a fate attached to our race, which extends beyond its bounds even to our years, we women of the house of Tantalus are fit subjects for ravishment ?' For the fate of race,' cf. note on iv. 53.—' Errat :' of this word, Lennep says, 'nihili est,' but I cannot agree with him. 'Errat' gives excellent sense : Ovid here puts himself in the Greek point of view, which often regarded some πρώταρχος ἄτη as drawing down a calamity on future ages. Its evil influence might reasonably have expended itself long before, but still it goes on even beyond its bounds (errat), bringing misery on the devoted family in the same way from generation to generation. Ovid very likely had the word ἐξορίζεται, Eur. Hipp. 1381, in his mind, παλαιῶν προγενῆ τόρων ἐξορίζεται κακὸν οὐδὲ μέλλει.

70. This fine line, which Ovid repeats, Art. ii. 8, is borrowed from Propertius, I. ii. 20, 'Avecta externis Hippodamia rotis.' Hippodamia was daughter of Oenomaus, King of Elis, won in marriage by Pelops the Phrygian : hence ' peregrinis.'

71. *Castori*.] The elision of the long vowel at the end of this word was with Lachmann a chief argument against the authenticity of this Epistle. I will treat at greater length of his objections in the preface to this edition.

Reddita Mopsopia Taenaris urbe soror :]
Taenaris Idaeo trans aequora ab hospite rapta
  Argolicas pro se vertit in arma manus.
Vix equidem memini, memini tamen. Omnia luctus,   75
  Omnia solliciti plena timoris erant.
Flebat avus Phoebeque soror fratresque gemelli,
  Orabat superos Ledā suumque Iovem.
Ipsa ego, non longos etiam tum scissa capillos,   80
  Clamabam 'sine me, me sine, mater, abis ?'
Nam coniux aberat. Ne non Pelopeïa credar,
  Ecce Neoptolemo praeda parata fui.
Pelides utinam vitasset Apollinis arcus!
  Damnaret nati facta proterva pater.
Nec quondam placuit, nec nunc placuisset Achilli,   85
  Abducta viduum coniuge flere virum.
Quae mea caelestes iniuria fecit iniquos ?
  Quodve mihi miserae sidus obesse querar ?
Parva mea sine matre fui : pater arma ferebat :
  Et duo cum vivant, orba duobus eram.   90
Non tibi blanditias primis, mea mater, in annis
  Incerto dictas ore puella tuli :
Non ego captavi brevibus tua colla lacertis,

72, 73. *Taenaris* P, *Tyndaris* vulg.
77. *Phoebique soror* P, *flebatque* G libri plurimi. Corr. Meziriacus.
88. Ita P, et vulg. *quod mihi vae miserae* G, multi libri.

---

77. *Phoebeque soror.*] This is the restoration of Meziriacus followed by Heinsius from P, for 'flebat.' Eur. Iphig. in Aul. 49, ἐγένοντο Λήδᾳ Θεστιάδι τρεῖς παρθένοι Φοίβῃ Κλυταιμνήστρα τ' ἐμὴ σύναορος Ἑλένη τε. The existence of Phoebe, the sister of Helen and Clytaemnestra, has been strangely ignored by the commentators on Prop. 1. xiii. 30, 'Et Ledae partu gratior, una tribus,' which line has been in consequence misunderstood.

79. *Etiam tum.*] = etiamnum, i.e. 'still,' to be joined with 'non longos.' 'Having torn my hair, which was still short' (as being that of a child).

83. *Apollinis arcus.*] Achilles was, according to one account, shot by Apollo, assuming the guise of Paris. Vid. Hyg. Fab. 107.

90. *Vivant.*] Although the present tense is, in the first instance, due to the exigencies of the metre, it admits of explanation: for Menelaus and Helen are still alive. 'And though my father and mother are not yet dead, I was then an orphan.'

EP. VIII. HERMIONE ORESTAE.

Nec gremio sedi sarcina grata tuo :
Non cultus tibi cura mei, nec pacta marito 95
  Intravi thalamos matre parante novos.
Obvia prodieram reduci tibi—vera fatebor—
  Nec facies nobis nota parentis erat.
Te tamen esse Helenam, quod eras pulcherrima, sensi.
  Ipsa requirebas, quae tua nata foret. 100
Pars haec una mihi, coniux bene cessit Orestes :
  Is quoque, ni pro se pugnet, ademptus erit.
Pyrrhus habet captam reduce et victore parente.
  Hoc munus nobis diruta Troia tulit.
Cum tamen altus equis Titan radiantibus instat, 105
  Perfruor infelix liberiore malo.
Nox ubi me thalamis ululantem et acerba gementem
  Condidit, in maesto procubuique toro,
Pro somno lacrimis oculi fulguntur obortis,
  Quaque licet fugio sicut ab hoste viro. 110
Saepe malis stupeo, rerumque oblita locique
  Ignara tetigi Scyria membra manu :
Utque nefas sensi, male corpora tacta relinquo
  Et mihi pollutas credor habere manus.
Saepe Neoptolemi pro nomine nomen Orestis 115
  Exit, et errorem vocis ut omen amo.
Per genus infelix iuro generisque parentem,
  Qui freta, qui terras et sua regna quatit :
Per patris ossa tui, patrui mihi, quae tibi debent,

101. Ita G. *et minus, a nobis diruta Troia dedit* P. Ed. Naug. habet *et minus a nobis diruta Troia fuit.*
111. Ita G. *stuueo uerusque obl.* P.

---

101. 'I have been fortunate in one point only, namely, getting Orestes for a husband.' 'Bene cedere' = 'to turn out well.' 'Non ego per meritum, quoniam malo cessit, adoro.' x. 141. Hor. Sat. II. i. 31, 'neque, si male cesserat, usquam Decurrens alio, neque si bene.
106. *Liberiore.*] 'I enjoy greater freedom in my misery.'
112. *Scyria.*] Of Neoptolemus, born in Scyros.

Quod se sub tumulo fortiter ulta iacent: 120
Aut ego praemoriar, primoque exstinguar in aevo,
Aut ego Tantalidae Tantalis uxor ero.

EPISTOLA IX.

DEIANIRA HERCULI.

GRATULOR Oechaliam titulis accedere nostris:
Victorem victae succubuisse queror.
Fama Pelasgiadas subito pervenit in urbes
Decolor et factis infitianda tuis,
Quem numquam Iuno seriesque immensa laborum 5
Fregerit, huic Iolen inposuisse iugum.
Hoc velit Eurystheus, velit hoc germana Tonantis,
Lactaque sit vitae labe noverca tuae.
At non ille velit, cui nox—sic creditur—una

120. *Quod se* P *quod sic* G M.
121. Ita G, *ut ego praemorior priorque exuar in aevo* P, cuius librarius in hac epistola describenda solito plus dormitasse videtur.
1. *Vestris* Heins. et codd. nonnulli. Male.
4. *Discolor* codd. nonnulli: in eod. Apros. cum glossa, *priori famae tuae*.
5. *Ille venis* P G, *venit* vulg. *velit* multi libr. et ita corr Dammius. *Si creditur* G.
6. *Tanti* P G, *tanta* unus liber, Lenn., Jahn, Loers.

120. *Quod sc.*] 'That they have revenged themselves.' This is evidently the true reading, and not 'sic.' See note on 'induit illa pater,' vs. 50, supra.

IX.—Hercules had captured Oechalia in Euboea, and slain its king, Eurytus, of whose daughter Iole he became enamoured, and sent her to Trachis, where his wife Deianira was; he himself proceeding to the promontory of Cenaeum to sacrifice to Jupiter. On the arrival of Iole at Trachis, Deianira sent to Hercules the shirt, dipped in the blood of the centaur Nessus, which the latter had told her would act as a love-charm on her husband. After sending it she is supposed to write the following epistle to Hercules: and while writing it she learns that Hercules is perishing by the poison of the shirt. The Trachiniae of Sophocles is directly followed by Ovid. The ninth book of the Metamorphoses treats of the same circumstances.

1. Nostris was changed by Heinsius to 'vestris.' By what authority he made 'vestris' = 'tuis,' I know not. 'Nostris,' so far from being unsuitable, is used with much dignity by Deianira as the lawful wife of Hercules, and therefore the rightful sharer in his glories.

3. 'A foul report, which should be disowned by your actions, suddenly pervaded the Grecian cities.' 'Infitianda' is correctly explained by Loers: 'quam negari debeat esse famam factorum tuorum,' cf. Met. ii. 34; 'Progenies, Phaethon, haud infitianda parenti.'

7. Cf. Virg. ii. 104. 'Hoc Ithacus velit et magno mercentur Atridae.'

Non tanti, ut tantus conciperere, fuit. 10
Plus tibi quam Iuno, nocuit Venus : illa prem...
  Sustulit, haec humili sub pede colla tenet.
Respice vindicibus pacatum viribus orbem,
  Qua latam Nereus caerulus ambit humum.
Se tibi pax terrae, tibi se tuta aequora debent : 15
  Implesti meritis solis utramque domum.
Quod te laturum est, caelum prius ipse tulisti :
  Hercule supposito sidera fulsit Atlas.
Quid nisi notitia est misero quaesita pudori,
  Si cumulas turpi facta priora nota ? 20
Tene ferunt geminos pressisse tenaciter angues,
  Cum tener in cunis iam Iove dignus eras ?
Coepisti melius, quam desinis : ultima primis
  Cedunt : dissimiles hic vir et ille puer.
Quem non mille ferae, quem non Stheneleius hostis, 25
  Non potuit Iuno vincere, vincit amor.
At bene nupta feror, quia nominer Herculis uxor,
  Sitque socer rapidis qui tonat altus equis.

12. *Humilis* G.
15. *Tota* P G M. Heins. corr. *tuta* quod recepi. Vid. ad. vii. 71, supra.
19. Ita P *quid tibi—pudoris* G. Burmannus malebat *Quid nisi stultitia est sero quaesita pudori.*
20. *Stupri* P G M. Sed nescio quomodo displicet " *nota stupri.*" Et certe vim habent quae monuit Heusingerus, ' non stupratam Iolen, sed iugum ab Iolo acceptum Deianirae exprobrare.' Recepi Heinsii coni. *turpi* quae vel nulla vel minima mutatio est. *Si macula stupri notas* al. *Si maculas* al. *Si cumulo s.—notas,* al.
27. *Nominor* P G M. Corr. Heins. *Nominor* retinent Jahnus et Loersius: etiam Amarus qui *estque* quoque in sequenti protulit.

10. *Tanti ut.*] 'One night was not long enough for your begetting.' The notion of equivalence is not however lost, and therefore, 'tanti' is the proper reading, not 'tanta,' which can hardly be 'satis longa.'
13. *Vindicibus viribus.*] 'Your champion strength.' Met. ix. 241, 'timuere dei pro vindice terrae.
16. *Solis utramque domum.*] i. e. both east and west. Cf. Sen. Herc. Fur. 1061. ' Novit tuas utrasque domus.' Id. Herc. Oet. 3, Utraeque Phoebi sentiunt fulmen domus.'
19. 'What have you gained by all these achievements but notoriety added to your shame, if you finish off your great deeds with a disgraceful stain?' ' Quaesita' would naturally be ' quaesitum ;' but it is attracted to ' notitia.' ' Pudori' is governed by ' quaesita.' ' Cumulare,' ' to give the finishing touch to :' 'cumulus' is properly the top of a h ap; in measures, it denoted that which was given over and above. Vid. Festus, s. v. ' Auctarium.'
21. *Tene.*] Emphatic. 'Are you he of whom men say?' &c.
27. Those who read ' nominor' here, and 'sit' in the next line, must suppose a

Quam male inaequales veniunt ad aratra iuvenci,
 Tam premitur magno coniuge nupta minor. 30
Non honor est, sed onus species laesura ferentes.
 Siqua voles apte nubere, nube pari.
Vir mihi semper abest, et coniuge notior hospes,
 Monstraque terribiles persequiturque feras.
Ipsa domo vidua, votis operata pudicis,
 Torqueor, infesto ne vir ab hoste cadat.
Inter serpentes aprosque avidosque leones
 Iactor, et haesuros terna per ora canes.

31. *Ferentem* libri quidam.
35. *Domi* G, unde Heins. corr. *domi viduae.*
38. *Terna per ossa* P (ap. Jahn.). *Cerno per ora* G. Corr. Heins. multi libri habent *haesuros cerno per ossa* quam lect. longe pessimam revocavit Jahn. *Esuros* multi, et ita Heins.

subtle distinction: it was a fact that she was called the wife of Hercules; therefore 'nominor,' the indicative, is used: that Jupiter was her father-in-law was not quite such a certainty: it was the current hypothesis (see Met. ix. 24): therefore the subjunctive is used. See Madvig. § 357, b. 'I doubt whether such a distinction was intended: both verbs are properly in the subjunctive, because 'the reason is given according to the views of another party.' Madvig. § 357. 'Men say I am well married, because I am the wife of Hercules:' 'nominor' = 'ferar' = 'sim.' Vid. note on vi. 114.

29. 'Just as ill-matched bullocks take badly to the plough, so a lowly wife is oppressed by a high-born husband.'

31. *Non honor est sed onus species laesura ferentes.*] 'The state that will injure those who bear it is not an honour, but a burden.' There is an untranslateable play on παρονομασία in the words 'onus' and 'honor;' Cicero several times puns on the words 'onerati' and 'honorati.'

32. *Si qua voles apte nubere nube pari.*] Cf. Callimachus Epigr. i. 16, from which passage Ovid has borrowed this, as Ernesti remarked.

33. *Et coniuge notior hospes.*] 'Is better known to me as a guest than a husband.' Not 'a stranger is better known than my husband,' as 'vir' must be carried on to the next line, and therefore must be understood in this clause also.

35. *Operata.*] 'Operari' is generally used of offering up sacrifices, like ἔρδειν. Cf. Hor. Od. III. xiv. 6, 'Prodeat iustis operata sacris.' Here it is used of offering up prayers as a religious duty. For 'pudicis,' cf. vi. 73, 'adde preces castas.'

36 *Ne vir ab hoste cadat.*] Cf. Met. 192, 'Magna feres tacitas solacia mortis ad umbras, A tanto cecidisse viro.' Ovid uses 'a' or 'ab' with the ablative, not only with the agent after passive verbs, but even after adjectives and intransitive verbs, as here. Vid. ad x. 138.

37, 38. 'I keep tossing among serpents, boars, and lions, and dogs ready to fasten on one with triple mouths.' 'Jactor' is used with reference to the sleepless nights she spent tossing about as she thought of the horrid monsters her husband was engaged with. The Lernaean Hydra, the Erymanthian boar, the Nemeaean lion, and Cerberus, are referred to. There seems to be no sufficient reason for following Heinsius in changing 'haesuros' to 'Esuros.' See a passage in Met. i. 535, where a dog is described pursuing a hare: 'Alter, *inhaesuro similis* iam iamque tenere Sperat,' ix. 5. Lennep defends the use of 'per' in the construction, 'Esuros terna per ora,' by Lucian Hermot. c. 74, ᾔσθη διὰ τριῶν στομάτων—a defence which, of course, applies equally to 'haesuros.'

EP. IX. DEIANIRA HERCULI.

Me pecudum fibrae simulacraque inania somni
   Ominaque arcana nocte petita movent.   40
Aucupor infelix incertae murmura famae,   *catch*
   Speque timor dubia, spesque timore cadit.
Mater abest, queriturque deo placuisse potenti :
   Nec pater Amphitryon, nec puer Hyllus adest.
Arbiter Eurystheus irae Iunonis iniquae   45
   Sentitur nobis, iraque longa deae.
Haec mihi ferre parum ?   Peregrinos addis amores,
   Et mater de te quaelibet esse potest.
Non ego Partheniis temeratam vallibus Augen,
   Nec referam partus, Ormeni nympha, tuos :   50
Non tibi crimen erunt, Theutrantia turba, sorores,
   Quarum de populo nulla relicta tibi est.
Una, recens crimen, referetur adultera nobis,
   Unde ego sum Lydo facta noverca Lamo.
Maeandros, terris totiens errator in isdem,   55
   Qui lassas in se saepe retorquet aquas,

---

53. *Referentur* P *referetur* G. Edd. ante Heins. *refertur* (adv. metro) aut *defertur* Heins. protulit *praefertur* e suis codd.
55. *Maeandros ter totiens erratur in isdem* P. *Maeandros totiens qui terris errat in isdem* G : corr. Heins.
56. *Lassas* P G, *lapsas* vulg.

39, 40. Deianira refers to three methods of divination she resorted to for the purpose of discovering whether Hercules was well: by means of the entrails of cattle, the interpretation of dreams, and magical arts. The last were usually applied to in 'the mysterious night.'

41. *Aucupor.*] 'I catch at every whisper of uncertain rumour.' Cf. Sen. Theb. 361, ' Hic aucupabor verba rumoris vagi.'

42. The reader need hardly be reminded of the lines, which must surely have been inspired from this passage: ' Our very hopes belied our fears, our fears our hopes belied,' &c. The Deathbed, by Thomas Hood.

45. 'Eurystheus, minister of the wrath of angry Juno.' 'Arbiter,' from the old form ' ar – bio' = ' adeo,' had three meanings closely connected with its derivation. (1.) 'a spectator;' (2.) ' an arbitrator or judge ;' (3.) ' a manager or master,' cf. ' arbiter Hadriae,' ' arbiter bibendi,' &c.

It is in the last sense the word is used here.

46. *Sentitur.*] 'Sentire aliquoties significat magno suo damno aliquid experiri,' Ruhnken, who quotes Sen. Oed. 471, ' Regna securigeri Bacchum sensere Lycurgi :' Petron. 139, ' Innonem Pelias sensit.'

49–54. ' I do not intend to speak of your amours with Auge, Astydamia, and the fifty daughters of Thespius : I will content myself with mentioning one recent case only : that of Omphale.' Auge was daughter of Aleus, King of Arcadia, mother of Telephus, by Hercules. Astydamia was daughter of Amyntor, and granddaughter of Ormenus : she bore Ctesippus to Hercules. The fifty daughters of Thespius, son of Theutras, bore fifty sons to Hercules. Lamus was son of Hercules, by the Lydian Queen Omphale, concerning whom, vide Class Dict.

Vidit in Herculeo suspensa monilia collo
  Illo, cui caelum sarcina parva fuit.
Non puduit fortes auro cohibere lacertos,
  Et solidis gemmas opposuisse toris?   60
Nempe sub his animam pestis Nemeaea lacertis
  Edidit, unde humerus tegmina laevus habet.
Ausus es hirsutos mitra redimire capillos:
  Aptior Herculeae populus alba comae.
Nec te Maeonia lascivae more puellae   65
  Incingi zona dedecuisse putas?
Non tibi succurrit crudi Diomedis imago,
  Efferus humana qui dape pavit equas?
Si te vidisset cultu Busiris in isto,
  Huic victor victo nempe pudendus eras.   70

58. *Illo* P G *collo*, unus Heins. Lenn. Eleganter sane.
66. *Dedecuisse pudet* P G. Corr. Heins. qui haec scripsit "codd. nonnulli *putes*: certe puduit jam praecesserat. Rem. Am. 410: 'Et nihil est quod se dedecuisse putant.'" Nec facile explicanda est constructio verborum 'incingi dedecuisse pudet.'
70. Quaerendi signum post h. v. habent M. et Iahn. quod jure damnat Loers.

---

56. The river Maeander, famous for its winding course, rose in southern Phrygia, and formed the boundary between Lydia and Caria, till it fell into the Icarian sea. The reading 'lassas' is defended by Burmann against 'lapsas' by Met. i. 582, 'Moxque amnes alii, qui qua tulit impetus illos, In mare deducunt *fessas erroribus undas*;' and by Lucan. v. 466, 'Neuter (amnis) longo se gurgite *lassat*.'

59. *Non puduit.*] 'Were you not ashamed to confine your strong arms with golden bracelets, and to place jewels on your brawny muscles?' I prefer the interrogative form here, as it occurs twice below, 75, 89.

61. *Nempe.*] 'Verily.' This word is not ironical here, but denotes, as it sometimes does, strong affirmation. 'These were the very arms that slew the Nemean lion.' Cf. iv. 144, 'Hiscere nempe tibi terra roganda fuit,' and 70, infra.

63. *Mitra.*] The turban was looked upon by the Romans as characteristic of the Phrygians and Lydians. Servius ad Aen. ix. 616, 'Mitra proprie Lydorum fuit.' Cf. Juv. iii. 66.

64. *Populus alba.*] Cf. Theoc. ii. 121, κρατὶ δ᾽ ἔχων λεύκαν Ἡρακλέος ἱερὸν ἔρνος. Virg. Ecl. vii. 61, 'Populus Alcidae gratissima,' where Conington: 'The story was, that Leuce was a nymph beloved by Pluto, who caused a white poplar to grow up in the shades after her death; and that Hercules, on his way from the infernal regions, made himself a garland from its leaves.'

67. Diomedes, King of Thrace, who fed his horses on human flesh; Busiris, King of Egypt, and son of Poseidon, who sacrificed all foreigners that visited Egypt; and Antaeus, a Libyan giant and wrestler, son of Earth, who remained invincible as long as he was in contact with his mother Earth, were all slain by Hercules.

70. *Nempe.*] See note on v. 61, supra. Merkel and Jahn point this verse interrogatively; but I do not think the sense is thereby improved.

EP. IX. DEIANIRA HERCULI. 83

Detrahat Antaeus duro redimicula collo,
  Ne pigeat molli succubuisse viro.
Inter Ioniacas calathum tenuisse puellas
  Diceris, et dominae pertimuisse minas.
Non fugis, Alcide, victricem mille laborum 75
  Rasilibus calathis imposuisse manum,   *polished*
Crassaque robusto deducis pollice fila,
  Aequaque formosae pensa rependis erae?
A! quoties, digitis dum torques stamina duris,
  Praevalidae fusos comminuere manus. 80
Crederis infelix scuticae tremefactus habenis
  Ante pedes dominae pertimuisse minas.
Eximiis pompis praeconia summa triumphi
  Factaque narrabas dissimulanda tibi:

78. Pro *formosae* codd. nonnulli habent: *famosae*.
81-84. Scribit M: "vss. 81, 83, in margine P a ma. sec. adiciuntur: vetus aliquis librarius in libro qui pentametros non reductos haberet describendo aberravit in *hexametro* 82 a voce *dominae* in v. 74, adjecti deinde ante aetatem G codicis duo hexametri duobus pentametris." Argute ille quidem: sed discrepat recensio Iahni, qui scribit: "totum distichon (81, 82), una cum sequenti (83, 84), a textu cod. Put. abest et in margine tantum legitur." Incertus igitur de scriptura P nolo conjecturam facere. Credo tamen 'Dominae pertimuisse minas' in ambobus versibus (74, 82), sana esse nullo modo posse. Sed in priore loco spuria magis quam in posteriore, ut M placet, mihi videntur: nam postulabantur in 74, verba qualia in Am. II. ii. 226, leguntur: Inter Ioniacas calathum tenuisse puellas creditur *et lanas excoluisse rudes*, potius quam *dominae pertimuisse minas*.
83. *Pompas immania semina laudum* P ma. sec.

---

73. The 'calathus,' was a basket in which the balls of wool, prepared for spinning, was held. 'Rasiles,' in v. 76, denotes that these baskets were made of 'scraped,' 'smooth,' osiers or twigs. Cf. Catull. lxiv. 319, 'Ante pedes autem conductis mollia lanae Vellera virgati custodibant calathisci.'
77. Hercules' hands were so big and clumsy that the threads he spun were coarse, 'crassa.' 'Deduco,' used of drawing the thread out of the 'glomus,' which was wound round the 'colus,' or 'distaff,' by means of the 'fusus,' or 'spindle.' This was set spinning round to form the 'stamina,' or 'threads,' vss. 79, 80. The 'fusi' were delicate in make, and often got broken by the hands of Hercules, which were 'too strong.'

81, 83. Vid. Ad. Crit. Verse 83, as it stands in the text, or in the margin of P, is an absurd piece of patchwork, more like the despairing effort of a modern schoolboy to complete his verses than Ovid's style. 'Praeconia,' and 'pompae,' and 'triumphus,' were favourite expressions of Ovid, no doubt, and well known as such to the composer, whoever he was: but the poet would not have given us such emblazonry all in one line. Besides 'praeconia narrare' is not Latin: 'praeconia facere,' is the usual and Ovidian expression. Vid. xvi. 139. Am. III. xii. 9. Pont. I. i. 55, etc., nor indeed would 'to narrate a proclamation' be English. The reading of P by a later hand 'Eximiis pompis immania semina laudum' is equally bad.

Scilicet immanes elisos faucibus hydros 85
　Infantem caudis involuisse manum :
Ut Tegeaeus aper cupressifero Erymantho
　Incubet, et vasto pondere laedat humum.
Non tibi Threiciis adfixa penatibus ora,
　Non hominum pingues caede tacentur equae : 90
Prodigiumque triplex, armenti dives Hiberi
　Geryones, quamvis in tribus unus erat :
Inque canes totidem trunco digestus ab uno
　Cerberus implicitis angue minante comis :
Quaeque redundabat fecundo vulnere serpens 95
　Fertilis et damnis dives ab ipsa suis,
Quique inter laevumque latus laevumque lacertum
　Praegrave compressa fauce pependit onus :
Et male confisum pedibus formaque bimembri
　Pulsum Thessalicis agmen equestre iugis. 100
Haec tu Sidonio potes insignitus amictu
　Dicere ? non cultu lingua retenta silet ?

86. *Caudis* P G.　*Cunis*, al.　*Nodis* Heins.
88. *Incubet—laedat* P ; *incubat—laedit* G M.
96. Ita P ; *ditior ipsa* G.

85, 86. 'Namely that throttled serpents had wound their tails round your infant hand.' The fable of the serpents sent by Juno to destroy Hercules in his cradle is given by Theocritus Idyll. xxiv. The 30th line of that Idyll, quoted by Lennep, seems to me to support 'caudis' against 'cunis,' or 'nodis :' τῷ δ' αὖτε σπείραισιν ἑλισσέσθην περὶ παῖδα. Cf. also. Met. v. 361, where, of a serpent struggling with an eagle it is said, 'alligat, et cauda spatiantes implicat alas,' a passage also quoted by Lennep, who, however, gives the preference to the reading 'cunis,' on the ground that 'sollemnis' in hac historia est mentio cunarum.' Cf. Met. ix. 67, ' Cunarum labor est angues superare mearum.' 'Elisa,' is regularly used of strangling, squeezing to death. Cf. Met. ix. 197, ' His elisa iacet pestis Nemeaea lacertis.' Hence 'elidere collum' was substituted by Bentley for 'laedere collum,' Hor. Od. III. xxvii 60.

87. The range of Erymanthus was in the north-east, and Tegea was in the south-west of Arcadia, so Tegeeus must be used generally for 'Arcadian.' The hiatus in 'cupressifero' is repeated in 131, 133, and 141 infra. These were evidently considered elegances rather than licenses. Cf. viii. 71, note.

88. *Laedat.*} 'Dints the ground.' Cf. Juv. iii. 272, ' quanto percussum pondere signent Et laedant silicem.'

96. *Dives ab ipsa suis.*} Cf. Art. iii. 668, 'indicio prodor ab ipse meo,' and thus repeatedly.

97. Antaeus, who had to be held in air by Hercules, to prevent his touching his mother Earth.

EP. IX. DEIANIRA HERCULI.

Se quoque nympha tuis oneravit Iardanis armis,
    Et tulit e capto nota tropaea viro.
I nunc, tolle animos et fortia gesta recense,   105
    Quod tu non esses iure, vir illa fuit.
Qua tanto minor es, quanto te, maxime rerum,
    Quam quos vicisti, vincere maius erat.
Illi procedit rerum mensura tuarum :
    Cede bonis: heres laudis amica tuae.   110

103. *Ornavit* P G, *oneravit* al.   *Dardanis* edd. vett.
106. *Quem tu* P.

---

103. Omphale was the daughter of Iardanus. 'Oneravit' is so peculiarly appropriate, and so often confounded with 'ornavit' in MSS., that I read it with some later ones. The 'arma' are the club and bow and arrows: 'the nota tropaea' in v. 104, are the same as 'spolia leonis,' v. 113, the lion's skin.

104. 'That which you were not by right, namely, a man, she was.' Loers wrongly makes 'quod' = 'quia :' it is of course the relative, in apposition to the antecedent of vir understood.

109. 110. *Illi procedit.*] 'To her accrues the sum total of your property: resign your goods : your mistress has succeeded to your fame.' This difficult passage has been slurred over by the commentators. It forms one of the many metaphors derived from legal phraseology found in Ovid, which no doubt he became acquainted with when filling a post in the centumvirate. Ruhnken and Loers briefly say the metaphor in v. 109 is drawn from military affairs, because 'aera procedere militibus dicebantur.' But it is perfectly clear that there is no military metaphor whatever, and that one and the same legal metaphor runs through both lines. The process known as 'cessio bonorum,' was the origin of the metaphor in both lines, not in the latter only, as the commentators would have us believe. The process in its simplest form was this: when a man found he had more debts than he could hope to pay, he handed over his property to his creditors. There was an ancient gloss describing the 'cessio bonorum' (See Dict. Ant. s. v. Bonorum cessio), thus : ' Cedere bonis est *ab universitate rerum suarum* recedere. These words are remarkable, as they were probably the very legal form Ovid was thinking of when he wrote the words ' Illi procedit rerum mensura tuarum,' almost the identical words, except that 'universitas' is expressed by 'mensura,' which very probably was itself a legal term, meaning the same thing. 'Heres laudis amica tuae,' is a continuation of the same metaphor, for it was possible to alienate the right of inheritance also by the form of ' bonorum cessio' (Dict. Ant. s. v. Heres.) Ovid's meaning, expressed more freely, is this : ' The glory that once was yours has passed to her, your conqueror: bankrupt as you are in reputation, you may as well formally declare yourself so, and appoint your mistress the heir to the fame that once was your rightful inheritance.' ' Procedere' was a legal term used 'de iis quae in utilitatem alicuius cedunt, prosunt, iuvant :' Forcellini. Hence, it was said of a creditor who was ' de facto' receiver of his debtor's income, and the ' bonorum cessio' made him so ' de iure.' The words ' aera procedere militibus,' Liv. v. 7, was only one out of the many possible applications of the phrase.—' Mensura rerum :' we have ' census mensura' in Juv. xiv. 316, which, although ' mensura' there bears a somewhat different meaning from that in the passage before us, seems to show that the word was regularly used when speaking of the amount of a man's fortune—as we would say ' the inventory,' which probably took place in a 'cessio bonorum.'

O pudor! hirsuti costas exuta leonis
   Aspera texerunt vellera molle latus.
Falleris et nescis: non sunt spolia illa leonis,
   Sed tua: tuque feri victor es, illa tui.
Femina tela tulit Lernaeis atra venenis,   115
   Ferre gravem lana vix satis apta colum,
Instruxitque manum clava domitrice ferarum,
   Vidit et in speculo coniugis arma sui.
Haec tamen audieram: licuit non credere famae,
   Et venit ad sensus mollis ab aure dolor.   120
Ante meos oculos adducitur advena pelex,
   Nec mihi, quae patior, dissimulare licet.
Non sinis averti: mediam captiva per urbem
   Invitis oculis aspicienda venit.
Nec venit incultis captarum more capillis,   125
   Fortunam vultu fassa decente suam.
Ingreditur late lato spectabilis auro,
   Qualiter in Phrygia tu quoque cultus eras.

111. *Costas* P G, *costis* vulg.
126. *Fassa tegente* P; *fassa tegendo* G; Lennepii coniecturam edidi.

---

120. 'Pain that proceeds from the ear comes soft to the senses' (i. e. compared with that which is derived from being an eye-witness). Cf. Hor. A. P. 130, 'Segnius irritant animos demissa per aurem,' etc.

121. *Pelex.*] Iole, daughter of Eurytus, King of Oechalia, sent by Hercules to Trachis, where Deianira was.

123. 'You do not allow me to turn my eyes away from the sight of your shame.'

126. *Fortunam vultu fassa decente suam.*] 'Confessing her ill-fortune by a face becoming it.' I have adopted without hesitation Lennep's emendation 'decente' for 'tegente' as it stands in P (according to the recension given by Merkel), and in some other MSS. 'A face becoming her fortune' would be a sad one (cf. Juv. x. 136, 'tristis captivus in arcu'), not a proud one, as Iole's was. The strongest defence of 'decente' is given by Lennep in the passage he cites in support of it. Trist. I. i. 3, 4 (ad librum suum), 'Vade sed incultus qualem *decet* exulis esse: Infelix habitum temporis huius habe'—a passage which would go to support 'cultu,' instead of 'vultu,' were there any need to change the latter. As for the ordinary reading 'tegendo,' 'confessing her fortune by hiding her face,' there may be urged against it—(1.) After all it is not found in the best MS., according to the latest recension: (2) Ovid nowhere else shortens -*do* in the gerund; nor can any passage be quoted from any Augustan poet where it is shortened, except a solitary one in Tibullus III. vi. 3, 'Aufer et ipse meum pariter medicando dolorem,' where 'medicando' has long been given up as corrupt. It has been emended with probability by Heinsius: 'Aufer et ipse meum patera medicante dolorem.'

EP. IX. DEIANIRA HERCULI.

Dat vultum populo sublimis ut Hercule victo.
Oechaliam vivo stare parente putes. 130
Forsitan et pulsa Aetolide Deianira
Nomine deposito pelicis uxor erit:
Eurytidosque Ioles atque Aonii Alcidae
Turpia famosus corpora iunget Hymen.
Mens fugit admonitu, frigusque perambulat artus, 135
Et iacet in gremio languida facta manus.
Me quoque cum multis, sed me sine crimine amasti.
Ne pigeat, pugnae bis tibi causa fui.
Cornua flens legit ripis Achelous in undis,
Truncaque limosa tempora mersit aqua. 140
Semivir occubuit in letifero Eveno
Nessus, et infecit sanguis equinus aquas.
Sed quid ego haec refero? scribenti nuntia venit
Fama, virum tunicae tabo perire meae.
Ei mihi, quid feci? quo me furor egit amantem? 145
Impia quid dubitas Deianira mori?
An tuus in media coniux lacerabitur Oeta,
Tu sceleris tanti causa superstes eris?

129. *Sublime sub Hercule victo* P G, codd. plurimi. *Sublimis ab,* unus et alter. Nostram edd. vett. nisi quod puncto sublato ad sequentem referunt. Vulgatam defendunt Heins. Loers.
133. *Et insanii Alcidae* P, *atque insani Alcidae* G vulg. M versum obelo notavit, deinde in addendis pro *insani* conjecit *Aonii* quod in ed. Tauchn. nuper recepit Riesius, conjiciens ipse *Ismeni* vel *Inachii.*
141. *In letifero veneno* P *in letiferoque veneno* G: corr. Heins. Pleraeque edd. vett: *vi lerniferoque veneno.*

129, 130. *Dat vultum.*] 'She throws haughty looks upon the people, proud as though she had conquered Hercules: you would suppose her native town was still standing, and her father alive.' 'Sublimis ab Hercule victo' would mean, according to Burmann, 'proud owing to the conquest of Hercules,' 'ab' denoting the result. I have seen no satisfactory defence of 'sublime sub Hercule v.;' nor can I understand it.
133, *Aonii.*] Cf. Met. ix. 112, and see Adn. Crit. 'Aonius' is 'Boeotian;' Hercules was so called from the fact that he was born at Thebes.
138. The contest between the river-god Achelous and Hercules for the hand of Deianira, is described in Met. ix. 'Legit:' 'picked up his horns:' one of the horns of Achelous was broken off by Hercules. According to Ovid, Met. l. c., the Naiads filled this horn with flowers and fruit, and it became the horn of plenty.
141. Evenus was a river flowing through Aetolia into the Corinthian gulf. For the Centaur Nessus, and the story of the death of Hercules, cf. Met. ix. 120, sqq., and Class. Dict.

Siquid adhuc habeo facti, cur Herculis uxor
  Credar, coniugii mors mihi pignus erit.   150
Tu quoque cognosces in me, Meleagre, sororem.
  Impia quid dubitas Deianira mori?
Heu devota domus! solio sedet Agrius alto:
  Oenea desertum nuda senecta premit:
Exulat ignotis Tydeus germanus in oris: 155
  Alter fatali vivus in igne fuit:
Exegit ferrum sua per praecordia mater.
  Impia quid dubitas Deianira mori?
Deprecor hoc unum per iura sacerrima lecti,
  Ne videar fatis insidiata tuis.   160
Nessus ut est avidum percussus arundine pectus,
  'Hic' dixit 'vires sanguis amoris habet.'
Illita Nesseo misi tibi texta veneno.
  Impia quid dubitas Deianira mori?
Iamque vale, seniorque pater germanaque Gorge,   165
  Et patria et patriae frater adempte tuae,
Et tu lux oculis hodierna novissima nostris,
  Virque,—sed o possis!—et puer Hylle, vale!

153. *Acrius* P *acrior* G. Corr. Micyllus.

---

149. 'If I have ever in my life done anything worthy of the wife of Hercules, Death itself shall be the final proof of my being his true spouse.'

151. *Tu quoque cognosces in me, Meleagre, sororem.*] i. e. 'as my death will show you I am Hercules' wife, it will show you I am your true sister,' by proving that I share your bravery. Cf. Met. ix. 149, 'Quid si me Meleagre tuam nemor esse sororem Forte paro facinus.'

152. *Impia quid dubitas Deianira mori.*] This is the only passage in the Heroides where there is a recurring burden. This fact, however, so far from being an argument against the authenticity of the Epistle, is an argument in its favour, as no imitator would have ventured to introduce anything unusual with Ovid himself. The only other passage in the writings of Ovid, where a refrain occurs, is in Am. i. 6, where the words, 'Excute poste seram,' are reiterated. Among the Greek poets we meet with the refrain occasionally in Aeschylus and Euripides, but chiefly in Theocritus, whom Catullus and Virgil have imitated.

153. *Heu devota domus!*] See notes on iv. 53, viii. 65. Oeneus, king of Pleuron and Calydon, was husband of Althaea, father of Meleager, Tydeus, Deianira, Gorge, and others. He was deprived of his kingdom by his brother, Agrius: Tydeus was banished on account of a murder, and went to Argos: Althaea slew herself after causing the death of Meleager, by consuming the brand on which his life depended. Hence 'fatali in igne vivus.'

168. *Sed o possis.*] i. e. valere.

EPISTOLA X.

ARIADNE THESEO.

{Mitius inveni quam te genus omne ferarum.
  Credita non ulli quam tibi peius eram}
Quae legis, ex illo, Theseu, tibi litore mitto,
  Unde tuam sine me vela tulere ratem:
In quo me somnusque meus male prodidit et tu, 5
  Per facinus somnis insidiate meis.   *having leaped*
Tempus erat, vitrea quo primum terra pruina
  Spargitur et tectae fronde queruntur aves:
Incertum vigilans, a somno languida, movi
  Thesea prensuras semisupina manus: 10
Nullus erat, referoque manus, iterumque retempto,
  Perque torum moveo brachia: nullus erat.
Excussere metus somnum: conterrita surgo,

6. *Per facinus* P G. *Pro facinus* al. edd. vett.
9. Ita G *an somno* al. *somno languenta* P.
10. *Pressuras* G *semisopita*, adv. metro P G. Corr. Heins.

X.—From Ariadne to Theseus. The Epistle is supposed to be written from the island of Naxos or Dia, where Theseus abandoned Ariadne on his return from Crete, where he had slain the Minotaur by her aid. The Epistle is one of considerable beauty.

1, 2. 'I have found the whole race of brutes more kind than you: I could not have fared worse in the power of any beast than in yours.' These lines certainly have the appearance of being the prefix of a late hand, as the poem seems properly to begin at vs. 3: but, as regards the lines themselves, I cannot agree with Micyllus, who said, 'Ili versus putidi sunt neque quidquam Ovidianae facilitatis atque elegantiae habentes. I agree with him that 'ulli' is 'any beast,' not 'any man,' as Loers takes it. 'Eram' poetic for 'essem.'

6. *Per facinus.*] Cf. Ibis 568, 'Per facinus soror est cui sua facta parens.'

9. *Incertum vigilans.*] 'Only half awake.' Cf. Hor. Sat. II. v. 100, 'Certum vigilans,' 'wide awake.' Stat. Theb. v. 129, 'Turbidus, incertumque oculis vigiluntibus.' For 'a somno languida,' cf. vs. 138, infra.

10. *Semisupina.*] 'Turning on my side.' 'Supinus' = ὕπτιος, properly 'lying on the back.' The word occurs again in Am. I. xiv. 20, Art. iii. 788.

Membraque sunt viduo praecipitata toro.
Protinus adductis sonuerunt pectora palmis, 15
Utque erat e somno turbida, rapta coma est.
Luna fuit: specto, siquid nisi litora cernam:
Quod videant oculi, nil nisi litus habent.
Nunc huc, nunc illuc, et utroque sine ordine curro.
Alta puellares tardat arena pedes. 20
Interea toto clamanti litore 'Theseu!'
Reddebant nomen concava saxa tuum:
Et quoties ego te, toties locus ipse vocabat.
Ipse locus miserae ferre volebat opem.
Mons fuit: apparent frutices in vertice rari: 25
Hinc scopulus raucis pendet adesus aquis:
Ascendo, vires animus dabat, atque ita late
Aequora prospectu metior alta meo.
Inde ego, nam ventis quoque sum crudelibus usa,
Vidi praecipiti carbasa tenta noto. 30
Aut vidi, aut tamquam quae me vidisse putarem,
Frigidior glacie semianimisque fui.
Nec languere diu patitur dolor: excitor illo,
Excitor et summa Thesea voce voco.
'Quo fugis?' exclamo 'scelerate revertere Theseu, 35
Flecte ratem! numerum non habet illa suum.'

26. *Hinc* G *nunc* P M.
27. Ita G (nisi quod *putavi*) et P, ut videtur, sub ras. Vulgo legitur: *aut vidi aut certe cum me.* Pro *certe* al. *etiam*, quod edidit Loers. Iahn. cum Heusingeris dedit *Ut vidi, aut certe cum.*

15. *Adductis.*] i. e. 'Ad pectora ductis.' Cf. vs. 104, infra; 'Fila per adductas saepe recepta manus:' and Trist. IV. ii. 5, 'adducta collum percussa securi.'
26. *Hinc pendet.*] So join. 'On it there hangs, suspended over the deep, a rock eaten into by the hoarse waves.'
30. *Praecipiti.*] Cf. Hor. Od. I. iii. 12, 'Praecipitem Africum.' Met. xi. 481, 'Praeceps Eurus.'
31. *Aut vidi aut tamquam quae me vidisse putarem.*] 'I either saw it, or at least,

like one who thought she had seen it, I turned colder than ice,' &c. I have adopted Merkel's reading, although I am hardly satisfied with it. For '*putarem*' is not wanted if '*tamquam*' is the reading: '*tamquam quae viderem*' would be sufficient: 'I either really saw it, or, as though I saw it,' &c. The construction is a very peculiar one, equivalent to '*tamquam quae se vidisse putaret.*'
36. *Numerum.*] i: q: πλήρωμα, full complement of sailors and passengers.

Haec ego. Quod voci deerat, plangore replebam:
　Verbera cum verbis mixta fuere meis.
Si non audires, ut saltem cernere posses,
　Iactatae late signa dedere manus. 40
Candidaque imposui longae velamina virgae,
　Scilicet oblitos admonitura mei.
Iamque oculis ereptus eras. Tum denique flevi.
　Torpuerant molles ante dolore genae.
Quid potius facerent, quam me mea lumina flerent, 45
　Postquam desierant vela videre tua?
Aut ego diffusis erravi sola capillis,
　Qualis ab Ogygio concita Baccha deo:
Aut mare prospiciens in saxo frigida sedi,
　Quamque lapis sedes, tam lapis ipsa fui. 50
Saepe torum repeto, qui nos acceperat ambos,
　Sed non acceptos exhibiturus erat, (*legal*)
Et tua, quae possum, pro te vestigia tango,
　Strataque quae membris intepuere tuis.
Incumbo, lacrimisque toro manante profusis 55
　'Pressimus' exclamo 'te duo, redde duos.
Venimus huc ambo, cur non discedimus ambo?
　Perfide, pars nostri, lectule, maior ubi est?'

40. *Iactatae* P G, *iactantes* unus liber.
46. *Desierant* G, *desieram* P.

---

37. *Replebam*.] Cf. note on 'implesti,' vi. 58. 'Plangore' is 'beating of the bosom.'
40. *Iactatae late*.] Ruhnken, who prefers 'iactantes,' for the sake of euphony, must take 'signa' twice—'Signa autem intellige mappam, vel simile quid in altum iactatum,' and he quotes Am. III. ii. 74. But Ariadne evidently first waved her hands, and then resorted to this kind of signalling, which is described in the following verse.
44. 'Genae' are here 'the eyes,' as in Her. xx. 206, and elsewhere in poetry.
48. *Ogygio deo*.] 'The Theban god,' i. e. Bacchus. Ogyges is said to have been an ancient King of Boeotia.
50. *Quamque lapis sedes tam lapis ipsa fui*.] Literally, 'And I was much as a stone myself, as the stone which was my seat.'
52. *Exhibiturus erat*.] This expression is probably used here with a legal reference to the *actio ad exhibendum* the object of which was to compel a person to produce an article of property, which was being sued for, for fear of its being fraudulently made away with in the meantime. See Dict. Ant. s. v. 'Exhibendum, Actio ad.' Translate: 'The bed which had received us both, but which was destined never to make good its receipt.' Cf. Her. xvii. 194, 'In non exhibitis utraque lusa toris.'
53. *Quae possum*.] i. e. 'quae (una) tui possum tangere.' Cf. viii. 3, 'Quod potui, renui.'

Quid faciam? quo sola ferar? vacat insula cultu.
Non hominum video, non ego facta boum. 60
Omne latus terrae cingit mare: navita nusquam,
Nulla per ambiguas puppis itura vias.
Finge dari comitesque mihi ventosque ratemque,
Quid sequar? Accessus terra paterna negat.
Ut rate felici pacata per aequora labar, 65
Temperet ut ventos Aeolus, exul ero.
Non ego te, Crete centum digesta per urbes,
Aspiciam, puero cognita terra Iovi.
At pater et tellus iusto regnata parenti
Prodita sunt facto, nomina cara, meo, 70
Cum tibi, ne victor tecto morerere recurvo,
Quae regerent passus, pro duce fila dedi:
Cum mihi dicebas ' per ego ipsa pericula iuro,
Te fore, dum nostrum vivet uterque, meam.'
Vivimus, et non sum, Theseu, tua: si modo vivit 75
Femina periuri fraude sepulta viri.
Me quoque qua fratrem, mactasses, improbe, clava,
Esset quam dederas, morte soluta fides.
Nunc ego non tantum quae sum passura, recordor,
Sed quaecumque potest ulla relicta pati. 80
Occurrunt animo pereundi mille figurae:
Morsque minus poenae quam mora mortis habet.

75. *Vivis* P G M: dubito anne recte. Nam sententia generalis est ut docet v. *femina*: et mutatio ad secundam personam librario alicui debetur ad Thesea verba referenti. Denique, quamvis sit ἐμφατικωτέρον ut ait Burm. se ipsam Ariadnen alloqui, tales translationes non sunt Ovidiani moris. *Vivit* multi codd. et edd. vett.

---

60. *Non hominum video non ego facta boum.*] Hom. Od. x. 98, 'Ἔνθα μὲν οὔτε βοῶν οὔτ' ἀνέρων φαίνετο ἔργα.
62. *Ambiguas vias.*] 'Perilous paths of the sea.' 'Ambiguus' and 'dubius,' especially the latter, are often used of the dangers of the deep. Cf. xviii. 52. Trist. I. xi. 13; Art. ii. 514, and passim.
65. *Ut rate felici pacata per aequora labar.*] Cf. Prop. IV. xvii. 2. 'Da mihi pacato vela secunda pater'—a line which has, in my opinion, been completely misunderstood. 'Pacato' is there used as 'tranquillo' often is = ' on a calm sea.' It is generally taken to agree with ' mihi,' which gives poor sense.
73. *Per.*] This word in adjurations is often separated from its case by a pronoun, probably in imitation of the similar usage in Greek with regard to πρός (πρός σε γονάτων, etc). Cf. Virg. Aen. iv. 314; Tibull. I. v. 7.

Iam iam venturos aut hac aut suspicor illac,
Qui lanient avido viscera dente, lupos.
Forsitan et fulvos tellus alat ista leones. 85
Quis scit, an et saevam tigrida Dia ferat?
Et freta dicuntur magnas expellere phocas.
Quis vetat et gladios per latus ire meum?
Tantum ne religer dura captiva catena,
Neve traham serva grandia pensa manu : 90
Cui pater est Minos, cui mater filia Phoebi,
Quodque magis memini, quae tibi pacta fui.
Si mare, si terras porrectaque litora vidi,
Multa mihi terrae, multa minantur aquae.
Caelum restabat : timeo simulacra deorum. 95

86. *Quis scit an haec tigrides insula habet* P, vitiose. *Quis scit an haec saevas tigridas insula habet* G, libri plurimi. Audiendus est vir ille clarissimus Heinsius, qui haec scripsit de hoc loco : 'Dicam quod sentio. Puto ultimam in *tigrides* aut *tigridas* syllabam absorpsisse vocem quae sequebatur, *Dia* videlicet, cuius glossema fuerit τὸ *insula*. Deinde pro *habet* exaratum primo corrupte fuisse *bacet* vel quid simile, unde *habet* sit fac um. Lego igitur, *quis scit at et saeva tigride Dia vacet.*' Certe vocem *Dia* loco sui glossematis *insula* restituendum nullus dubito. De ceteris incertum Emendatio tamen Auctoris Elect. Eton. magis arridet quam Heinsiana cujus vestigiis ingreditur : *Quis scit an et saevam tigrida Dia ferat.* Hodie quidem in Elect. Eton. profertur *an et saevas tigridas intus alat* cum *habet* in priore versu.
87. *Magnas* P G, *magnos* codd. plurimi. *Phoca* fem. generis est (φωκή). Virg. G. iii. 543 : iv. 432.

86. *Quis scit an et saevam tigrida Dia ferat?*] 'Who knows whether or no Naxos breeds a fierce tiger as well?' 'Dia' was the ancient name of Naxos, and is often used in poetry. Ovid uses it elsewhere : Met. iii. 690, Ibid. viii. 174 : in the latter passage when describing the desertion of Ariadne. One would have, therefore, expected to meet the word in this poem. Most certainly, if even there was a gloss, 'insula' in the ordinary reading was a gloss on 'Dia ;' 'da,' the last syllable of 'tigrida,' was thereupon confounded with 'Dia,' which was omitted, and 'insula' admitted by the next copyist : and finally the line was remodelled to suit 'insula,' by changing 'tigrida' to 'tigridas,' and 'ferat,' or whatever the last word was, to 'habet.' The vulgate cannot stand for a moment : the subjunctive is demanded after 'scit an,' and 'insula habet' in the end of a pentameter cannot be tolerated. To Hein-sius belongs the merit of first making this restoration, which, incredible to relate, has not been adopted by a single modern editor.

95. The commentators are pretty well agreed that there is something wrong here. Burmann thought vs. 95 was spurious, and that the genuine line which described the island as deserted was lost. Lennep considered vs. 94 and 95 both interpolations, and that the sense is complete if we reject them. I see no valid reason for supposing any corruption. The mention of 'ferae' in 96 was quite sufficient to account for the 'sive colunt viri' of the following line, without supposing any more detailed description of the deserted state of the island. The 'simulacra deorum' are phantoms, supposed divine, seen by Ariadne hovering in the air at twilight, and at night. Cf. xiii. 111, 'Excutior somno simulacraque noctis adoro.' Am. I. vi. 9, 'At quondam

Destituor rapidis praeda cibusque feris.
Sive colunt habitantque viri, diffidimus illis:
 Externos didici laesa timere viros.
Viveret Androgeos utinam, nec facta luisses
 Impia funeribus, Cecropi terra, tuis: 100
Nec tua mactasset nodoso stipite, Theseu,
 Ardua parte virum dextera, parte bovem:
Nec tibi quae reditus monstrarent, fila dedissem
 Fila per adductas saepe recepta manus.
Non equidem miror, si stat victoria tecum,   105
 Strataque Cretaeam belua texit humum.
Non poterant figi praecordia ferrea cornu:
 Ut te non tegeres, pectore tutus eras.
Illic tu silices, illic adamanta tulisti:
 Illic qui silices, Thesea, vincat, habes.   110
Crudeles somni, quid me tenuistis inertem?
 Aut semel aeterna nocte premenda fui.
Vos quoque crudeles, venti, nimiumque parati,
 Flaminaque in lacrimas officiosa meas.
Dextera crudelis, quae me fratremque necavit,   115
 Et data poscenti, nomen inane, fides.
In me iurarunt somnus ventusque fidesque.
 Prodita sum causis una puella tribus.
Ergo ego nec lacrimas matris moritura videbo,
 Nec mea qui digitis lumina condat, erit?   120

106. Ita G, *belua stravit* P.
112. *Aut* P, *ut* G.

noctem simulacraque vana timebam.' Lennep would explain 'simulacra,' if the line were sound, as referring to Bacchus, and his thiasus, already seen hovering about the island. This would have been more clearly expressed, evidently.
 99. *Androgeos*, son of Minos, slain by the Athenians, to atone for whose death they sent their annual human tribute to the Minotaur.
 102. *Ardua.*] ' raised on high.'
 104. 'A clew often gathered up by your hands drawn towards you.' Any one who has seen a man hauling in a rope will understand 'adductas' and 'recepta.'
 112. *Aut.*] The meaning of the distich is: 'I should never have slept at all, or else I should have slept for ever,' and 'aut' is used as if the sentence had taken that form. 'Semel' = εἰσάπαξ, 'once for all.'
 114. *In lacrimas.*) See note on iv. 16, ' In mea vota.'
 116. *Fides.*] Supply ' crudelis.'

EP. X. ARIADNE THESEO.

Spiritus infelix peregrinas ibit in auras,
  Nec positos artus unguet amica manus?
Ossa superstabunt volucres inhumata marinae?
  Haec sunt officiis digna sepulchra meis?
Ibis Cecropios portus, patriaque receptus   125
  Cum steteris urbis celsus in arce tuae,   *(emended)*
Et bene narraris letum taurique virique
  Sectaque per dubias saxea tecta vias,
Me quoque narrato sola tellure relictam:
  Non ego sum titulis subripienda tuis.   130
Nec pater est Aegeus, nec tu Pittheïdos Aethrae
  Filius: auctores saxa fretumque tui.
Di facerent, ut me summa de puppe videres:

126. *Cum steteris turbes celsus in aure tuae* P pr. man: *urbis celsus in arce* P sec. man. *Cum steteris turbae celsus in ore tuae* G (nisi quod *dum*) M, plerique edd. rec. Sed verba *in ore turbae* minime conveniunt res gestas narranti: *in aure* quamvis rarior sit locutio postulabatur ut est in P, et ita restituendum si *turbae* legas. Sed valde dubitari potest annon rectum sit id quod P a. man. correctoris habet *urbis celsus in arce* quod recepit Burm.
129. *Solam* P G. Corr. Micyllus.

126. *Cum steteris.*] 'When you shall stand on high in the citadel of your native town.' Cf. vii. 20, supra, 'Et videas populos altus ab arce tuos.' A line so similar to this, that it seems to establish Burmann's reading, which I have adopted. The corruption in P is easily accounted for: it is 'turbes:' some copyist, ignorant or forgetting that *ris*, the second person singular of the future perfect, is generally long, wrote 'tu urbis' for 'urbis' = which became 'turbes,' then 'turbae.' Ovid nearly always lengthened *ris* in second sing. of the future perfect. Thus we have 'vitaris,' xiii. 67, 'reddideris,' Am. iv. 31, 'biberis,' Ib. 32, all futures: but 'impleveris,' Trist. II. 323, is the perfect subjunctive. See a complete list in Ramsay's Latin Prosody, pp. 75, 76. There are one or two exceptions, but the general rule is as I have stated. Probably originally there was a radical distinction between the future perfect in ro, ris, rit (we have fuerit, dederit, both futures in Ennius), rimus, ritis, and the perf. subj., which in –rim, ris, rimus, ritis: but the tenses gradually became confused. 'Turbae in aure' might possibly stand for 'in the hearing of your followers,' though the phrase 'in aure' is uncommon: but 'celsus stare in ore turbae' is, it seems to me, nonsense. 'In ore populi' means 'to be talked about by the people:' yet the commentators, though reading 'ore,' seem to understand it of Theseus relating his adventures. The only thing in favour of 'turbae' is the fact that it is a favourite expression of Ovid's, = 'retinue,' 'suite,' Cf. Am. I. i. 6, 'Pieridum vates non tua turba sumus.' But this is not quite the meaning it ought to have here, as it should refer to the general population of Athens. Professor Maguire suggests it may mean 'your democracy' = $\pi\lambda\hat{\eta}\theta o\varsigma$, ($\dot{a}\nu a\chi o\acute{o}\nu\omega\varsigma$), but I hardly think that was intended by Ovid.

127. *Narraris.*] As Loers remarks, the idea seems to be taken from the account given in the temple of Bellona to the senate by a victorious imperator previous to a triumph.

128. *Saxea tecta.*] i. e. the labyrinth, 'cut into puzzling paths.'

129. *Sola tellure.*] 'A lonely land.' Cf. xi. 84, 'In solis destitui locis.'

130. Cf. ii. 74.

Movisset vultus maesta figura tuos.
Nunc quoque non oculis, sed qua potes, aspice mente   135
　Haerentem scopulo, quem vaga pulsat aqua :
Aspice demissos lugentis more capillos
　Et tunicas lacrimis sicut ab imbre graves.
Corpus ut impulsae segetes aquilonibus horret,
　Litteraque articulo pressa tremente labat.   140
Non te per meritum, quoniam male cessit, adoro :
　Debita sit facto gratia nulla meo :
Sed nec poena quidem. Si non ego causa salutis,
　Non tamen est, cur sis tu mihi causa necis.
Has tibi plangendo lugubria pectora lassas   145
　Infelix tendo trans freta longa manus :
Hos tibi, qui superant, ostendo maesta capillos :
　Per lacrimas oro, quas tua facta movent :
Flecte ratem, Theseu, versoque relabere velo :
　Si prius occidero, tu tamen ossa feres.   150

149. *Vento* P G M. libri omnes praeter Basil. qui habet *relo* quod verum est. Vertere ventum Theseus non poterat. Et *vento* ex *movent* in *-vent* desinente ortum est, quod viros doctos latuit.

---

136. *Haerentem scopulo.*] 'Haerentem' does not imply that she was clinging to the rock, or that there was any danger of her being washed off by the waves. 'Haerere' is poetically used to describe the appearance her figure would present at a distance, fastened, as it were, to the rock. Cf. Prop. III. xxii. 27, 'Illic aspicies scopulis haerere sorores.'

138. *Ab imbre graves.*] 'Heavy with rain.' Ovid's use of the ablative with 'a' or 'ab' is peculiar. We have in the epistles many instances where the preposition is used, where it would not be expected : for instance, 'solvi ab laetitia,' xiii. 16. 'Notari a labe,'iv. 32 : 'oblitus a caede,' xi. 2 ; 'a somno languida,'x. 10 : and many others. On the other hand, he sometimes leaves out the preposition where it would be expected, as xii. 162, 'Deseror coniuge.' In such passages as 'ab imbre gravis,' 'a somno languida,' the preposition may be explained as denoting the result: 'heavy after rain,' 'languid after sleep.' But this explanation will not suit all the passages. Professor Maguire has kindly communicated to me his views on this subject; and they are, I believe, sound, although, owing to poetic license, the distinction he lays down may not be always observed. The usage, he says, appears to be : the ablative of the agent may be used without a preposition—(1.) Where the person is ἔμψυχον ὄργανον : as in Luc. vii. 402, 'vincto fossore coluntur Hesperiae segetes.' Cic. de Sen. 13, delectabatur funali et tibicine (2.) Where the person is regarded only as a means to an end, as Juv. xiii. 124, 'Curentur dubii medicis maioribus aegri.' So 'deseror coniuge' calls attention to the result: while 'deseror a coniuge' would call attention to the act of desertion. So in Fast. i. 415, 6, 'Priapus Lotide captus erat,' the abl. means that he was caught by her beauty : 'a Lotide' would mean that he was caught by her allurements. On the other hand, a thing takes the preposition to mark peculiar activity. See this subject further developed by Professor Maguire, in the Journal of Philology, vol. iii.

149. *Versoque relabere velo.*] Vid Adn. Crit., and compare xiii. 132. 'Dum licet Inachiae vertite vela rates.'

EPISTOLA XI.

CANACE MACAREO.

Siqua tamen caecis errabunt scripta lituris,
    Oblitus a dominae caede libellus erit.
Dextra tenet calamum, strictum tenet altera ferrum
    Et iacet in gremio charta soluta meo :
Haec est Aeolidos fratri scribentis imago.   5
    Sic videor duro posse placere patri.
Ipse necis cuperem nostrae spectator adesset,
    Auctorisque oculis exigeretur opus.
Ut ferus est multoque suis truculentior euris,
    Spectasset siccis vulnera nostra genis.   10
Scilicet est aliquid, cum saevis vivere ventis :

1. *Errabunt* libri omnes. *Enabunt* nuper edidit Riesius, *haerebunt* Muellerus : quarum ineptiarum melior est coniectura Riesiana, quae rideri saltem possit.
    9. *Utque ferus multoque* G.

XI.—The following epistle is supposed to be written by Canace, daughter of Aeolus, to her own brother Macareus. Though the subject is painful, the poem is perhaps the most highly finished of all the Epistles, and is much admired by Lindemann, and other German critics. The author probably followed the Aeolus of Euripides, a tragedy severely censured by Aristophanes in the Clouds, on the score of immorality of plot.

1, 2. 'But if my writing is found confused with blots, it is the blood of its author with which the letter will be blotted.' 'Tamen :' another remarkable instance of the abruptness courted by the poet in beginning these epistles : so 'at' in the opening of the next epistle. The words are imitated from Prop. V. iii. 3.

4. *Charta soluta.*] i. e. a scroll of parchment unfolded for writing on. We have 'charta soluta,' of untying a paper parcel in Iuv. xiii. 116.

7, 8. 'I would that he himself were here to look on at my death, and that so the deed might be done to the satisfaction of him who is the author of it.' 'Exigere opus' technically means to examine a piece of work to see that it is correctly done. Cf. Tac. Germ. 7, 'exigere plagas,' 'to demand a strict account of their wounds.' Cic. Verr. i. 51, 'ad perpendiculum columnas exigere.' So the common phrase 'sarta tecta exigere,' to require buildings to be kept in good repair.' 'Spectator' also, in 7, is used with reference to the sense it often bears of 'examiner,' 'approver.'

9, 10. *Ut ferus est.*] 'Cruel one that he is, and fiercer than his own winds, he would have gazed on my wounds without a tear.'

11. *Est aliquid.*] 'It has great effect.' A common phrase. Cf. iii. 131. 'Est aliquid collum solitis tetigisse lacertis.' The meaning is that Aeolus by living with the winds has become assimilated to their disposition.

Ingenio populi convenit illo sui.
Ille Noto Zephyroque et Sithonio Aquiloni
    Imperat, et pinnis, Eure proterve, tuis.
Imperat heu! ventis, tumidae non imperat irae: 15
    Possidet et vitiis regna minora suis.
Quid iuvat admotam per avorum nomina caelo
    Inter cognatos posse referre Iovem?
Num minus infestum, funebria munera, ferrum
    Feminea teneo, non mea tela, manu?   20
O utinam, Macareu, quae nos commisit in unum,
    Venisset leto serior hora meo!
Cur umquam plus me, frater, quam frater, amasti,
    Et tibi non debet quod soror esse, fui?
Ipsa quoque incalui, qualemque audire solebam,   25
    Nescio quem sensi corde tepente deum.
Fugerat ora color, macies adduxerat artus:
    Sumebant minimos ora coacta cibos:
Nec somni faciles, et nox erat annua nobis,
    Et gemitum nullo laesa dolore dabam: 30
Nec, cur haec facerem, poteram mihi reddere causam,
    Nec noram, quid amans esset: at illud eram.
Prima malum nutrix animo praesensit anili,
    Prima mihi nutrix 'Aeoli,' dixit 'amas.'
Erubui, gremioque pudor deiecit ocellos.   35
    Haec satis in tacita signa fatentis erant.

17, 18. 'What is the use of my reaching heaven by ancestral pedigree, and being able to reckon Jove among my kindred?' Aeolus was son of Hellen, son of Jove, according to one account.

19. *Num minus.*] So xvii. 230. xviii. 171.

25. *Qualemque.*] Sc. potentem, Loers. But that is surely not the only meaning—all the attributes of love, as she had heard it described, were now felt by her.

27. *Adduxerat.*] 'Had pinched.' 'Adduco' is often used of the pinching, contracting effect of famine. Cf. Met. iii. 397.

28. *Ora coacta.*] 'Compelled to eat.' So 'invito crescit in ore cibus,' xvi. 226. Burmann and Ruhnken wrongly take 'coacta' in the same sense as 'adduxerat' in the preceding line = 'contracta, minora facta per maciem.'

35. *Gremio.*] This is apparently the poetical use of the dative for 'ad gremium.' Cf. Am. I. viii. 37, 'Cum bene deiectis gremio spectaris ocellis.' It may however be the abl., like 'iugulo demittere ferrum,' xiv. 5.

Iamque tumescebant vitiati pondera ventris,
　　Aegraque furtivum membra gravabat onus.
Quas mihi non herbas, quae non medicamina nutrix
　　Attulit audaci supposuitque manu, 40
Ut penitus nostris—hoc te celavimus unum—
　　Visceribus crescens excuteretur onus!
Ah! nimium vivax admotis restitit infans
　　Artibus, et tecto tutus ab hoste fuit.
Iam novies erat orta soror pulcherrima Phoebi, 45
　　Denaque luciferos Luna movebat equos:
Nescia, quae faceret subitos mihi causa dolores,
　　Et rudis ad partus et nova miles eram.
Nec tenui vocem. 'Quid,' ait, 'tua crimina prodis?'
　　Oraque clamantis conscia pressit anus. 50
Quid faciam infelix? gemitus dolor edere cogit,
　　Sed timor et nutrix et pudor ipse vetant.
Contineo gemitus elapsaque verba reprendo
　　Et cogor lacrimas conbibere ipsa meas.
Mors erat ante oculos, et opem Lucina negabat: 55
　　Et grave, si morerer, mors quoque crimen erat:
Cum super incumbens scissa tunicaque comaque
　　Pressa refovisti pectora nostra tuis,
Et mihi 'Vive, soror, soror o carissima,' aisti,
　　'Vive nec unius corpore perde duos! 60
Spes bona det vires, fratri nam nupta futura es.
　　Illius, de quo mater, et uxor eris.'
Mortua, credo mihi, tamen ad tua verba revixi:
　　Et positum est uteri crimen onusque mei.
Quid tibi grataris? media sedet Aeolus aula: 65

37. Heins. coni: *tumescebam pondere.*
44. *Tecto* P *tectis* G *tectus tutus* vulg.
46. *Nonaque* P.　*Denaque* G.
53. *Continuo* P G. Corr. Aldus.
56. *Si morior* G ma. sec.　*Si morior* G. ma. pr. *simreor* P, *si morerer* vulg. quod verum est.
61. Ita G. In P antiqua scriptura erasa. *Fratri es nam nupta futura* P, ma. sec.

Crimina sunt oculis subripienda patris.
Frugibus infantem ramisque albentis olivae
  Et levibus vittis sedula celat anus,
Fictaque sacra facit, dicitque precantia verba :
  Dat populus sacris, dat pater ipse viam. 70
Iam prope limen erat : patrias vagitus ad aures
  Venit, et indicio proditur ille suo.
Eripit infantem mentitaque sacra revelat
  Aeolus : insana regia voce sonat.
Ut mare fit tremulum, tenui cum stringitur aura, 75
✶ Ut quatitur tepido fraxina virga noto,
Sic mea vibrari pallentia membra videres :
  Quassus ab imposito corpore lectus erat.
Irruit et nostrum vulgat clamore pudorem,
  Et vix a misero continet ore manus. 80
Ipsa nihil praeter lacrimas pudibunda profudi.
  Torpuerat gelido lingua retenta metu.

67. *Frugibus* P *frondibus* G M, vulg.
72. *Ille* P *ipse* G. Recte *ille* : infans proditur, non vagitus.
76. *Fraxinacies virga* P *fraxina virga* rell. omnes. Unde vitium in P ortum sit, nescio. Aut in *fraxinacies* latet vera lectio, *fraxinus icta*, vel simile quid, *virga* a correctore addito : aut *fraxina virga* verum est, et in *fraxinacies* latet adiectivum *fraxinacea* a librario aliquo procusum ad normam vocum *malvaceus, oleaceus,* ut illustraret *fraxina* quod ut adiectivum nusquam alibi occurrit.
82. *Gelida manu* P.

---

67. *Frugibus.*] 'Ears of corn,' as Lennep takes it, comparing Met. x. 433. Heinsius understood it to mean the 'mola salsa,' or sacrificial cake : but this evidently could not have been used for the purpose of concealing the child.
75. *Stringitur.*] 'Stringere' is often used of the wind just ruffling the surface of the water. Cf. Am. I. vii. 56. So of a bird skimming the surface, Met. xi. 733.
76. *Fraxina virga.*] It is curious that the common reading 'fraxina virga' has hitherto passed unchallenged, though there there are two objections to it ; (1) No such adjective as 'fraxinus' is known, save from this one passage. True we have 'faginus' and 'fagineus:' but then we have no noun 'faginus' that the adj. would be confused with. More to the point is the existence of 'Romulus,' as an adj. beside 'Romuleus.' (2) 'Fraxina virga' is not the reading of P, nor does the corruption there easily admit of the supposition that it is derived from 'fraxina virga.' Vid. Adn. crit. I was at one time inclined to suggest 'fraxinus icta.' Cf. El. in Mort. Drus. 101, '(nives) Zephyris et solibus ictae.' x. 139, 'Corpus, ut impulsae segetes Aquilonibus, horret.' But on the whole I assent to the soundness of the received ἅπαξ λεγόμενον.
82. The curious reading of P, 'gelida retenta manu' was evidently derived from 'manus' in 80. 'Lingua retenta metu' occurs again in Am. I. vii. 20. Cf. also ix. 102.

Iamque dari parvum canibusque avibusque nepotem
  Iusserat, in solis destituique locis.
Vagitus dedit ille miser: sensisse putares: 85
  Quaque suum poterat voce rogabat avum.
Quid mihi tunc animi credis, germane, fuisse—
  Nam potes ex animo colligere ipse tuo—
Cum mea me coram silvas inimicus in altas
  Viscera montanis ferret edenda lupis ? 90
Exierat thalamo. Tunc demum pectora plangi
  Contigit inque meas unguibus ire genas.
Interea patrius vultu maerente satelles
  Venit, et indignos edidit ore sonos:
'Aeolus hunc ensem mittit tibi'—tradidit ensem— 95
  'Et iubet ex merito scire, quid iste velit.'
Scimus, et utemur violento fortiter ense.
  Pectoribus condam dona paterna meis.
His mea muneribus, genitor, connubia donas ?
  Hac tua dote, pater, filia dives erit ? 100
Tolle procul deceptae faces, Hymenaee, maritas,
  Et fuge turbato tecta nefanda pede.
Ferte faces in me, quas fertis, Erinyes atrae,
  Ac meus ex isto luceat igne rogus.
Nubite felices Parca meliore sorores, 105
  Amissae memores sed tamen este mei.
Quid puer admisit tam paucis editus horis ?
  Quo laesit facto vix bene natus avum ?
Si potuit meruisse necem, meruisse putetur:

104. *At* P *et* G *ac* M.
106. *Amissae* P G *admissi* codd. longe plurimi.

---

84. *Solis locis.*] Cf. 'sola tellure,' x. 129.
99. *Ex merito.*] 'And he bids you infer from your conduct, what it (the sword) means.' It is probable that the scene here depicted, and the lament that follows, are drawn from the Aeolus of Euripides, as Lennep has remarked.
101. *Maritas.*] Here the adj. as often. Cf. iv. 134.
108. *Vix bene natus*]. For 'bene,' 'thoroughly,' cf. vii. 90, and xii., 37, note.

102 HEROIDES.

Ah! miser admisso plectitur illo meo! *fault* 110
Nate, dolor matris, rapidarum praeda ferarum,
  Ei mihi, natali dilacerate tuo :
Nate, parum fausti miserabile pignus amoris :
  Haec tibi prima dies, haec tibi summa fuit.
Non mihi te licuit lacrimis perfundere iustis, 115
  In tua non tonsas ferre sepulchra comas :
Non super incubui, non oscula frigida carpsi.
  Diripiunt avidae viscera nostra ferae.
Ipsa quoque infantis cum vulnere prosequar umbras,
  Nec mater fuero dicta, nec orba diu. 120
Tu tamen, o! frustra miserae sperate sorori,
  Sparsa, precor, nati collige membra tui,
Et refer ad matrem socioque inpone sepulchro,
  Urnaque nos habeat quamlibet arta duos.
Vive memor nostri, lacrimasque in vulnera funde, 125
  Neve reformida corpus amantis amans.
[Tu, rogo, dilectae nimium mandata sororis
  Perfer : mandatis perfruar ipsa patris.]

127. Hoc distichon quod in P a ma. sec. scriptum est Heinsius merito spurium duxit.

---

110. *Plectitur.*] 'He is punished for my fault.' The word 'plecti' is most properly used of undeserved or vicarious suffering. Cf. Hor. Ep. I. ii. 14, 'Quidquid delirant reges plectuntur Achivi.' Ter. Phorm. I. iv. 43, 'Tu iam lites audies : ego plectar pendens.' Ov. Trist. III. v. 49, 'Inscia quod crimen viderunt lumina, plector.' Cf. Her. xxi. 54.

111. *Rapidarum.*] Cf. vii. 142, note.

127, 128. The last two lines are certainly spurious. If they are allowed to stand, they must be supposed to be addressed by Canace to an attendant. As regards the shortening of the *o* in 'rogo' it is to be noticed that Ovid allowed himself this licence chiefly in common disyllabic words like 'peto,' 'nego,' 'volo,' and of course 'puto.' This is, however, a licence which the student must not imitate except in the case of the parenthetical 'puto' where *o* is always short. Next to 'puto' 'peto' occurs most often with *o* short of the other verbs : but even it is only shortened four or five times. There are only one or two instances at most of any other verb with $\breve{o}$ final, and none in the genuine Heroides save pet$\breve{o}$ in xii. 197. The only trisyllabic verb with *o* shortened in the genuine works of Ovid is 'confero,' but that occurs in the Epistles from Pontus, an avowedly careless composition. The occurrence of 'rependo,' Her. xv. 32, 'desino,' xviii. 203, is one argument against the authenticity of the Epistles they occur in. See notes on V. 59, ix. 126, and Ramsay's Latin Prosody, p. 57.

EPISTOLA XII.

MEDEA IASONI.

At tibi Colchorum, memini, regina vacavi,
 Ars mea, cum peteres, ut tibi ferret opem.
Tunc quae dispensant mortalia fila sorores
 Debuerant fusos evoluisse meos.
Tum potui Medea mori bene. Quidquid ab illo   5
 Produxi vitae tempore, poena fuit.

1. *At* P, *ut* G.
3. *Facta* P, *fata* G, *fila* multi codd. et Heins.
6. *Vitam* P G M : male, ut opinor. Librarius, accusativum quaerens, *vitam* intulit. *Vitae* multi libri.

XII. The Argonautics of Apollonius, as well as the Medea, furnished the poet with most of his materials for the following poem, which I consider second to none of the epistles of Ovid, although pronounced by Lachmann and Merkel unworthy of him or of any of his friends. The narrative, it is true, rather preponderates over the sentiment: but many fine passages occur. Ovid does not seem to have borrowed much from Euripides, though he knew his play, for it reminds us here and there of the Medea: he could not draw a poetical picture of a cunning and ferocious woman: accordingly here, as in his Dido, he softens the features of the portrait presented to him to copy.

1. 'But when I was Queen of Colchis I hearkened to your prayers.' The beginning is excellent : Medea at once takes up her theme, the ingratitude of Jason. 'At' is just the particle to lead 'in medias res,' as it implies a reference to a previous current of thoughts, like 'sic, in vii. 1. Thus 'at' is a common exordium where indignation is intended, the indignant speaker refusing to waste words or thoughts logically antecedent to the sentiment expressed, but which he knows he calls up in his hearers' minds, without expressing them. Virg. Aen. ii. 535, 'At tibi pro scelere exclamat pro talibus ausis Di si qua est caelo pietas quae talia curet Persolvant grates dignas.' Hor. Epod. v. 1, 'At O deorum quicquid in coelo regit Terras et humanum genus,' etc. Cf. Met. xii. 366, 'Hunc procul ut foedo disiectum vulnere Peleus Vidit, At inferias iuvenum gratissime Crantor Accipe, ait.' This compendious use of 'at' is like the use of ἀλλά in Greek. Thus in oracles ἀλλά is used to cut short introductory matter. Herod. i. 55, 'Ἀλλ' ὅταν ἡμίονος βασιλεὺς Μήδοισι γένηται.

3. 'Then the sisters who arrange our threads of life,' etc. The fact that Juvenal says, 'dispenso filum,' iii. 287, in some degree supports 'fila' against the other reading 'fata.' Heinsius quoted El. in Ob. Maecen. 'Nestoris annosi vixisses saecula si me Dispensata tibi stamina nente forent.' 'Fila sororum' also occurs in Am. I. iii. 17.

Ei mihi! cur umquam iuvenalibus acta lacertis
  Phrixeam petiit Pelias arbor ovem?
Cur umquam Colchi Magnetida vidimus Argon,
  Turbaque Phasiacam Graia bibistis aquam?   10
Cur mihi plus aequo flavi placuere capilli
  Et decor et linguae gratia ficta tuae?
Aut semel in nostras quoniam nova puppis arenas
  Venerat, audaces attuleratque viros,
Isset anhelatos non praemedicatus in ignes   15
  Immemor Aesonides oraque adunca boum,
Semina sevisset, totidem quot semina et hostes,
  Et caderet cultu cultor ab ipse suo.
Quantum perfidiae tecum, scelerate, perisset,
  Dempta forent capiti quam mala multa meo!   20
Est aliqua ingrato meritum exprobrare voluptas:
  Hac fruar, haec de te gaudia sola feram.
Iussus inexpertam Colchos advertere puppim,

13. *Aut* P G, *at* vulg.
16. *Adusta* unus liber.
17. *Semina* .... (*sensisset* ma. sec. *sevisset* fuisse ma. pr. opinatur Heins.) *totidem que et seminat et hostes* P. *Semina iecisset totidem quod seminat hostes* G, *totidem sumpsisset et hostes* G ma. sec. Heins. voluit *Semina iecisset totidem iecisset et hostes*. M edidit *semina sevisset totidem sevisset et hostes*. Meam coniecturam edidi.

---

7. *Pelias arbor.*] Eur. Med. 3, μηδ' ἐν ναπαισι Πηλίου πεσεῖν ποτε Τμηθεῖσα πεύκη κ.τ.λ. Cf. 'Pelias hasta,' iii. 126.
12. *Linguae gratia.*] This is the Euripidean conception of Jason's character. Med. 582, γλώσσῃ γὰρ αὐχῶν τἄδικ' εὖ περιστελεῖν. κ.τ.λ.
13. *Aut—isset.*] For a similar instance of 'aut' following a sentence with 'cur' or 'quid,' see x. 111. 'Crudeles somni quid me tenuistis inertem? Aut semel aeterna nocte premenda fui.' The interrogative sentence is equivalent to the first member of a disjunctive proposition. 'Either the Argo ought not have come to Colchis at all, or Jason should have been allowed to perish.'—'Nova:' the Argo was the first ship ever built. Speaking of a poem on the Argonautic expedition written by Varro Atacinus, Ovid asks, Am. I. xv. 21, 'Varronem primamque ratem quae nesciet aetas?' In Tac. Agric. 24, 'Agricola nave prima transgressus' may mean that Agricola's was the first ship that ever was seen in the Frith. — 'Non praemedicatus,' 'without previous anointing:' alluding to the φάρμακον, given by Medea to Jason. Cf. Apoll. iii. 1033.—'Immemor' is 'heedless,' 'without consideration.' The variant 'adusta' for 'adunca' is supported by vs. 44, 93.
17. *Totidem quot semina et hostes.*] 'And a foe in every seed.' Such I have no doubt was the reading of P, in spite of the somewhat unusual elision.
21. *Est aliqua ingrato meritum exprobrare voluptas.*] Cf. Eur. Med. 473, ἐγώ τε γὰρ λέξασα κουφισθήσομαι Ψυχὴν κακῶς σε καὶ σὺ λυπήσει κλύων.

EP. XII. MEDEA IASONI.

Intrasti patriae regna beata meae.
Hoc illic Medea fuit, nova nupta quod hic est. 25
Quam pater est illi, tam mihi dives erat.
Hic Ephyren bimarem, Scythia tenus ille nivosa
Omne tenet, Ponti qua plaga laeva iacet.
Accipit hospitio iuvenes Aeeta Pelasgos,
Et premitis pictos corpora Graia toros. 30
Tunc ego te vidi, tunc coepi scire, quid esses.
Illa fuit mentis prima ruina meae.
Et vidi et perii, nec notis ignibus arsi,

25. *Fuit* P G *fui* M et vulg.
31. *Quis esses* P G *quid* plurimi.
33. *Et vidi et perii* P G. Egnatius corr; *ut vidi ut perii* quod Heinsio quoque placuit.

---

24. *Beata.*] 'Wealthy.' The story of the quest of the golden fleece is a mythical embodiment of the early explorations of the Greeks for gold in the countries east of the Euxine. The inhabitants of those countries are still said to collect the gold-dust in the River Rion (Phasis) by means of a fleece.

25–28. *Ephyren bimarem.*] Ephyre was an ancient name of Corinth, to which the epithet ' bimaris' is frequently applied. Met. vi. 419; Hor. Od. 14.—Cf. iv. 106. *Scythia — iacet.* Ovid places Scythia on the west of the Euxine, or the left looking at an ordinary map. When banished there he sometimes plays on the double sense of 'sinistra,' applying it to Scythia: Cf. Trist. v. 14, ' Scythici vere terra sinistra freti.' ' Omne' as well as 'omnia' in geographical descriptions is sometimes used without a noun. Stat. Theb. vii. 15, ' omne quod Isthmius umbo Distinct;' Florus, ' omne intra Iberum et Tanain' (quoted by Heinsius). ' Omne' is incorrectly joined with Ponti in the Delphin Ed. The meaning is that Aeetes' dominions extended along the north of the Euxine till they reached Scythia on the left or west side of that sea.

29, 30. ' Aeeta' is the Greek Epic nominative of the Aeolic dialect. The use of the expression ' corpora,' like ' turba' above, 10, while it increases the vividness of the picture, seems also to express the fact, that before Medea's eyes singled out Jason from his fellows, she made no distinction between the individual Argonauts. They were to her 'a crowd of Greeks,' 'so many Greek figures.' ' Pictos' means ' covered with embroidery.'

31. *Tunc coepi scire quid esses.*] 'Then I first began to feel your power:' i. e. your power of kindling love. Cf. Pont. i. 7, ' Certe ego cum primum potui sentire quid essem.' ' Quis,' the reading of P, can hardly bear the meaning which is evidently intended.

33. *Et vidi et perii.*] Most readers will at first sight be disposed to agree with Heinsius, who proposed ' ut vidi, ut perii,' from the well-known passage in Virg. Ed. viii. 41, ' Ut vidi, ut perii, ut me malus abstulit error,' where the Greek idiom is literally rendered from Theocr. iii. 41, Ὡς ἴδεν ὡς ἐμάνη ὡς ἐς βαθὺν ἅλετ' ἔρωτα. But two arguments against the change may be adduced (besides authority of MSS.) one negative, the other positive. Ovid is not consciously a verbal copyist, and would have studiously avoided adopting without change an idiom peculiarly stamped as the property of Virgil: and secondly, as Loers has remarked, ' et vidi' after a previous ' vidi' is in accordance with Ovidian diction. Cf. v. 43, ' Flenti discedens——*Et flesti* et nostros vidisti flentis ocellos.' v. 154, ' auxilium tu mihi

Ardet ut ad magnos pinea taeda deos.
Et formosus eras, et me mea fata trahebant. 35
Abstulerant oculi lumina nostra tui.
Perfide, sensisti; quis enim bene celat amorem?
Eminet indicio prodita flamma suo.
Dicitur interea tibi lex, ut dura ferorum
Insolito premeres vomere colla boum. 40
Martis erant tauri plus quam per cornua saevi,
Quorum terribilis spiritus ignis erat:
Aere pedes solidi, praetentaque naribus aera,
Nigra per adflatus haec quoque facta suos.
Semina praeterea populos genitura inermis 45
Spargere devota lata per arva manu,
Qui peterent natis secum tua corpora telis:
Illa est agricolae messis iniqua suo.
Lumina custodis, succumbere nescia somno,
Ultimus est aliqua decipere arte labor. 50
Dixerat Aeetes: maesti consurgitis omnes,

39. *Dicitur interea tibi rex* P, *dixerat interea tibi rex* G. Corr. Heins.

ferro *potes. Et potes* et merui.' Fast. v. 528, 'Coniugio, *dixi*, sola fruere meo. *Et dixi* et servo.'—'Nec notis ignibus arsi:' 'and I burned with no ordinary fires: (but) like a pine torch kindled at a sacrifice.' The simile is somewhat different in Apollonius iii. 592 sqq.

36. *Abstulerant*.] 'Captivated.' Cf. Virg. Aen. iv. 29, 'Ille meos primus qui me sibi iunxit amores Abstulit; ille habeat secum servetque sepulchro:' where 'abstulit meos amores' is 'he won my heart,' and not as Conington explains it, 'has carried with him to the grave.' In the passage from Lucan, which he adduces, the meaning of 'abstulit' is defined by 'ad Manes.' There should be no comma after 'meos,' as 'primus' refers at least as much to 'abstulit' as to 'iunxit.'

37. *Bene*.] = 'well,' in the sense of 'completely.' So often, especially in the phrase 'vix bene.' Cf. vi. 24, 'tactum vix bene limen erat.' xi. 108,

'vix bene natus.' Fast. v. 278, 'Vix bene desieram.'

39, 40. *Lex*.] 'The ordeal,' or conditions on which Jason should win the fleece. So 'lex' and 'leges' are often used. Cf. xvi. 26, 'Nostra per has leges audacia fortiter isset.' Met. x. 571, 'Praemia veloci coniux thalamique dabuntur: mors pretium tardis: ea lex certaminis esto.' So passim. The imperf. 'premeres' in 40 is admitted because 'dicitur' is the historical present, and equivalent to 'dicta est.'

43. *Aere*.] The oxen were the work of Hephaestus, made by him for Aeetes. Τοὶ ἄρ' ἐνὶ μεγάροισι Κυταιίου Αἰήταο Τεχνήεις Ἥφαιστος ἐμήσατο θέσκιλα ἔργα. Καὶ οἱ χαλκόποδας ταύρους κάμε χάλκεα δὲ σφέων ἦν στόματ' ἐκ δὲ πυρὸς δεινὸν σέλας ἀμπνείεσκον. Apoll. iii. 228. sqq.—'Praetentus:' 'praetendi' dicuntur quae adversus vim muniunt et tegunt. Lucan ix. 673, 'Defenduntque caput praetentis crinibus hydri.' Ruhnken.

EP. XII. MEDEA IASONI.

Mensaque purpureos deserit alta toros.
Quam tibi tunc longe regnum dotale Creusae
  Et socer et magni nata Creontis erant?
Tristis abis, oculis abeuntem prosequor udis, 55
  Et dixit tenui murmure lingua 'vale!'
Ut positum tetigi thalamo male saucia lectum,
  Acta est per lacrimas nox mihi, quanta fuit.
Ante oculos taurique meos segestesque nefandae,
  Ante meos oculos pervigil anguis erat. 60
Hinc amor, hinc timor est. Ipsum timor auget amorem.
  Mane erat: est thalamo cara recepta soror.
Disiectamque comas adversaque in ora iacentem
  Invenit, et lacrimis omnia plena meis.
Orat opem Minyis: petit altera, et altera habebat: 65
  Aesonio iuveni quod rogat illa, damus.
Est nemus et piceis et frondibus ilicis atrum,
  Vix illuc radiis solis adire licet.

---

62. *Est* reposui pro *et* quod exhibent codd. omnes.
63. *Adversa* P G *aversa* vulg.
65. Ita G ma. sec. et multi codd. *Habebit* P G ma. pr. et codd. plurimi. Fr. Heusinger scripsit *petit altera et altera*: "*habebit,*" Heinsius coni: *orat opem Minyis soror altera, at altera flevit.*

---

52. *Mensa—deserit.*] The ancient tables were of small size, and it was usual to bring them with the dishes on them to the couches of the guests. Hence the phrases 'mensam apponere,' 'mensam removere.'

53. 'How far off then was Creusa's dowry-realm for you?' Creusa is called Glauce by Apollodorus and others.

57, 58. The poem here closely follows Apollonius iii. 665. sqq. 'Saucius' is often used of the wound of love. Am. II. i. 7. Virg. Aen. iv. 1. 'Nox, quanta fuit,' is 'the live-long night.' Cf. iii. 49, 'quantus erat.' Met. iv. 657, 'Quantus erat, mons factus Atlas.'

62. *Soror.*] Chalciope, who was mother of Argus and his brethren by Phryxus. They had gone from Colchis to Greece to try and recover the possessions of their grandfather Athamas and afterwards joined in the Argonautic expedition. It was at the request of Argus that Chalciope interceded with Medea. Apollon. iii. 610. sqq.

63. *Adversa in ora iacentem.*] i. q. 'pronam iacentem,' 'Adversa' is to a certain extent otiose: it means 'turned towards the bed.' Apollonius has Λέκτροισι πρηνὴς ἐνικάππεσεν εἰλιχθεῖσα.

65. *Petit altera et altera habebat.*] 'One sister sues, the other held the power to grant.' This is the interpretation of Lennep. He quoted Pont. II. viii. 54, where the countenance of Augustus is said 'habere auxilium.' But 'vulnus' is there read for 'vultus' in Merkel's edition. Still I think the passage before us may well bear Lennep's rendering. Of the emendations that have been proposed, I prefer 'flebat' for 'habebat.'

HEROIDES.

Sunt in eo—fuerant certo—delubra Dianae:
Aurea barbarica stat dea facta manu. 70
Noscis, an exciderunt mecum loca ? Venimus illuc:
Orsus es infido sic prior ore loqui :
' Ius tibi et arbitrium nostrae fortuna salutis
Tradidit, inque tua est vitaque morsque manu.
Perdere posse sat est, siquem iuvet ipsa potestas : 75
Sed tibi servatus gloria maior ero.
Per mala nostra precor, quorum potes esse levamen,
Per genus et numen cuncta videntis avi,
Per triplices vultus arcanaque sacra Dianae,
Et si forte aliquos gens habet ista deos, 80
O virgo, miserere mei, miserere meorum :
Effice me meritis tempus in omne tuum !
Quod si forte virum non dedignare Pelasgum—
Sed mihi tam faciles unde meosque deos ?—
Spiritus ante meus tenues vanescat in auras, 85
Quam thalamo, nisi tu, nupta sit ulla meo :
Conscia sit Iuno, sacris praefecta maritis,

69. Ita PG *Fuerantque diu* multi codd.
71. *Noscis* G, in P rasura : *nostin* fuisse credit Heins. *Nescio an exciderint* codd. plurimi : *exiderant* G, *exciderunt* P sub. ras. ut videtur.
75. *Perdere posse . . . . dest si* P, *sat est* rell. codd. *Iuret* P *iuvat* G. *Ipsa* PG, *ista* multi libri.
84. *Arbitror unde deos* G.

---

69. *Delubra Dianae.*] Called the temple of Hecate, whose priestess Medea was, in the Argonautics of Apollon. iii. 915.

75. *Perdere posse sat est, si quem iuret ipsa potestas.*] The sentiment is like Juv. x. 96, ' Et qui nolunt occidere quemquam Posse volunt.'

78. *Avi.*] The Sun, father of Aeetes. 'Numen :' see note on iii. 105.

79, 80. 'Aliquos' according to Ruhnken is = ' alios quos,' ' any other gods.' He claims this meaning for 'aliquid' in Ter. Heaut. I. i. 15, ' fodere aut arare aut aliquid facere,'' digging, or ploughing, or doing something else.' But 'aliquid' is there simply ' something or other,' and the meaning here is, ' I implore you by Diana (who I know is *your* individual patroness), and also by the patron deities of your *race*, if such there be.'

81. ' But how shall I find deities so propitious and favourable to me?' 'Unde' is often used with an accusative, a verb like 'inveniam' being understood. Hor. Sat. II. vii. 116, 'Unde mihi lapidem? Quorsum est opus? Unde sagittas.' Ibid. v. 102, ' Unde mihi tam fortem tamque fidelem ?' Lucan vii. 28, ' Unde pares somnos populis, noctemque beatam ?' ' Meos' is predicative, = ' on my side.' Ruhnken quotes ii. 126, in illustration, but he mistakes the meaning of the latter passage.

Et dea, marmorea cuius in aede sumus!'
Haec animum—et quota pars haec sunt?—movere puellae
  Simplicis, et dextrae dextera iuncta meae.   90
Vidi etiam lacrimas. An pars est fraudis in illis?
  Sic cito sum verbis capta puella tuis.
Iungis et aeripedes inadusto corpore tauros,
  Et solidam iusso vomere findis humum.
Arva venenatis pro semine dentibus imples: 95
  Nascitur et gladios scutaque miles habet.
Ipsa ego, quae dederam medicamina, pallida sedi,
  Cum vidi subitos arma tenere viros:
Donec terrigenae—facinus mirabile!—fratres
  Inter se strictas conseruere manus.   100
Insopor ecce draco squamis crepitantibus horrens
  Sibilat, et torto pectore verrit humum.
Dotis opes ubi erant? ubi erat tibi regia coniux,
  Quique maris gemini distinet Isthmos aquas?
Illa ego, quae tibi sum nunc denique barbara facta,   105
  Nunc tibi sum pauper, nunc tibi visa nocens,
Flammea subduxi medicato lumina somno,
  Et tibi, quae raperes, vellera tuta dedi.
Proditus est genitor, regnum patriamque reliqui,
  Munus in exilio quodlibet esse tuli.   110

96. *Habet* P G, *habens* codd. plurimi.
99. *Mirabile* P, *miserabile* G et codd. reliqui.
100. Ita G, *inter constrictas* P.
101. *Insopor ecce vigil* P G M, *pervigil ecce draco* codd. plurimi. *Insopor ecce draco* ego: credo *vigil* glossema ad v. *insopor* scriptum fuisse.
110. *Quodlibet* P, cod. plurimi: *quod licet* G, *quolibet* codd. Trev. et ita edidit Burm.

99, 100. *Mirabile.*] All the MSS. except Puteaneus have 'miserabile,' a very unsuitable reflection for Medea to make.— 'Strictas manus:' so Am. I. vi. 14, Trist. V. ii. 30. Cf. Hor. I. vi. 18, 'strictis unguibus' ap. Bentl. For the construction, cf. Liv. xxi. 1; 'haud ignotas belli artes inter se, sed expertas primo Punico conserebant bello.'

110. 'I considered it to be the greatest boon to live in exile,' so long as I should be with you, she means. 'For so that I your company may have, I ask no more,' says our own ballad. 'Quodlibet' in the sense of 'as large as you please,' is defended by the corresponding use of 'quamlibet,' as in Am. II. xviii. 14, 'huic operi quamlibet aptus eram.' Seneca, Ovid's greatest imitator, has, Med. 492, 'Poenam putavi, munus, ut video, est fuga.'

Virginitas facta est peregini praeda latronis.
  Optima cum cara matre relicta soror.
At non te fugiens sine me, germane, reliqui.
  Deficit hoc uno littera nostra loco.
Quod facere ausa mea est, non audet scribere dextra.   115
  Sic ego, sed tecum, dilaceranda fui.
Nec tamen extimui—quid enim post illa timerem?—
  Credere me pelago femina, tamque nocens.
Numen ubi est? ubi di? meritas subeamus in alto,
  Tu fraudis poenas, credulitatis ego.   120
Compressos utinam Symplegades elisissent,
  Nostraque adhaererent ossibus ossa tuis,
Aut nos Scylla rapax canibus mersisset edendos!
  Debuit ingratis Scylla nocere viris.
Quaeque vomit totidem fluctus totidemque resorbet,   125
  Nos quoque Trinacriae supposuisset aquae!
Sospes ad Haemonias victorque reverteris urbes:
  Ponitur ad patrios aurea lana deos.
Quid referam Peliae natas pietate nocentes

118. *Iamque nocens* dicitur esse in libris omnibus praeter Francof. *Tamque* Burm. et M. Verissimo.
123. *Misisset* P G M. Correxi ego.

---

113. *Germane.*] Absyrtus cf. vi. 129.
118. *Tamque nocens.*] Respicit ad opinionem veterum qui credebant, nusquam vindictam divinam esse praesentiorem, quam in mari, si scelerati se illi commiterent. Ruhnken. Cf. vii 57, 'Perfidiae poenas exigit iste locus.'
121-126. The Argonauts after the murder of Absyrtus by Medea were driven by tempests round the world until they were purified of the murder by Circe in Ausonia. —'Elisissent:' 'elidere' is regularly used of crushing, squeezing to death. Cf. ix. 85, note.
123, 124. *Mersisset.*] I have substituted this word for 'misisset.' The change appears to me to be certain: 'quoque supposuisset' said of Charybdis in 126, implies that a word of the same meaning as 'supposuisset' had preceded, and we have in Met. xiv. 73, said of this same Scylla, 'Mox eadem Teucras fuerat *mersura* cari-
nas.' So also Met. xiv. 482. Am. II. xvi. 25. There were two Scyllas in mythology, who are here confounded, as elsewhere. Scylla! the sea-monster opposite Charybdis was once a beautiful maiden, daughter of Phorcus, who was transformed by Circe, cf. Met. xiv.: the other Scylla was the daughter of Nisus, King of Megara. When Minos King of Crete was at war with Nisus, Scylla fell in love with Minos, and deprived Nisus of the tuft of purple hair on which his life depended. Minos after his victory drowned Scylla in the Saronic gulf: hence 'ingratis viris' refers to the conduct of Minos.
127. *Haemonias.*] Thessalian, from Mt. Haemus.
129. *Pietate nocentes.*] 'Guilty in their very affection,' which led them to cut off and boil their father Pelias, in the hope of renewing his youth by the charms of Medea.

EP. XII. MEDEA IASONI.

Caesaque virginea membra paterna manu ? 130
Ut culpent alii, tibi me laudare necesse est,
 Pro quo sum toties esse coacta nocens.
Ausus es—o! iusto desunt sua verba dolori—
 Ausus es 'Aesonia' dicere 'cede domo!'
Iussa domo cessi, natis comitata duobus 135
 Et, qui me sequitur semper, amore tui.
Ut subito nostras Hymen cantatus ad aures
 Venit, et accenso lampades igne micant,
Tibiaque effundit socialia carmina vobis,
 At mihi funerea flebiliora tuba, 140
Pertimui, nec adhuc tantum scelus esse putabam :
 Sed tamen in toto pectore frigus erat.
Turba ruunt, et 'Hymen' clamant, 'Hymenaee' frequentant.
 Quo propior vox haec, hoc mihi peius erat.
Diversi flebant servi, lacrimasque tegebant. 145
 Quis vellet tanti nuntius esse mali ?
Me quoque, quidquid erat, potius nescire iuvabat :
 Sed tamquam scirem, mens mea tristis erat.
Cum clamore Pheres iussus, studioque videndi

149. *Cum minor e pueris iussus studioque videndi* P G et codd. plurimi. Pro *iussus* multi libri habent *iussu*, duo *lusu*, unus *visu*, unus *missus*. Burm. coni: *iussus studione :* Lenn. *lusu* vel *lusus studione ;* Heins. *casu studione*, Locis *lusu studioque ;* M *lusus*

131, 132. 'Though others blame me, you must praise me, you for whose sake I was forced so often to commit deeds of guilt.'
134. *Cede domo.*] A Roman formula of divorce. Other formulae were 'Res tuas tibi habeto :' 'res tuas tibi agito.'
136. There is in most editions, and rightly, a full stop at the end of this verse. Jahn prints a comma, and makes a full stop at the end of 140. But Medea here closes the subject of the divorce, and begins the description of the marriage with Creusa. Verses 141, 142, on the apodosis to 'ut subito,' etc. It is plain from 145–150 that Medea was in the palace during the scene here depicted.
139, 140. *Socialia carmina.*] 'The marriage song.' Cf. iv. 62. The 'tibia' was used at weddings, tho 'tuba' at funerals. Prop. II. vii. 12, 'Tibia funesta tristior

illa tuba.'
143. *Frequentant.*] 'Repeat.' Ruhnken quotes Auct. ad Herenn. iii. 24, 'primas quasque partes in animo frequenta,' ' go over repeatedly in your mind.' Sen. Consol. ad Marc. 3, 'memoriam alterius retinere ac frequentare.' Cf. also xiv. 29, ' Comitum clamore frequentes.'
144. *Hoc mihi peius erat.*] 'The more I felt sick at heart.' The vague dread of some unknown coming evil produces this feeling. 'But you'd not believe how ill all's here about my heart.' Hamlet, Act V. sc. 2.
145. *Diversi flebant servi.*] 'The slaves wept, withdrawing into different places.' 'Diversus' often implies motion. Cf. xix. 167 : ' Nos quoque diversi medium coeamus in aequor,' Liv. x. 33, ' Diversi consules discedunt.'
149, 150. ' When Pheres incited by the shouting, and the desire of seeing (the pro-

Constitit ad geminae limina prima foris :   150
'Hinc mihi, mater, abi! pompam pater' inquit 'Iason
studioque. Inveterato morbo laborat versus, cui qui levi curatione se auxilium laturos
sperant nihil aliud facere mihi videntur nisi θρηνεῖν ἐπῳδὰς πρὸς τομῶντι πήμητι.
De Mermero et Pherete, natis Medeae ex Iasone susceptis, cf. Apollod. i. 27. Glossema *minor natu* vel simile quid ad nomen *Pheres* (*peres* fortasse vel *peris*) scriptum
erat : cetera quis non videt? Argumentis quae in comm. dedi id solum adiungam,
quod nihil ieiunius esse potest quam uxorem ad maritum de filio, communi pignore,
scribentem, eius nomen tanquam oblitam reticere.

cession), stood still near the outer threshold of the hall-door.' Pheres was the younger of Medea's two sons by Jason. Apoll. Bibl. I. ix. 27, τούς τε παῖδας οὓς εἶχεν ἐξ Ἰάσονος Μέρμερον καὶ Φέρητα ἀπέκτεινε. I do not wish any one to acquiesce in this emendation, who is satisfied with any of the readings hitherto proposed. These, however, are all unsatisfactory in the highest degree. To examine them in detail—(1.) The reading of P, and most MSS., which was also the old vulgate, as ' Cum minor o pueris iussus, studioque videndi.' This was objected to by Heinsius and Lennep, and well it might be : for, not to dwell on the fact that this must have been a self-willed boy, for it is distinctly implied that he would not have stood at the threshold, had not his desire of seeing the procession coincided with a sense of the duty of obedience, Lennep's objection is fatal : who ordered him to stand at the threshold ? ' Ecquis hic iussisse fingatur, rem celare studentibus domesticis, nec ipsa matre, quid illud esset vehementer scire cupiente ?' Besides there is something that jars greatly on the ear in the construction, perhaps the mixing of a strongly objective and external motive (iussus) with a subjective one (studio). (2.) Some MSS. have '*lusu*' for '*iussus,*' and this is adopted by Loers. But this is not sense. I have the same objection to it that I have to (3.) *lusus studioque videndi,* the hyperbaton adopted by Merkel—namely, that if the boy considered it sport to stand at a door, his notion of sport was incredibly rudimentary. For in no possible way can '*lusu*' or '*lusus*' mean 'enjoyment of the spectacle,' 'the fun,' as we would say, which I suppose is the meaning attached to it by Merkel and Loers. '*Lusus*' in Ovid is always '*play*,' and that of an active kind, except in its metaphorical use of '*lusus amoris.*' The other readings proposed are not likely to find favour. In defence of my own conjecture I would observe—first, that it is very likely that Ovid would mention the names of Medea's children. He is very fond of exhibiting his research in the matter of the names of relations of his chief characters: thus he has brought to light Phoebe, sister of Helen, known to us as such from only one other passage, viii. 77 : he mentions Gorge, sister of Deianira, ix. 165 : Alcimede, mother of Jason, vi. 105 ; and finally, Idyia and Chalciope, mother and sister of Medea, xvii. 32. True, he generally states their relationship on introducing them to the reader, 'germana Gorge,' ' Alcimede mater tua,' ' Phoebe soror,' etc. But in this case the children have already been introduced, 135, supra, ' natis comitata duobus;' and therefore even a person ignorant of their names might conclude that one of the children was referred to by the name Pheres. It is not then, I think, improbable that Ovid, who knew Apollodorus well, here introduced the name Pheres. ' Minor o pueris' is a gloss on Pheres: or, more likely, the result of a combination of a gloss ' minor natu.' written over ' Pheres,' with the word ' Pheres' itself, which an ignorant transcriber changed into ' pueris,' to which word it bore a strong resemblance in the archetype ; in fact, the words would look exactly the same, if carelessly written. ' Minor o pueris' then must go out, and ' Pheres' come in. But how to supply the remainder of the line ? Now, ' studioque videndi' clearly shows that, in the first part of the line, some other abl. corresponding to ' studio' was expressed. If ' iussus' is to stand (and there is no reason why it should not) ' clamore' probably was the word, and it has this in its favour, that its final syllables ' more' may well have been turned into ' minor o,' while the first syllable may have been confounded with ' cum.' With ' iussus clamore' cf. ' clamor vocat.' Hor. Od. III. xxiv. 46, and ' Nocturnusque vocat

EP. XII. MEDEA IASONI.

Ducit, et adiunctos aureus urget equos.'
Protinus abscissa planxi mea pectora veste,
 Tuta nec a digitis ora fuere meis.
Ire animus mediae suadebat in agmina turbae, 155
 Sertaque compositis demere rapta comis.
Vix me continui, quin sic laniata capillos
 Clamarem 'meus est' iniceremque manus.
Laese pater gaude. Colchi gaudete relicti.
 Inferias umbrae fratris habete mei. 160
Deseror, amissis regno patriaque domoque,
 Coniuge, qui nobis omnia solus erat.
Serpentes igitur potui taurosque furentes,
 Unum non potui perdomuisse virum.
Quaeque feros populi doctis medicatibus ignes 165
 Non valeo flammas effugere ipsa meas.
Ipsi me cantus herbaeque artesque relinquunt.
 Nil dea, nil Hecates sacra potentis agunt.
Non mihi grata dies. Noctes vigilantur amarae,
 Et tener a misero pectore somnus abit. 170
Quae me non possum, potui sopire draconem.
 Utilior cuivis quam mihi cura mea est.

152. *Ducet* P, *ducit* codd. plurimi.
170. *Nec teneram misero pectore somnus habet* P G et multi libri, *ram* P ma. sec. in ras. *Nec tener in misero pectore somnus adest* vulg. M edidit *nec tener in misero pectore somnus habet*, quod vix Latinum, certe non est Ovidianum. Meam coniecturam edidi.

---

clamore Cithaeron,' Vir. Aen. iv. 303. If any one should prefer 'Cum lusuque Phoreas lassus,' I should not much object : 'lassus' resembles 'iussus;' and the fact of 'lusu' being like 'lassus' may have disposed the remodeller of the line to omit one of these words.

151. *Hinc mihi mater abi.*] 'Come this way, mother!' 'Si per invisum mora ianitorem Fiat, *abito*,' ' *Come* away.' Hor. Od. III. xiv. 24; Met. iii. 454. 'Quisquis es, huc exi!'

157, 158. *Sic.*] οὕτως, 'Just as I was,' with my hair all torn. Cf. xiii. 137, 'Troasin invideo quae sic lacrimosa suorum Funera conspicient, nec procul hostis erit:'

where 'sic' seems to mean 'without stirring,' 'just as they are.' Loers here joins 'sic' with 'clamarem' wrongly.—'Iniceremque manus:' cf. viii.

160. 'Shades of Absyrtus, receive your appeasing sacrifice'—namely, my misfortunes.

162. *Coniuge.*] See note on x. 138.

163. *Igitur.*] 'And so.' In Greek the line might begin δράκοντ' ἄρ' ὡς ἔοικε καὶ ταύρων βίαν. 'Ergo' is more common in this sense.

170. *Et tener a misero pectore somnus abit.*] 'And tender sleep flies from my wretched breast.' Thus I have restored the passage from Trist. IV. iii. 22,

Quos ego servavi, pelex amplectitur artus,
  Et nostri fructus illa laboris habet.
Forsitan et, stultae dum te iactare maritae   175
  Quaeris et iniustis auribus apta loqui,
In faciem moresque meos nova crimina fingas.
  Rideat et vitiis laeta sit illa meis.
Rideat, et Tyrio iaceat sublimis in ostro:
  Flebit, et ardores vincet adusta meos!   180
Dum ferrum flammaeque aderunt sucusque veneni,
  Hostis Medeae nullus inultus erit.
Quod si forte preces praecordia ferrea tangunt,
  Nunc animis audi verba minora meis.
Tam tibi sum supplex, quam tu mihi saepe fuisti: 185
  Nec moror ante tuos procubuisse pedes.
Si tibi sum vilis, communis respice natos:
  Saeviet in partus dira noverca meos.
Et nimium similes tibi sunt, et imagine tangor,
  Et quoties video, lumina nostra madent.   190
Per superos oro, per avitae lumina flammae,
  Per meritum et natos, pignora nostra, duos:
Redde torum, pro quo tot res insana reliqui:
  Adde fidem dictis, auxiliumque refer.
Non ego te imploro contra taurosque virosque,   195
  Utque tua serpens victa quiescat ope.

185. *Nam* P G. : corr. Heins.—*quam* P, *quod* G et vulg.

'Lenis ab admonito pectore somnus abit:' and Pont. III. ii. 12, 'Pulsus et e trepido pectore somnus abit.' Vid. Adn. Crit. The reading of Merkel, 'Nec tener in misero pectore somnus habet,' where 'habet' = 'dwells' cannot stand, as Ovid never uses 'habet' in this rare sense, which is found, I believe, only once or twice in Plautus. The corruption in P arose from the similarity of 'abit' to 'habet,' four lines farther down. The latter word was substituted for the former: and then 'et' was changed to 'nec,' to make sense (without doing so), 'tener a misero' being also mistaken for 'teneram misero.' The erasure in the last syllable of 'teneram' clearly points to the reading in the text. 'Tener' is applied to 'somnus' by Ovid, Art. ii. 546.

180. *Adusta*.] Cf. Eur. Med. 1135, sqq., where an account of the burning of Creusa by the magic robe and crown sent her by Medea is given at length.

184. 'Listen to prayers too abject for my high spirit,' ταπεινοτέρας ἢ κατὰ τὸν ἐμὸν θυμόν.

EP. XII. MEDEA IASONI.

Te peto, quem merui, quem nobis ipse dedisti,
   Cum quo sum pariter facta parente parens.
Dos ubi sit, quaeris? Campo numeravimus illo,
   Qui tibi laturo vellus arandus erat.   200
Aureus ille aries villo spectabilis aureo,
   Dos mea: quam dicam si tibi 'redde,' neges.
Dos mea tu sospes. Dos est mea Graia iuventus:
   I nunc, Sisyphias, improbe, confer opes.
Quod vivis, quod habes nuptam socerumque potentis,   205
   Hoc ipsum, ingratus quod potes esse, meum est.
Quos equidem actutum —sed quid praedicere poenam
   Attinet? Ingentis parturit ira minas.
Quo feret ira, sequar. Facti fortasse pigebit.
   Et piget infido consuluisse viro.   210
Viderit ista deus, qui nunc mea pectora versat.
   Nescio quid certe mens mea maius agit.

205. *Potentem* G et libri omnes praeter P.

---

197. *Te peto quem merui.*] 'I sue for yourself, whom I have earned.' Cf. 82, supra, 'Effice me meritis tempus in omne tuum.'

199. *Numerarimus.*] 'I paid it down.' 'Numerare' is the technical word for paying down in money, opposed to paying by draft, 'perscribere.'

204. *Sisyphias opes.*] The wealth of Corinth, of which Sisyphus was said to be the founder.

206. 'It is owing to me that you have it in your power to be ungrateful:' a line worthy of being quoted, and thoroughly Ovidian in spirit.

211. *Viderit ista Deus, qui nunc mea pectora versat.*] 'Let God who now agitates my heart see to that'—namely, the consequences of what I am about to do: referring to 'facti fortasse pigebit' in 209. Ruhnken observes that 'viderit' is often used when the speaker declares his intention of persevering in a design, and leaving the consequences to others. Heinsius on Pont. I. ii. 9, quotes many instances of this usage. Art. iii. 671, 'Viderit utilitas: ego coepta fideliter edam;' ii. 'Viderit Atrides: Helenen ego crimine solvo.' Petron. 61, 'Videris tamen' inquit: 'non oro tui similis.' We have almost the same idiom in English: S. Matt. xxvii. 4, 'What is that to us? See thou to that.'

EPISTOLA XIII.

LAODAMIA PROTESILAO.

Mittit, et optat amans, quo mittitur, ire salutem,
  Haemonis Haemonio Laodamia viro.
Aulide te fama est vento retinente morari:
  A! me cum fugeres, hic ubi ventus erat?
Tum freta debuerant vestris obsistere remis. 5
  Illud erat saevis utile tempus aquis.
Oscula plura viro mandataque plura dedissem:
  Et sunt quae volui dicere multa tibi.
Raptus ea hinc praeceps, et qui tua vela vocaret,
  Quem cuperent nautae, non ego, ventus erat. 10

8. *Multa* P G, *plura* vulg.

XIII.—Supposed to be addressed by Laodamia to Protesilaus, while detained with the Grecian fleet at Aulis. The account given by Homer of Protesilaus is as follows, Il. ii. 695, sqq.:—

οἱ δ' εἶχον Φυλάκην καὶ Πύρασον ἀνθεμόεντα
Δήμητρος τέμενος Ἰτωνά τε μητέρα μήλων
Ἀγχίαλόν τ' Ἀντρῶν' ἠδὲ Πτελεὸν λεχεποίην,
Τῶν αὖ Πρωτεσίλαος ἀρήϊος ἡγεμόνευεν
Ζωὸς ἐών· τότε δ' ἤδη ἔχεν κάτα γαῖα μέλαινα,
Τοῦ δὲ καὶ ἀμφιδρυφὴς ἄλοχος Φυλάκῃ ἐλέλειπτο
Καὶ δόμος ἡμιτελής· τὸν δ' ἔκτανε Δάρδανος ἀνήρ
Νηὸς ἀποθρῴσκοντα πολὺ πρώτιστον Ἀχαιῶν.

The Δάρδανος ἀνήρ, who slew Protesilaus, is in the later legend said to have been Hector. Cf. Hyg. Fab. 103; Ovid Met. xii. 67: vs. 65 of this Epistle. I have stated in the preface to this edition the grounds for believing that this epistle is not from the pen of Ovid. It has considerable merit, though the sentiments are rather drawn out.

1, 2. *Mittit, et optat amans, quo mittitur, iro salutem.*] There is a choice between two interpretations: 'Mittit amans salutem, et optat (salutem) iro quo mittitur,' and ' Mittit amans salutem et optat (ipsa) iro quo mittitur salus.' The latter is the least nonsensical of the two, and is something like xviii. 1: ' Mittit Abydenus quam mallet ferre salutem:' but from the form of the line I think the former is evidently intended; and that sense is supported by Pont. III. ii. 2, '(Quam legis a nobis missam tibi, Cotta, salutem Missa sit ut vere perveniatque precor.' 'Haemonis' is 'Thessalian,' xii. 12.

9. *Hinc.*] From Thessaly to join the Grecian fleet at Aulis.

EP. XIII. LAODAMIA PROTESILAO.

Ventus erat nautis aptus, non aptus amanti :
 Solvor ab amplexu, Protesilae, tuo,
Linguaque mandantis verba imperfecta reliquit :
 Vix illud potui dicere triste vale.
Incubuit Boreas, abreptaque vela tetendit :   15
 Iamque meus longe Protesilaus erat.
Dum potui spectare virum, spectare iuvabat :
 Sumque tuos oculos usque secuta meis.
Ut te non poteram, poteram tua vela videre,
 Vela diu vultus detinuere meos.   20
At postquam nec te, nec vela fugacia vidi,
 Et quod spectarem, nil nisi pontus erat,
Lux quoque tecum abiit, tenebrisque exsanguis obortis
 Succiduo dicor procubuisse genu.
Vix socer Iphiclus, vix me grandaevus Acastus,   25
 Vix mater gelida maesta refecit aqua.
Officium fecere pium, sed inutile nobis.
 Indignor miserae non licuisse mori.
Ut rediit animus, pariter rediere dolores.
 Pectora legitimus casta momordit amor.   30
Nec mihi pectendos cura est praebere capillos,
 Nec libet aurata corpora veste tegi.
Ut quas pampinea tetigisse Bicorniger hasta
 Creditur, huc illuc, qua furor egit, eo.

13. *Mandantis* P G, *mandatis* multi libri, quare Heins. voluit *mandatrix*.
29. *Ut rediit animus* P *utque animus rediit* G, et vulg.

---

15. *Incubuit*.] 'Proprium verbum de vehementi flatu ventorum.' Ruhnken.
23, 24. 'The light of day fled along with you, and darkness rising to my eyes, they tell me that I fell with tottering knees.' 'Obortis:' cf. 'lacrimis obortis' passim. 'Succiduo:' Met. x. 458, 'Poplite succiduo genua intremuere.'—'Dicor:' cf. iv. 51, 'Namque mihi referunt, cum se furor ille remisit, omnia.'
25. *Acastus*.] Father of Laodamia: he was son of Pelias, who was killed by his daughters through Medea's deceit.
29. *Ut rediit animus*.] The last syllable of 'rediit' is lengthened by the caesural pause. This caesural lengthening is very common in Ovid, especially in the perfects of compounds of 'eo :' see Ramsay's Latin Prosody, p. 109.
33. Cf. iv. 47, 'Nunc feror ut Bacchi furiis Eleleides actae.' ' Pampinea hasta' is the thyrsus or wand of Bacchus, called κισσινὸν βέλος, Eur. Bacch. 25; but here spoken of as entwined with vine leaves (pampinus). So Met. iii. 667, ' Pampineis agitat velatam frondibus hastam.' Val. Flacc. ii. 269, ' Pampineamque quatit ventosis ictibus hastam.' Pro-

118   HEROIDES.

Conveniunt matres Phylaceïdes, et mihi clamant   35
  'Induo regales, Laodamia, sinus!'
Scilicet ipsa geram saturatas murice lanas,
  Bella sub Iliacis moenibus ille gerat?
Ipsa comas pectar, galea caput ille prematur:
  Ipsa novas vestes, dura vir arma ferat?   40
Qua possum, squalore tuos imitata labores
  Dicar, et haec belli tempora tristis agam.
Dyspari Priamide, damno formose tuorum,
  Tam sis hostis iners, quam malus hospes cras.
Aut te Taenariae faciem culpasse maritae,   45
  Aut illi vellem displicuisse tuam.

35. Heins. conj. *Phylleides..*
37. *Vestes* G : *laenas* Burm.
41. *Qua* P G, *quo* vulg.
43. *Dux Pari* P G et vulg., *Dispari* cod. Sarrav. et pro var. lect. Reg. Δύσπαρι ed. Vinc. Corr. Hubertinus.

---

fessor Tyrrell, in his edition of the Bacchae, on v. 25, restoring μέλος of the MSS., remarks, that the thyrsus is never called a weapon (βέλος) by Euripides: and generally this applies to the Greek conception of the sacred wand, though an occasional use of it as a weapon was not excluded, Bacch. 761; on the other hand, it is often described as a weapon, and that of a deadly kind, by the Roman poets: cf. the passages quoted above, in which it is called 'hasta,' and the following, quoted by Professor Ramsay, Cat. lxiv. 257, 'Horum parstecta quatiebant cuspide thyrsos.' Sen. H. F., 'Tectam virenti cuspidem thyrso ferens.' Cf. Hor. Od. II. xix. 8, 'Gravi metuende thyrso.'—Bicorniger: Bacchus is represented with horns of a bull, or a ram, on coins. The figure is of eastern origin, symbolising the elation produced by intoxication. Cf. Hor. Od. III. xxi. 18, 'Addis cornua pauperi.' Eur. Bacch. 100, ταυρόκερων θεόν. 'Tetigisse' expresses both the actual touch of the thyrsus, and the frenzy communicated thereby, like 'contactus,' ix. 50.

35, 36. *Phylaceides.*] 'Phylace' was a town in Thessaly, the native place of Protesilaus. Hence Laodamia is called 'coniux Phylaceia,' Trist. V. xiv. 40,

and the shade of Protesilaus is called 'umbra Phylaceis,' Stat. Sylv. V. iii. 273. Phylaceides, the patronymic of Protesilaus, from his grandfather Phylacus, must not be confounded with this word. Heinsius has a long note on this passage, proposing 'Phylleides' from 'Phyllus,' another town in Thessaly. He quotes Art. iii. 783, 'Nec tibi turpe puta crinem, ut Phylleia mater, Solvere, et effusis colla reflecte comis:' where he believes 'Phylleia mater' to mean Laodamia, comparing Art. iii. 137, 138, 'Longa probat facies capitis discrimina puri: Sic erat ornatis Laodamia comis.' Both words seem to have been used. 'Sinus,' 'robes,' generally only the part of the robe covering the bosom.

41. *Squalore.*] 'Squalor' is especially used of signs of mourning displayed by wearing old and filthy dresses, unkempt hair, etc. It is often joined with 'sordes,' which has the same meaning; also with 'luctus' and 'maestitia.' Cic., Sest. 14, 'Erat in luctu senatus: squalebat civitas, publico consilio mutata veste'

43. *Dyspari.*] 'Unhappy Paris!' Hom. Il. iii. 39; xiii. 769: Δύσπαρι εἶδος ἄριστε γυναιμανὲς ἠπεροπευτά. So Euripides calls Paris δυσπαρις, Hec. 925.

EP. XIII. LAODAMIA PROTESILAO.

Tu, qui pro rapta nimium, Menelae, laboras,
   Ei mihi, quam multis flebilis ultor eris!
Di, precor, a nobis omen removete sinistrum,
   Et sua det reduci vir meus arma Iovi. *"the restorer"* 50
Sed timeo, quoties subiit miserabile bellum :
   More nivis lacrimae solo madentis eunt.
Ilion et Tenedos Simoisque et Xanthus et Ide
   Nomina sunt ipso paene timenda sono.
Nec rapere ausurus, nisi se defendere posset,   55
   Hospes erat. Vires noverat ille suas.
Venerat, ut fama est, multo spectabilis auro,
   Quique suo Phrygias corpore ferret opes,
Classe virisque potens, per quae fera bella geruntur.
   Et sequitur regni pars quota quemque sui?   60
His ego te victam, consors Ledaea gemellis,
   Suspicor: haec Danais posse nocere puto.
[Hectora nescio quem timeo : Paris Hectora dixit
   Ferrea sanguinea bella movere manu.]
Hectora, quisquis is est, si sum tibi cara, caveto :   65
   Signatum memori pectore nomen habe.

60. *Quota quemque* P, et vulg.: *quotaquaeque* G et multi libri. P pro div. lect. *quotacumque sui.*
63. Hoc distichon mihi spurium videtur. Unde enim quae dixisset Paris scire Laodamia potuit?

---

60. *Redux.*] = 'reducens.' 'Jove the restorer.' This active sense of 'redux' is rare, but occurs two or three times. Cf. Ep. Sabin. i. 78; Mart. viii. 65; 'Fortuna Redux,' cf. Id. x. 70. So often in inscriptions. —' Det arma Jovi :' alluding to the custom of discharged or retired soldiers 'suspending their arms in temples.' Hor. Od. iii. 26, 'Nunc arma defunctumque bello Barbiton hic paries habebit.' Cf. Id. Ep. I. i. 5; and Ovid Trist. IV. viii. 21.

58. *Quique suo Phrygias corpore ferret opes.*] 'Who displayed the wealth of Phrygia on his person' (in magnificent apparel, etc.) Cf. Art iii. 172, where a similar expression occurs in a slightly different sense, 'Quis furor est census corpore ferre suos.' 'Bearing their birthright proudly on their backs.' Shaksp. K. John, Act ii. Sc. i.

60. *Et sequitur regni pars quota quemque sui.*] 'What a small part of their subjects was the retinue that followed each chief.' The proposition is not general, I think, as Ramsay takes it : 'how small a proportion of the whole force of a kingdom is wont to attend a prince upon such an occasion.' I think it refers to the following, of the chieftains Paris may be supposed to have had in his train.

63. These lines are intended to refer to Paris' words to Helen, xvi. 365, 6 : 'Omnia si dederis numquid dabis Hectora fratrem? Unus is innumeri militis instar habet :' but they are probably spurious.

Hunc ubi vitaris, alios vitare memento,
  Et multos illic Hectoras esse puta:
Et facito ut dicas, quoties pugnare parabis,
  'Parcere me iussit Laodamia sibi.' 70
Si cadere Argolico fas est sub milite Troiam,
  Te quoque non ullum vulnus habente cadat.
Pugnet et adversos tendat Menelaus in hostis: 73
Hostibus e mediis nupta petenda viro est. 76
Causa tua est dispar. Tu tantum vivere pugna,
  Inque pios dominae posse redire sinus.
Parcite, Dardanidae, de tot, precor, hostibus uni,
  Ne meus ex illo corpore sanguis eat. 80
Non est, quem deceat nudo concurrere ferro,
  Saevaque in oppositos pectora ferro viros.
Fortius ille potest multo, quam pugnat, amare.
  Bella gerant alii: Protesilaus amet.
Nunc fateor, volui revocare, animusque ferebat. 85
  Substitit auspicii lingua timore mali.
Cum foribus velles ad Troiam exire paternis,
  Pes tuus offenso limine signa dedit.

73. Post h. v. in plurimis libr. sequuntur : *Ut rapiat Paridi quam Paris ante sibi Irruat et causa quem vincit vincat et armis :* desunt in P G.
77. *Tantum voluere* P.
83. Ita P G, *qui pugnat amore* libri plurimi.
89. Heins. coni. *ut vidi ut gemui.*

---

68. *Hectoras.*] Cf. the well-known expressions, 'Caesari multos Marios iuesse,' Suet. Caes. 1. ' Sint Maecenates non deerunt, Flacce, Marones.' Mart. viii. 41.

77. *Vivere pugna.*] ' Struggle to live.' ' Pugno' is often joined with an infinitive in Ovid, meaning to struggle hard. Cf. Met. ix. 351; Rem. 122. ' Repugno' is used with an inf. in the opposite sense: cf. Her. xvii. 137, ' amare repugno.'

85–89. To call any one back on the eve of departure on a journey was considered a very bad omen both among Greeks and Romans. The daughter of Polycrates incurred her father's displeasure by saying ill-omened words (possibly words of recall) to him on his departure to visit Orestes: Herod. ii. 124, ταύτην ἰδοῦσα τὴν ὄψιν παντοίῃ ἐγίνετο μὴ ἀποδημῆσαι τὸν Πολυκράτεα παρὰ τὸν Ὀροίτεα, καὶ δὴ καὶ ἰόντος αὐτοῦ ἐπὶ τὴν πεντηκόντερον ἐφημίζετο. Ὁ δὲ οἱ ἠπείλησε ἢν σῶς ἀπονοστήσῃ πολλόν μιν χρόνον παρθενεύεσθαι. Another bad omen was to stumble at the threshold when leaving the house. So Am. I. xii. 2, 'Omina sunt aliquid: modo quum discedere vellet, Ad limen digitos restitit icta Nape.' Laodamia here tried to avert the bad omen by accepting it as a good sign.

EP. XIII. LAODAMIA PROTESILAO.

Vt vidi, ingemui tacitoque in pectore dixi
   'Signa reversuri sint, precor, ista viri!'   90
Haec tibi nunc refero, ne sis animosus in armis.
   Fac meus in ventos hic timor omnis eat.
Sors quoque nescio quem fato designat iniquo,
   Qui primus Danaum Troada tangat humum.
Infelix, quae prima virum lugebit ademptum!   95
   Di faciant ne tu strenuus esse velis!
Inter mille rates tua sit millesima puppis,
   Iamque fatigatas ultima verset aquas.
Hoc quoque praemoneo: de nave novissimus exi:
   Non est, quo properas, terra paterna tibi.   100
Cum venies, remoque move veloque carinam,
   Inque tuo celerem litore siste gradum!
Sive latet Phoebus, seu terris altior exstat,
   Tu mihi luce dolor, tu mihi nocte venis:
Nocte tamen quam luce magis: nox grata puellis,   105
   Quarum subpositus colla lacertus habet.
Aucupor in lecto mendaces caelibe somnos.
   Dum careo veris, gaudia falsa iuvant.
Sed tua cur nobis pallens occurrit imago?

     100. *Properes* P G *properas* libri duo..

---

93. *Sors.*] The oracle which declared to the Greeks at Aulis that the first Greek who landed on the shore of Pisa would be slain. Protesilaus devoted himself and was slain by Hector. Loers quotes a translation by Ausonius of a Greek epigram, from which it appears that Ulysses jumped out first, but on to his shield, so as not to touch Trojan soil: 'Fatale adscriptum nomen mihi Protesilao; Nam primus Danaum bello obii Phrygio, Audaci ingressus Sigeia litora saltu, Captus pellacis Lartiadae insidiis; Qui ne Troianae premeret pede litora terrae; Ipse super proprium desiluit clypeum. Quid queror? hoc letum iam tum mea fata canebant, Tale mihi nomen cum pater imposuit.' In these lines the writer hints at what he supposes to be the derivation of the name Protesilaus, viz.

πρῶτος—λαῶν.

98. *Iamque fatigatas.*] These words must be joined together: the waters which by that time (ἤδη) will have been as it were wearied, owing to the perpetual rowing.

101. *Remo veloque.*] 'Remis velisque,' or remis ventisque,' became a Latin proverb for doing anything with all one's might. Cf. Cic. Tusc. iii. 11, 'Res . . . . omni contentione, velis, ut ita dicam remisque, fugienda.' Id. Fam. xii. 25, 'ventis remis in patriam omni festinatione properavi.' These passages are quoted by Conington on Virg. Aen. iii. 563, where he might have added the passage in the text to the one he quotes from Plautus, 'remigio veloque' to prove that the true reading is 'remis ventisque' and not 'ventis remisque.'

HEROIDES.

Cur venit, a verbis muta, querella latens ?   110
Excutior somno, simulacraque noctis adoro :
Nulla caret fumo Thessalis ara meo :
Tura damus, lacrimamque super, qua sparsa relucet,
Ut solet adfuso surgere flamma mero.
Quando ego, te reducem cupidis amplexa lacertis,   115

110. *Cur venit a verbis multa querela tuis* libri omnes, pessime, praeter optimum P qui loco unice subvenit exhibens *tens pro tuis*. Manifestum est *latens* primo fuisse, deinde primam syllabam *la* a voce *querela* in *la* quoque exeunte absorptam fuisse. Correxi ego: tum pro *multa* reposui *muta*. Forsitan tamen legendum *Cur venit ah! verbis multa querela latens ?*
113. *Quaesare lucet* a man. pri. correctum *quis ara relucet* P, *quae sparsa relucet* G, *lacrimasque super quae sparsa relucent* vulg. Corr. Heins. D. Heins. voluit *lacrimasque super queis ara relucet*.
114. *A fuso* G, multi libri, *effuso* al.

---

110. *Cur venit, a verbis muta, querella latens ?*] 'Why does a dark complaint, unexpressed in words, reach my ears?' The reading hitherto adopted without question, 'cur venit a verbis multa querela tuis,' cannot stand, for two reasons—(1.) It does not account for the corruption 'querela tens' in P, the only MS. of any value. (2.) It is not Latin, or rather, it is not sense to say, 'querella venit a verbis,' 'a complaint comes from words.' I can find no parallel to it. My emendation 'latens' merely supposes 'la,' the first syllable, to have been omitted, coming after another 'la' at the end of 'querela.' This, as I have repeatedly remarked, is the most characteristic error of the codex Puteaneus. I may here give a complete list of the false readings thereby produced, as far as I am aware: we find 'nisi' for 'nisi si,' iv. 3; 'hanc' for 'hanc hanc,' vi. 132; 'Troas invideo' for 'Troasin invideo,' infra, 137; 'cunctas' for 'cunctatas,' xvii. 260; and in the present instance, 'querela tens' for 'querela latens.' 'Latens' = 'obscure,' 'ambiguous,' is several times used by Ovid: Cf. Met. ix. 527. 'Apta minister Tempora nactus adit traditque latentia verba.' Fast. ii. 705. 'Illic Tarquinius mandata latentia nati Accipit, et virga lilia summa metit.' Cf. also Cic. de Orat. ii. 66, 'Arguta etiam significatio est quum parva re et saepe verbo res obscura et latens significatur.' Also, it is to be noticed, a word like 'latens' is wanted here: for if the phantom of Protesilaus had expressed himself clearly in words, Laodamia would have been more certain of his fate, and the vagueness of her apprehensions would have been exchanged for loud lamentations. The change 'muta' for 'multa' is not a violent one, and these words are sometimes confounded in MSS, as was to be expected. The idiom 'muta a verbis' is supported by Cic. Att. viii. 14, 'Omnino intelligo, nullum fuisse tempus post has fugas et formidines, quod magis debuerit mutum esse a litteris' = 'silent in point of letters,' a common use of 'a' or 'ab.' This reading also agrees with the sense often given by Ovid to 'querella,' and 'queror,' viz. : 'a plaintive *inarticulate* cry:' Cf. Met. xiv. 99, where it is said of the Cercopes transformed into apes by Jupiter : 'abstulit usum Verborum et natae dira in periuria linguae: *Posse queri* tantum rauco stridore reliquit:' and so xi. 734, of the transformed Alcyone, 'Dumque volat, maesto similem *plenumque querellae* Ora dedere sonum tenui crepitantia rostro.' Met. ii. 665, 'Talia dicenti pars est extrema querellae Intellecta parum confusaque verba fuerunt.' I confess I am not so convinced of the necessity of changing 'multa' to 'muta,' as 'tuis' to 'latens :' but I have no doubt whatever of the truth of the latter reading. Could 'latens a verbis' be joined together, and rendered, 'refusing to be expressed in words?' We have 'a caede latentem' in Ibis, 625.

Languida laetitia solvar ab ipsa mea?
Quando erit, ut lecto mecum bene iunctus in uno
  Militiae referas splendida facta tuae?
Quae mihi dum refores, quamvis audire iuvabit,
  Multa tamen rapies oscula, multa dabis.   120
Semper in his apte narrantia verba resistunt:
  Promptior est dulci lingua refecta mora.
Sed cum Troia subit, subeunt ventique fretumque,
  Spes bona sollicito victa timore cadit.
Hoc quoque, quod venti prohibent exire carinas,   125
  Me movet: invitis ire paratis aquis.
Quis velit in patriam vento prohibente reverti?
  A patria pelago vela vetante datis!
Ipse suam non praebet iter Neptunus ad urbem.
  Quo ruitis? Vestras quisque redite domos!   130
Quo ruitis, Danai? Ventos audite vetantes!
  Non subiti casus, numinis ista mora est.
Quid petitur tanto nisi turpis adultera bello?
  Dum licet, Inachiae, vertite vela, rates!

116. *Tristitia* multi libri.
122. *Refere* P *referre* G M vulg. *retenta* libri quatuor. Ego reposui *refecta* quod certissimum mihi videtur.

---

117. *Bene iunctus.*] 'Closely joined.' Cf. xii. 37, note.
122. 'The tongue is more fluent when refreshed by a pleasant pause.' I have restored 'refecta' for 'referre' ('referre' in P) for many good reasons—(1.) The violent instrumental ablative the ordinary reading offends the ear: 'the tongue is more prompt to recount by means of a pleasant pause.' (2.) 'Referre' is evidently induced by the preceding 'referes,' and 'referas:' the single 'r' in P points to this. (3.) 'Promptus' is often used absolutely of fluent speech. Juv. iii. 24, 'Sermo promptus et Isaeo torrentior:' and in Fast. iv. 310, 'prompta' absolutely, is joined with 'lingua,' as here: 'Cultus et ornatis varie prodisse capillis Obfuit, ad rigidos promptaque lingua senes.' 'Her (Claudia's) dress, and the adornment of her hair, told against her, and her tongue too glib in answering back the reproofs of grave old men' (not, surely, as Paley understands it, 'pertly conversing with grave old men,' whose age she thought would secure her from blame. But this is not the point). (4.) 'Mora' is often joined with 'reficio' by Ovid, as the regular method of recruiting, refreshing. Fast. iv. 610, 'Haud secus indoluit quam si modo rapta fuisset Maesta parens longa vixque refecta mora est.' vii. 175 — 'laniataque classis Postulat exiguas semirefecta moras.' (5.) The regular construction of 'promptus' requires 'ad referendum.' Lastly, and perhaps most important of all, can 'referre' be used absolutely = 'to tell stories'?
134. *Inachiae.*] 'Argive,' 'Grecian.' 'Inachus' was the mythical founder of Argos.

Sed quid ago ? revoco ? revocaminis omen abesto, 135
 Blandaque compositas aura secundet aquas.
Troasin invideo, quae sic lacrimosa suorum
 Funera conspicient, nec procul hostis erit.
Ipsa suis manibus forti nova nupta marito
 Imponet galeam barbaraque arma dabit. 140
Arma dabit, dumque arma dabit, simul oscula sumet:—
 Hoc genus officii dulce duobus erit—
Producetque virum, dabit et mandata reverti,
 Et dicet 'referas ista fac arma Iovi!'
Ille, ferens dominae mandata recentia secum, 145
 Pugnabit caute, respicietque domum.
Exuet haec reduci clipeum, galeamque resolvet,
 Excipietque suo corpora lassa sinu.
Nos sumus incertae, nos anxius omnia cogit,
 Quae possunt fieri, facta putare timor. 150
Dum tamen arma geres diverso miles in orbe,
 Quae referat vultus est mihi cera tuos.
Illi blanditias, illi tibi debita verba

135. Turbant codd. *Sed quid ego revoco. . . .omen* P supra ras. man. sec. scriptum *revocantis et.* G habet *ago revocans ? omen revocantis abesto.* Vulgo codd. recc. habent *Sed quid ego revoco haec ? omen revocantis abesto.* Merkelianam coniecturam edidi.
137. *Troas invideo* P, *Troadas invideo* G rell. codd. Corr. Salmasius et post illum Heins. Vid. ad vi. 31 et conf. v. 110, supra.—*Si* P, errore sollenni, *sic* G et vulg. Lehrsius coni. *quamvis*, quod recepit Riesius: ridicule.

---

137. *Troasin invideo.*] Vid. Adn. Crit., and note on 110, supra. Professor Ramsay calls 'Troasin' a *conjecture* of Heinsius: if it be a conjecture, it would be hard indeed to say what is a restoration.
143. *Producet.*] προπέμψει, 'will escort on their way to the field.' Cf. Prop. v. 189, 'Dixi ego, quum geminos produceret Arria natos.' Shakspeare, Henry V., Act II. Sc. iii. 'Prithee honey-sweet husband, let me *bring thee* to Staines,' says Pistol's wife to her husband when on his way to the 'Gallia wars.'
144. *Fac.*] On the quantity of this word see note on ii. 98.—' Sic :' see note on xii. 157.
152. *Cera.*] This description of Laodamia dressing up a doll, and nursing it, consoling herself by imagining it to represent the absent Protesilaus, is unspeakably silly. Hyginus (Fab. 104) speaks of an image made by Laodamia to represent Protesilaus; but with this important difference, that it was after his death. 'Laodamia, Acasti filia, amisso coniuge cum tres horas consumpsisset, quas a dis petierat, fletum et dolorem pati non potuit. Itaque fecit simulacrum cereum simile Protesilai coniugis, et in thalamis posuit sub simulatione sacrorum et cum colere coepit.' This does not differ very much from the worship paid by Dido to the shrine of Sychaeus, vii. 99.

EP. XIII. LAODAMIA PROTESILAO.

Dicimus, amplexus accipit illa meos.
Crede mihi, plus est, quam quod videatur, imago: 155
  Adde sonum cerae, Protesilaus erit.
Hanc specto teneoque sinu pro coniuge vero,
  Et, tamquam possit verba referre, queror.
Per reditus corpusque tuum, mea numina, iuro,
  Perque pares animi coniugiique faces, 160
[Perque, quod ut videam canis albere capillis,
  Quod tecum possis ipse referre, caput,]
Me tibi venturam comitem, quocumque vocaris,
  Sive—quod heu timeo, sive superstes eris.
Ultima mandato claudetur epistula parvo: 165
  Si tibi cura mei, sit tibi cura tui !

161-162. Hoc distichon uncis ut spurium inclusi.
162. Pro *quod* Ileius. maluit *huc* vel *o*.

---

159. *Queror*.] 'I make my plaint to it as though it could reply.'
160. *Perque pares animi coniugiique faces*.] This is rather a difficult line to translate, though the meaning is clear. 'By the marriage torch whose fires are ever felt by my constant soul.'
161. *Ut*.] = 'utinam,' if the reading be sound. I can find no other instance in the writings attributed to Ovid of 'ut' used in this sense. It is common enough in the writings of the Comedians. But the next verse is so absurd that the distich, which is not wanted, is very likely spurious.
164. *Sive—quod heu timeo*.] i. e. 'sive mortuus eris.' The aposiopesis is intentional, in order to prevent the unlucky omen, which speaking of death would involve. Loers says, absurdly, it appears to me, this is not the meaning, and that an unlucky omen is contained in the words 'superstes eris,' just as much as there would be in 'mortuus eris.' That is not true. He says the aposiopesis is merely 'vehementioris expressio doloris.' This is hardly an explanation.

EPISTOLA XIV.

HYPERMNESTRA LYNCEO.

Mittit Hypermnestra de tot modo fratribus uni :
 Cetera nuptarum crimine turba iacet.
Clausa domo teneor gravibusque coercita vinclis :
 Est mihi supplicii causa fuisse piam.
Quod manus extimuit iugulo demittere ferrum, 5
 Sum rea : lauderer, si scelus ausa forem.
Esse ream praestat, quam sic placuisse parenti.
 Non piget iumunes caedis habere manus.

1. *Hypermestra* P, ubique.
5. *Dimittere* P G et vulg : *demittere* odd. vett.

XIV.—Aegyptus and Danaus were twin brothers, sons of Belus : by whom Arabia was given to Aegyptus, Libya to Danaus. Aegyptus conquered the country called after his name, and settled there. Aegyptus had fifty sons, Danaus fifty daughters. Danaus, having reason to fear the sons of Aegyptus, fled with his daughters to Argos, where they were hospitably received by the king of the country called by Aeschylus, and the author of this epistle, v. 23, Pelasgus, v. 23, but by Apollodorus, Gelanor. The fifty sons of Aegyptus pursued Danaus and demanded his daughters in marriage. Danaus consented, but ordered all the brides to slay their husbands on the night after the wedding. They all obeyed except Hypermnestra, married to Lynceus, who allowed Lynceus to escape. The other daughters were purified of the murder by Hermes and Athena at the command of Jupiter. Danaus afterwards forgave Hypermnestra, and allowed her to become the wife of Lynceus. Such is the myth as given by Apollodorus. The author of this epistle differs from it in one or two points. He alludes to a war between Danaus and Aegyptus, vs. 111, ending in the defeat of the former, of which nothing is said in the ordinary legend. He makes the forty-nine murderesses to perish by a retributive justice of which we hear nothing elsewhere, vs. 116, 117. Lachmann rejects the epistle, as not by Ovid. L. Mueller's opinion, as I have shown on vs. 105, 109, 111, rests on grounds which make it utterly worthless. I have discussed the question of the authenticity of the epistle more fully in the Preface to this edition.

1, 2. 'Hypermnestra sends this letter to the only survivor of her cousins, who were lately so many. The rest lie low through the crime of their brides.' 'Mittit' without an accusative 'epistolam,' or 'salutem' is uncommon : I have not been able to find another instance of it in Ovid. 'Fratribus:' 'frater' is used throughout the epistle for 'cousin,' as in Ep. viii. 'Frater' properly included both the 'frater germanus,' and the 'frater patruelis.' So ἀδελφός is used.

EP. IV. HYPERMNESTRA LYNCEO.

Me pater igne licet, quem non violavimus, urat,
Quaeque aderant sacris, tendat in ora faces: 10
Aut illo iugulet, quem non bene tradidit ensem, *(attracted in)*
Ut, qua non cecidit vir nece, nupta cadam:
Non tamen, ut dicant morientia 'paenitet' ora,
Efficiet: non est, quam piget esse piam.
Paeniteat sceleris Danaum saevasque sorores. *(acc.)*   15
Hic solet eventus facta nefanda sequi.
Cor pavet admonitu temeratae sanguine noctis,
Et subitus dextrae praepedit ossa tremor.
Quam tu caede putes fungi potuisse mariti,
Scribere de facta non sibi caede timet.   20
Sed tamen experiar. Modo facta crepuscula terris,
Ultima pars lucis, primaque noctis erat:
Ducimur Inachides magni sub tecta Pelasgi, *2½*.

   11. Ita P G : *ense* vulg.
   14. *Non sum* al : Heins. coni : *non es*.
   17. *Ossa* P G *orsa* Nauger. *ausa* Allenus.
   22. Ita vulg. : *noctis primaque lucis* P, edd. vett.

---

9. *Me pater—licet.*] This passage is an imitation, perhaps an unconscious one, of Horace, Od. III. xi. 45, sqq.: 'Me pater saevis oneret catenis,' etc. The fire intended is that on the marriage altar, cf. vs. 26, and the torches are the torches of the marriage procession.

11. *Ensem.*] Attracted into the case of relative 'quem.' So in iv. 1, 'Qua nisi tu dederis caritura est ipsa salute Mittit,' etc., 'salute' for 'salutem' is attracted into the case of 'qua.' The attraction of an antecedent into the case of the relative is commonly called inverse attraction.

14. *Non est, quam piget esse piam.*] 'She who is sorry for being righteous, is not really so.' The construction, 'Non est (pia), quam piget esse piam,' simple as it is, has puzzled some learned commentators: even Heinsius, apparently.

15, 16. 'Let Danaus and my cruel sisters repent : this result (viz., remorse) is wont to follow deeds of wickedness (not conduct like mine).' Cf. Her. xix. 86, 'Excitus hic fractis puppibus esse solet.'

17. 'My heart is affrighted at the recollection of that night profaned with blood, and a sudden tremor impedes my fingers.' I do not see sufficient reason for changing 'ossa,' the reading of all MSS., to 'orsa.' 'Orsa' would mean 'the words I begin to write.' 'Orsa' in a sense like this occurs in Virg. Aen. vii. 435, 'Hic iuvenis vatem irridens sic orsa vicissim Ore refert,' but the only parallel Conington quotes is Val. Flacc. v. 470. He might have added Stat. Theb. vii. 195. But in all these passages 'orsa' is used of words not writing. On the other hand ' ossa' is defended by x. 140, ' Litteraque articulo pressa tremente labat:' 'articulus,' properly a joint, then a finger, being here expressed by 'ossa dextrae.' If 'orsa' were the true reading, it ought to be found again in the writings attributed to Ovid, where every form of epistolary expression is so often repeated, but it does not recur.

23, 24. Inachides are the daughters of Danaus. The line of descent was Inachus, Io, Epaphus, Libya, Belus, Danaus. Pelasgus was the king of Argos at this

Et socer armatas accipit ipso nurus.
Undique conlucent praecinctae lampades auro : 25
Dantur in invitos impia tura focos :
Vulgus 'Hymen, Hymenaee' vocant : fugit illo vocantes :
Ipsa Iovis coniux cessit ab urbe sua.
Ecce mero dubii, comitum clamore frequentes,
Flore novo madidas impediente comas, 30
In thalamos laeti, thalamos, sua busta, feruntur,
Strataque corporibus, funere digna, premunt.
Iamque cibo vinoque graves somnoque iacebant,
Securumque quies alta per Argos erat :
Circum me gemitus morientum audire videbar : 35
Et tamen audieram, quodque verebar, erat.

24. *Ipse* P G, *ille* multi libri : *aede* unus.
32. *Funera* unus liber. Prorsus insolens mihi videtur locutio *funere digna* pro *funeri aptiora*. Non hic solum limam desiderat epistola, quam tamen non temere ab Ovidio abiudicandam in praef. huius ed. disputavi.
36. *Audibam* P *audieram* G.

---

time in the legend as given by Aesch. Supp. 247, according to the probable reading of Canter, and we find in Apoll. l. ii. 1, iii. 7, that Pelasgus was the name of an ancient Peloponnesian prince, although according to him the name of the king of Argos at this time was Gelanor ii. 1. 'Socer' must be Aegyptus, and in this respect the writer differs from both Apollodorus and Aeschylus, who do not represent Aegyptus as coming to Argos with his daughters. Euripides, however, agrees with our author here : in the beginning of his play Archelaus ap. Aristoph. Ran. 1207, he says—
Αἴγυπτος ὡς ὁ πλεῖστος ἔσπαρται λόγος
σὺν παισὶ πεντήκοντα ναυτίλῳ πλάτῃ
Ἄργος κατασχών : and so Schol. ad Eur. Hec. 887.

28. *Ipsa Iovis coniux.*] Argos was the principal seat of the worship of Juno. Hor. Od. l. vii. 8, Virg. Aen. i. 24. The absence of Juno is mentioned, because she ought to be present as patroness of the marriage τελεία, 'pronuba.'

29, 30. *Mero dubii*] 'Staggering with wine.' 'Dubius' is applied to the foot of fortune, Pont. iv. 32, and is often used of ships tost at sea.—'Clamore frequentes' is undoubtedly the right reading, though, as Loers says, it is 'paullo dictum audacius' for 'clamore frequenti.' The bridegroom's hair was steeped in unguents, and wreathed with flowers according to wedding custom.

31, 32. 'They rush joyfully into the marriage chambers, destined to be their tombs, and with their bodies press the beds, more suitable for death (than marriage).' 'Feruntur' evidently points to the intoxication of the bridegrooms : they 'tumbled' into the chambers, 'carried thither' as it were by their unsteady legs, rather than walking. The nominat. before 'feruntur' must be supplied : this is, however, only a slight blemish compared with the extraordinary expression ' funere digna,' which I can hardly bring myself to believe Ovid wrote, for 'digniora cadaveribus premi.' 'Funere digna' is properly 'deserving death,' and its use in the other sense is not at all defended by vi. 42, 'Faxque sub arsuros dignior iro rogos,' which is the meaning here intended. It may be Latin, but it is not Ovidian Latin.

35, 36. 'I seemed to hear all round me the groans of the dying : and, in fact

EP. XIV. HYPERMNESTRA LYNCEO.

Sanguis abit, mentemque calor corpusque relinquit,
    Inque novo iacui frigida facta toro.
Ut leni zephyro graciles vibrantur aristae,
    Frigida populeas ut quatit aura comas,   40
Aut sic, aut etiam tremui magis. Ipse iacebas,
    Quaeque tibi dederam, plena soporis erant.
Excussere metum violenti iussa parentis :
    Erigor, et capio tela tremente manu.
Non ego falsa loquar : ter acutum sustulit ensem,   45
    Ter male sublato recidit ense manus.
Admovi iugulo, sine me tibi vera fateri,
    Admovi iugulo tela paterna tuo :
Sed timor et pietas crudelibus obstitit ausis,
    Castaque mandatum dextra refugit opus.   50
Purpureos laniata sinus, laniata capillos
    Exiguo dixi talia verba sono :
'Saevus, Hypermnestra, pater est tibi : iussa parentis

---

42. *Vina soporis erant* P G M, et vulg. nisi quod plurimi codd. habent *dederant*. Ed. princ : *vinaque quae dederant signa soporis erant*. Nulla autem vina dederant nuptae maritis, qui semel ipsos in coena nuptiali invitavissent, et recepta lectio *vina soporis erant* cuius linguae sit nescio. Non possum quin proferam id quod verum esse perspexi. De sopore qui coitu efficitur loquitur Hypermnestra, qua de re instar omnium licet conf. Stat. Theb. v. 73, 'nullus in amplexu sopor est.' *Vina* fuit glossema ad *quae* adscriptum a lectore nescioquo ingenuo qui non vidit *quae* amplexus innuere. Stabilitur haec emendatio loco carminis nequioris notae, Nasonis ut fertur, huic simillimo, in Priapeis, iii. 5 : 'Quodque Iovi dederat....Quod virgo prima cupido dat nocte marito.' Cf. v. 69, infra.

46. *Decidit* G, P ma. sec. et vulg. .... *etendit* P ma. pr. mendose : *recidit* Heins.

I had heard them, and what I feared was reality. 'Tamen' is used because '*ridebar*,' 'I *seemed* to hear,' expresses in some degree the unreality of her fancy : 'but it was true : I had really heard the groans.' For the pluperfect in cases of this sort cf. Met. ix. 782, 'visa dea est movisse suas, et moverat aras' ('in fact had moved').—'Erat:' i.e. 'that which existed in my fears also existed in fact,' viz. the murder of her brothers-in-law.

37. There is a zeugma in 'calor,' it being used in a metaphorical sense with 'mens' and literally with 'corpus,' which does not seem to me to be quite in Ovid's manner ; cf. Her. xvi. 25, where 'aestus' is similarly used in a double sense.

42. The meaning is that the embraces of the marriage bed were laden with slumber.

46. *Recidit*]. This is one of the words compounded with 're' which lengthen that syllable though naturally short. See Ramsay's Lat. Prosody, p. 134.

51. 'Sinus' means the folds of the robe over the bosom. Hypermnestra's dress was purple, the royal colour, cf. xiii. 36, 'regales sinus :' Fast. v. 28, 'purpureo sinu' the dress of 'maiestas.'

53–66. Hypermnestra here argues for and against the commission of the murder alternately.

Effice: germanis sit comes iste suis.
Femina sum et virgo, natura mitis et annis: 55
 Non faciunt molles ad fera tela manus.
Quin age, dumque iacet, fortes imitare sorores:
 Credibile est caesos omnibus esse viros.
Si manus haec aliquam posset committere caedem,
 Morte foret dominae sanguinolenta suae. 60
Aut meruere necem patruelia regna tenendo
 Quae tamen externis regna tenenda forent?
Finge viros meruisse mori, quid fecimus ipsae?
 Quo mihi commisso non licet esse piae?
Quid mihi cum ferro? quid bellica tela puellae? 65
 Aptior est digitis lana colusque meis.'

61. *Quo* P (ap. Iahn. et Heins.) *Non* G aut P (ap. Riesium et M. ut videtur) an al. *haud* al. *quid* vulg.
62. *Danda forent generis* M vulg. Hic versus in P ma. sec. tantum scriptus est. Reponendum censeo id quod habet cod. Gron: *quae tamen externis regna tenenda forent*. Probabile est librarium P propter *regna tenenda* in utroque versu alterum praetermisisse.
64. *Piae* P, *piam* vulg.

58. 'It is likely that by this time all my sisters have slain their husbands.' 'Omnibus' is here probably the dat. though the abl. without 'ab' is not out of accordance with Ovidian syntax; cf. note on x. 138. If 'omnibus' is the dat. it is what is called the ethical dat. or dat. of reference, 'they have each slain her *man*.'

61, 62. 'Or have they deserved death by seizing the kingdoms of their cousins, which kingdoms after all (tamen) must have been occupied by foreigners?' The reading of the MSS. 'danda forent generis' in 62, was with Lachmann one of his strongest grounds of objection to the authenticity of this epistle, inasmuch as Ovid nowhere else allows a trisyllabic ending to the pentameter, except in the Epistles from Pontus, which, as Ramsay remarks, were, together with the Tristia, 'composed while the poet was plunged in the deepest despondency, and bear tokens of less accurate revision than his other productions,' Lat. Prosody, p. 172. But, as Merkel remarks, the line is certainly corrupt. The reading of a late MS., which I have given, is tolerable. Ovid often repeats the same words for emphasis' sake, and emphasis is wanted here. The meaning is: 'if our cousins the sons of Aegyptus had not seized our lands, they must have passed to strangers,' to whom we might have been given in marriage. Hence 'generis' is a gloss which has made its way in and corrupted the line. 'Tamen' is 'in spite of your unwillingness.'

63, 64. 'Grant that they deserved death: what have we done that we should be forced to stain ourselves with the guilt of murder?'—'Piae:' The dative after 'licet esse' is the regular idiomatic construction, although the accus. is allowable: cf. Hor. Sat. ii. 19, 'at qui licet esse beatis.' Mart. IX. xii. 16. 'Nobis non licet esse tam disertis.' Ov. Met. viii. 406, 'licet eminus esse Fortibus.' So with 'esse contingit,' 'expedit,' 'necesse est,' etc. Vid. Donaldson's Lat. Gramm. §. 143. 1.

EP. XIV. HYPERMNESTRA LYNCEO.

Haec ego, dumque queror, lacrimae sua verba sequuntur,
  Dequo meis oculis in tua membra cadunt.
Dum petis amplexus sopitaque brachia iactas,
  Paene manus telo saucia facta tua est.   70
Iamque patrem famulosque patris lucemque timebam.
  Expulerunt somnos haec mea dicta tuos,
'Surge age, Belide, de tot modo fratribus unus!
  Nox tibi, ni properas, ista perennis erit.'
Territus exsurgis; fugit omnis inertia somni: 75
  Aspicis in timida fortia tela manu.
Quaerenti causam 'dum nox sinit, effuge' dixi :
  'Dum nox atra sinit.' Tu fugis, ipsa moror.
Mane erat, et Danaus generos ex caede iacentes
  Dinumerat : summae criminis unus abes.   80
Fert malo cognatae iacturam mortis in uno,
  Et queritur facti sanguinis esse parum.
Abstrahor a patriis pedibus, raptamque capillis,
  Haec meruit pietas praemia, carcer habet.
Scilicet ex illo Iunonia permanet ira,   85

72. *Expulerunt* P, *expulerant* vulg.
82. *Facti* P G, *factum* vulg., coni. Riesius *fusi*.
85–118. Hos versus Scaliger, D. Heins., alii spurios duxerunt. Frustra, ut N. Heins. videtur, et recte videtur. Nam in Aeschyli Supplicibus tragoedia quae huic carmini simile argumentum habet, pertractatur Ius fabula, quae notissimam digressionem Prometheo quoque intulit.

---

67. *Sua verba.*] i. e. 'verba quae lacrimas decent, i. e. querentia,' Loers.
72. *Expulerunt.*] ' So steterunt,' vii. 166. 'Praebuerunt,' ii. 142, and passim.
73. Hae as in 9, sqq. supra, the imitation of Horace l.c. is again apparent: 'Surge ne longus tibi somnus, unde Non times detur.' The student need scarcely to be told not to confound 'Belīdes,' a male descendant of Belus, with 'Belĭdes' (plur. of Belis) female descendant of the same, although Loers has done so in his note on this line. The daughters of Danaus are often called 'Belides :' cf. Met. iv. 463, 'Assidue repetunt, quas perdunt Belides undas.'
78. Merkel makes Hypermnestra's words go on to 'moror :' Jahn and most editors make them end at 'effuge.' Merkel is certainly wrong, as the latter clause of v. 78 evidently describes the flight of Lynceus. I regard 'sinit' in 78, as the end of H.'s words : emphasis is thus added to her entreaties to Lynceus to save himself. 'Fly! *while night, while black night allows it, fly.*'
79, 80, 'Day dawned, and Danaus counts his sons-in-law lying here and there in their blood (lit. after the murder): you are the only unit wanting to the sum of crime.'
81, 82. 'He takes ill the losing of one kinsman's murder, and complains that there has been too little blood shed.' 'In uno' = ' in the case of one.' ' Cognata mors' = 'mors cognati.' The phrase 'factus sanguis' occurs in Livy, ii. 30 : 'Plusque ibi sanguinis, promiscua omnium generum caede, quam in ipsa dimicatione factum.'
85. The digression on the wandering of Io, which here follows, is condemned

Quo bos ex homine est, ex bove facta dea.
At satis est poenae teneram mugisse puellam,
Nec, modo formosam, posse placere Iovi.
Adstitit in ripa liquidi nova vacca parentis,
Cornuaque in patriis non sua vidit aquis: 90
Conatoque queri mugitus edidit ore,
Territaque est forma, territa voce sua.
Quid furis, infelix? quid te miraris in unda?
Quid numeras factos ad nova membra pedes?
Illa Iovis magni pellex metuenda sorori, 95
Fronde levas nimiam caespitibusque famem :
Fonte bibis, spectasque tuam stupefacta figuram,
Et, te ne feriant quae geris arma, times.
Quaeque modo, ut posses etiam Iove digna videri,
Dives eras, nuda nuda recumbis humo. 100
Per mare, per terras cognataque flumina curris :
Dat mare, dant amnes, dat tibi terra viam.
Quae tibi causa fugae? Quid, Io, freta longa pererras?

91. *Conato* .... (P ap. M) *conata eloqui* ap. Heins. et Iahn. *et conata queri* vulg. *conataque queri* G *conatoque queri* M recte: ita Met. i. 637. Utrumque locum ulcus insedit, quod librarii *que* geminare neglexerunt, ut scribit Heins.
93. *Fugis* al. *Umbra* P.
95. *Illa* P G *ipsa* vulg.

---

as spurious by many who defend the authenticity of the rest of the poem : among the rest by Jos. Scaliger. As to the inappropriateness of the digression to the state of Hypermnestra, there can be only one opinion : but that does not prove Ovid was not its author. As Heinsius remarked, the Suppliants of Aeschylus, which was largely made use of by the author of this epistle (vid. ad. v. 13) is full of allusions to the story of Io ; cf. Aesch. Supp. 152 sqq. 287 sqq. The Prometheus, too, with its strange digression into this very myth, may have presented itself to the mind of the writer. ' Ex illo,' sc. ' tempore.'

86. *Bos.*] Io, daughter of Inachus, a mythical Argive king, also a river-god. vs. 89, was beloved by Jupiter and changed into a cow by Juno, and driven by a gadfly over land and sea until she arrived in Egypt, where she regained her own form on the banks of the Nile, and gave birth to Epaphus. She was deified after her death, and worshipped under the name of Isis.

94. ' Why do you count the feet made to match (ad) your new limbs ?' Io finds herself a quadruped to her astonishment.

95, 96. 'You who were once the famous rival feared by Juno, now appease your hunger with leaves and grass.'

99, 100. 'And you who were lately so rich that you might seem a mate for Jove, now lie bare on the bare ground.'

101. *Cognataque flumina.*] Rivers are said to be relations of Io, because she herself was daughter of the river-god Inachus.

EP. XIV. HYPERMNESTRA LYNCEO.

Non poteris vultus effugere ipsa tuos.
Inachi, quo properas? eadem sequerisque fugisque: 105
Tu tibi dux comiti, tu comes ipsa duci.
Per septem Nilus portus emissus in aequor
Exuit insanae pellicis ora bovis.
Ultima quid referam, quorum mihi cana senectus
Auctor? Dant anni, quod querar, ecce, mei. 110
Bella pater patruusque gerunt: regnoque domoque
Pellimur: eiectos ultimus orbis habet.
Ille ferox solio solus sceptroque potitur:
Cum sene nos inopi turba vagamur inops.
De fratrum populo pars exiguissima restat. 115
Quique dati leto, quaeque dedere, fleo.

108. *Bori* unus liber.
113. Hoc distichon 1ᵃ ma. sec. in margine tantum scriptum Lachmanno ansam dedit totius epistolae improbandae, propter *potitur*, cujus mediam syllabam Ovidius semper corripit.
116. *Restas* al.

---

105. *Eadem sequerisque fugisque.*] 'You pursue and flee from the same things,' viz., the form of a cow, especially the horns. See 97, 98 supra: and cf. Am. I. i. 21, 'exterrita cornibus Io.' It is almost incredible, that an industrious writer like L. Müller should suppose 'eadem' to be the nominative case here, and then challenge the passage as spurious because of the omission of 'te' after the verb. His other blunders on the passage are equally gross, see notes on 109, 111.

103. *Io.*] The first syllable of Io is always long in Greek, and elsewhere in Ovid, except in Ibis, 624: 'Quem memor a sacris nunc quoque pellit Io.' But licences in Ovid's later poems must by no means be here cited in defence of irregularities in his early poems: see note on v. 62, supra, and xi. 127, note: and the shortening of the first syllable of Io here seems to me to be the very strongest of the arguments that can be urged against the authenticity of the epistle.

107, 108. Literally: 'The Nile, which empties itself by seven channels into the sea, took away the face of the cow which belonged to the frenzied girl!' The allusion is to the legend that Io resumed her human form on the banks of the Nile.

The reading 'bovi' gives a different meaning: viz., 'that the Nile brought out the face of the girl from the cow,' beneath which it lay as it were concealed.

109, 110. 'Why should I speak of things far distant about which hoar antiquity is my informant: Io, my own times afford me subject for complaint.' 'Senectus' means the traditions handed down from antiquity. So 'vetustas' is more commonly used. Cf. Met. i. 400, 'quis hoc credat nisi sit pro teste vetustas.' Ruhnken prefers to take it as the abstract for the concrete = 'cani senes,' but I think the other explanation is correct, especially as 'canus' is often metaphorically used: cf. 'cana fides,' Virg. Aen. i. 296, 'cana iura,' Mart. i. 16: 'saecula cana,' Id. viii. 80. L. Müller, in his critique on this epistle in the Rheinische Museum, says Hypermnestra from this line suddenly appears transformed from a young to an old woman, showing that he totally misunderstood 'cana senectus.' In the next distich he thinks a war between Danaus and Aegyptus *after* the events related in this epistle is meant, whereas it evidently refers to their quarrels in Egypt before Danaus fled from that country. These mistakes are inexcusable

Nam mihi quot fratres, totidem periere sorores:
  Accipiat lacrimas utraque turba meas.
En ego, quod vivis, poenae crucianda reservor:
  Quid fiet sonti, cum rea laudis agar,   120
Et consanguineae quondam centesima turbae
  Infelix uno fratre manente cadam?
At tu, siqua piae, Lynceu, tibi cura sororis,
  Quaeque tibi tribui munera, dignus habes,
Vel fer opem, vel dede neci, defunctaque vita   125
  Corpora furtivis insuper adde rogis,
Et sepeli lacrimis perfusa fidelibus ossa,
  Sculptaque sint titulo nostra sepulchra brevi:
'Exul Hypermnestra., pretium pietatis iniquum,
  Quam mortem fratri depulit, ipsa tulit.'   130
Scribere plura libet, sed pondere lapsa catenae
  Est manus, et vires subtrahit ipse timor.

131. *Lapsa* M, *lassa* vulg., *pressa* G ap. Jahn.

---

in themselves, but it is altogether too bad that they should be made to furnish arguments against the authenticity of the epistle.

117. *Totidem periere sorores.*] The author here evidently forgets the legend. Nothing is said in it of any earthly retribution overtaking the forty-nine daughters of Danaus. On the contrary, they were purified from the murder by command of Jupiter. Others explain 'periere' to mean that Hyp.'s sisters are dead to her owing to their crime: but I think this forced, and the other explanation is in keeping with the general want of accuracy throughout the epistle.

120. *Quid fiet sonti cum rea laudis agar?*] 'What will be done to the guilty when I am put on my trial for a noble deed?' A fine line which could hardly have come from any pen but Ovid's. 'Reum agere,' 'to accuse,' is a common phrase.

126. *Furtivis.*] 'Constructed by stealth,' for fear of rousing the anger of Danaus. Antigone's burial of the body of Polynices, against the orders of Creon, was probably in the poet's mind.

129. *Exul.*] This also seems to refer to something not related in the ordinary legend, and indeed inconsistent with the whole tenor of the epistle. In fact, it must be conceded that there was considerable confusion in the mind of the author, whoever he was.

www.ingramcontent.com/pod-product-compliance
Lightning Source LLC
Chambersburg PA
CBHW032154160426
43197CB00008B/912